Joint Degrees, Dual Degrees, and International Research Collaborations

A Report on the CGS Graduate International Collaborations Project

COUNCIL OF GRADUATE SCHOOLS

JOINT DEGREES, DUAL DEGREES, AND INTERNATIONAL RESEARCH COLLABORATIONS:
A Report on the CGS
Graduate International Collaborations Project

Prepared for publication by: Daniel D. Denecke and Julia Kent with contributions by Gregory Anderson. This material is based upon work supported by the National Science Foundation under Grant No. DRL-0841399. Any opinions, findings, and conclusions or recommendations expressed in this material are those of the authors and do not necessarily reflect the views of the National Science Foundation.

ISBN (10-digit) 1-933042-27-3
ISBN (13-digit) 978-1-933042-27-5

Printed in the United States

TABLE OF CONTENTS

CONTENTS

PREFACE

nternational collaboration is an exciting new frontier for many North American universities. Greater international collaboration at the graduate level is indispensable to the advancement of scholarship and science. Participation in such collaborative work, whether through formal degree programs or through more informal research exchanges, also prepares students for a future in which research is destined to become truly global. There is extraordinary excitement surrounding the opportunities available to US and Canadian universities to partner with other institutions from around the world. This excitement is matched, however, by an equal amount of confusion. In order to help alleviate some of this confusion, the Council of Graduate Schools (CGS) has conducted research and hosted dialogues in recent years focused on advancing international collaboration. These activities have helped the North American graduate community to better orient itself in an area where some regions, such as Europe, have had the advantage of greater experience. Each event that CGS has facilitated, however, has also brought into the open serious questions upon which there is still no consensus and about which there has been a call for greater clarity: questions about definitions, values, and appropriate solutions to administrative challenges.

This publication is the result of an important CGS initiative to provide the graduate community with a clearer understanding of what is currently known about international collaborations at the graduate level, as well as what is valued, what the current gaps in our understanding are, and what areas call for greater clarification. Further dialogue is needed within the US and Canada to identify best practices in international collaboration appropriate to our own institutional contexts. This publication lays the groundwork for that subsequent work, but more remains to be done building upon this foundation to identify best practices. Further international dialogue is also needed to ensure that strategic institutional leaders of graduate education from around the world are apprised of trends and engaged in discussion about issues of mutual concern. CGS's development of the annual "Strategic Leaders Global Summit on Graduate Education" series is designed to help address that need. This publication and proceedings from last year's summit, now available as *Global Perspectives on Graduate International Collaborations (2010)*, may be seen as companion volumes that address similar issues from distinct geographical perspectives. CGS will continue to explore ways to serve the graduate community through efforts in both of these regional and international domains.

Some of the most important findings from the NSF-funded project described in this publication center on the importance of leadership in developing and sustaining effective international collaborations. It is my hope that this resource proves useful to all those who provide leadership in advancing their institution's internationalization efforts, including: graduate deans and senior leaders in graduate education from all countries who seek to better understand the issues facing American institutions as they engage in international collaboration; staff members from international offices and other campus units who seek information on issues specific to graduate (as opposed to undergraduate) degrees; faculty researchers (principal investigators and collaborators) with active international partnerships; policymakers who seek to better understand the inhibitors and facilitators of expanded US efforts in this area; and program officers at various organizations responsible for funding and assisting in the development of collaborations to ensure their success.

Debra W. Stewart
President
Council of Graduate Schools

ACKNOWLEDGMENTS

The authors are grateful to the National Science Foundation (NSF) for the REESE grant (DRL 0841399) that funded the Graduate International Collaborations Project and to Program Officer Carol Stoel for her helpful comments and support. Conversations with others at NSF proved particularly helpful in shedding light on issues faced in research collaborations where greater communication between graduate schools and researchers might prove helpful. For agreeing to discuss these issues with us, we thank John Tsapogas (who provided insights from the Office of International Science and Engineering) and Sonia Ortega (who discussed experiences from the GK-12 program).

Although we assured participants anonymity in the various activities associated with this project in order to encourage frank and open discussion, we thank each of the graduate deans and associate deans who contributed to a focus group on joint and dual degrees and a set of technical workshops on research collaborations. For their engaged participation in the latter, we especially thank the principal investigators and co-PIs from the NSF PIRE (Partnerships for International Research and Education) and IGERT (Integrative Graduate Education and Research Traineeship) programs who made special efforts to join us for the technical workshop discussions of international research collaborations described in Chapter Three.

Gregory J. Anderson, CGS/NSF Dean in Residence from September 2008 to August 2009, provided helpful input on the survey described in Chapter Two. A series of informal and exploratory semi-structured interviews that he conducted with many division directors and program directors throughout the NSF helped to inform this project's understanding of the challenges and concerns NSF has as it seeks to advance and support international collaboration. The authors thank all those NSF staff members who met with Dr. Anderson and provided such valuable input.

Other colleagues who deserve recognition for their contributions to this publication and the Graduate International Collaborations Project include: Sheila Kirby, Scott Naftel, and Nathan Bell for assistance in analyzing project data; Matthias Kuder and Ursula Lehmkuhl, who graciously shared extensive thoughts about Freie Universität Berlin's experience studying joint and dual degree phenomena in Europe and the US; Rajika Bhandari and Patricia Chow of the Institute of International Education (IIE), who offered helpful information about student mobility trends and data; Diana

Carlin, who provided input into the formative stages of this project and opportunities to discuss preliminary results with member deans; and last but not least, CGS President Debra Stewart, CGS staff members Robert Sowell, Joshua Mahler, Nathan Bell, and Lindsey Strain, and CGS member deans Debasish Dutta, Jacqueline Huntoon, Linda Lacey, Michelle Marks, and Allison Sekuler for their helpful comments on the draft manuscript and for sharing informational resources that enriched this project.

EXECUTIVE SUMMARY

ecent years have seen rapid growth in the number of international collaborative programs involving research and educational opportunities for graduate students. These opportunities include research collaborations between faculty as well as formal, dual or joint graduate degree programs between US institutions and international partners. Due to the interest in collaborations of both types, there have been many calls within the graduate community for national guidelines and best practices for their development and sustainability. The CGS Graduate International Collaborations Project, a first step in answering those calls, was designed to generate a clearer understanding of what is currently known and what is valued in international collaborations, what the current gaps in our understanding are, and what areas call for greater clarification.

The two major outcomes of this project are enhanced understanding of how graduate schools, faculty researchers, and other campus units work together throughout the process of international collaboration, and the identification of a number of specific national needs that can support the effectiveness of universities engaged in such collaborations. Below is a summary of key findings from the key research activities of this project, which included a survey, a set of focus group and technical workshop discussions, and related activities described in the introduction to this volume.

Benefits
Graduate international collaborations yield important benefits to US students, institutions, and state and local communities:

- *Impacts for Students* include more training and research opportunities, cultural perspective and skills required for international research projects.
- *Benefits for Faculty* include broader research networks and access to new knowledge, skills, and resources.
- *Impacts for Institutions* include broadened research capacities, enhanced powers to recruit talented international students and faculty, and a more visible and global research profile.

- *Broader Impacts for State and Local Communities*. When aligned with local and state priorities, international collaborations involving graduate research and/or education directly benefit state and local communities and economies.

Trends
Survey data and focus group discussions indicated trends in the following areas:

- *Institutional Leadership*
  The role of the graduate school and the graduate dean is changing: whereas in the past, graduate schools have primarily provided administrative support and "institutional good will," graduate deans now describe themselves as also playing increasingly strategic roles.

- *Motivations*
  The primary driver behind international collaborations at the graduate level is not revenue but rather academic and research motivations. These include attracting international students, responding to faculty interest, and strengthening academic research quality.

- *Key Challenges*
  The primary challenges to graduate international collaborations are: sustainability, securing adequate funding, recruiting students, negotiating an MOU, and deciding on fee structure. In the development of dual degrees, awarding students double credit for a single body of work is a key challenge. In the development of joint degrees, accreditation and approval processes pose a key challenge.

- *Funding Sources*
  - Primary funding sources for collaborative degree programs come from student fees, internal university budgets, and international sources.
  - There is strong evidence that US universities receive less funding for international research collaborations from the US federal government than they do from foreign sources.

- *Mobility*

  In general, more international students travel to US institutions to participate in international collaborative programs than domestic students travel to international institutions. However, a significant proportion of faculty travel for research or educational (i.e. non administrative) purposes.

Future Needs

US universities face significant barriers when pursuing sustainable international research and educational collaborations at the graduate level, including: limited federal and state resources that would support international collaboration, a lack of national guidance about how to measure and assess outcomes, and, where federal or state resources are available, limited guidance that would minimize costs, start-up time, and risk. Given their strong role in supporting and fostering sustainable international collaborations, graduate deans seek

- *Tools for Assessing Outcomes*

  Stronger evidence is needed of the extent to which, and in what ways, international collaborations benefit US domestic institutions, faculty researchers, graduate students, society and the economy. Tools and metrics can help institutions assess the broader impact of and quality of collaborations.

- *National Guidelines and Resources.*

  More resources are needed to support researchers who are pursuing, or who have obtained federal funds to create, international research and educational collaborations. Resources called for include: case studies, a database of international graduate degree collaborations, evidence-based best practices, and national guidelines.

I. International Collaboration in Graduate Education

The internationalization of higher education is a fast growing phenomenon. Evidence of this growth abounds. Over the past decade, the number of students who study outside their home country has been increasing dramatically, as has global competition for those students. Across Europe, massive reforms such as the Bologna Process are underway to promote greater comparability among European higher educational systems and greater mobility of talent. Meanwhile, universities around the world, including many in the United States, are moving quickly to develop new international collaborative degree programs such as joint and dual degrees at the graduate and undergraduate levels. Less highly structured research and educational exchanges between partnering institutions from different countries and regions are also becoming more common, especially as research networks become increasingly global in nature. And some institutions are building "brick and mortar" campuses abroad, which may help establish an institution's global identity and generate future revenue, but which may also involve greater initial investment and risk. The internationalization of graduate education comes in many different forms, and each of these forms brings opportunities as well as challenges for researchers and university leaders who strive to remain abreast of developments in other parts of the world and make strategic choices for their current students as well as those they seek to recruit.

In ensuring that international collaborations are successful, decision-makers and researchers alike require reliable and timely information about the scope and structure of collaborations between their home country's institutions and their international partners. They are also looking for guidelines and proven solutions to typical challenges. The US graduate community, however, has lacked information specific to the US graduate education context and has called for a common reference guide to fill this gap as they seek, in the long term, definitive guidelines and best practices in international collaboration. Building upon a grant from the National Science Foundation and upon prior international activities of the Council of Graduate Schools and its member universities, this book seeks to provide such a reference guide.

Because the Graduate International Collaborations Project was supported by an NSF grant, many of the examples provided in this book refer to STEM (science, technology, engineering, and mathematics) fields. Of course, US graduate international collaborations span the range of disciplines, and the majority of findings and issues discussed in this book are applicable to collaborations across the research disciplines. Taken together, the following chapters provide a comprehensive picture of the wide range of issues to be considered as institutions approach international collaborations for the first time, from a new direction, or in order to strengthen the collaborations they already have.

This introductory chapter presents an overview of the broader issues that surface around international collaboration: the benefits of international collaboration to students, institutions, and society; the US context for institutional collaboration with international partners; and the essential role of strategic leadership in support of such collaborations.

Chapter Two reviews the extant (mostly European) literature on joint and dual degrees. These degrees represent some of the most promising innovative degree structures for building sustainable relationships between institutions. Despite their promise, these structures have also resulted in great confusion given the lack of consensus on definitions and the sometimes significant administrative hurdles to be overcome.

Chapter Three presents findings from the CGS Graduate International Collaborations Project. Findings are discussed in three separate sections that represent three distinct project activities: (1) results of a CGS member survey on international collaborations that sought to shed light on some key, unanswered questions, such as: how are such degrees typically structured?, what policies are in place to support those degrees?, and what challenges or issues are typically encountered by degree type?; (2) analysis of focus group discussions that expanded upon issues identified in the survey and explored possible solutions to common challenges with graduate deans from North American institutions (US and Canada) that have developed joint and dual degree programs with international partners; and (3) a summary of discussions from a set of two technical workshops on international research collaborations involving principal investigators from NSF-funded grants programs and graduate deans at the host institutions. Together these participants discussed international research collaborations that are not necessarily housed in formal joint or dual degree programs but which constitute a large part of the US graduate education system's engagement in international collaborative research. There are still many questions that remain unanswered, and subsequent work remains to be done at the national level to assist universities in creating institutional environments for international collaborations to thrive and prosper.

Chapter Four discusses the gaps in our current understanding and national practice and defines next steps for national activities in the development of best practices and guidelines that would benefit the US graduate community. The NSF-funded Graduate International Collaborations Project was conceived to be an initial, synthesis phase project that could ultimately inform a larger, second-phase study to identify best practices and provide national guidelines for the development of collaborations, where appropriate and needed by the graduate community. The current publication therefore does not identify "best practices" per se as CGS defines them, i.e., as identified through a rigorous model of evidence-based assessments of pilot projects and case studies. Such activities are necessary and valuable but fell outside the parameters of the NSF grant that funded this project. The following chapters, especially Chapter Three and the appendix material, however, provide examples of solutions that universities participating in this study have found to be effective in solving some of the most common challenges.

The Benefits of International Collaboration
When considering options for international collaboration, one of the first questions that faculty and senior administrators raise is: what are the benefits? The investment of financial resources and time in institutionalizing formal collaborations with international partners can be significant. Therefore, all stakeholders should first seek to determine the value of the proposed collaboration to their institution's research, degree programs, and to the institution as a whole. Those who have been successful in launching or scaling up collaborations at the graduate level report a variety of typical benefits for students, institutions, and the broader public.

Student benefits
Graduate students and undergraduates may benefit in similar ways from participating in international collaborative programs and research exchanges, but there are also benefits that are unique to graduate study. Those benefits that are well documented for undergraduates and that may also extend to graduate students include:

- Personal development and enrichment,
- Enhanced career prospects and increased academic opportunities, and
- Enhanced cultural diplomacy skills (skills that may also benefit the institution.)[1]

In addition to these benefits that undergraduate and graduate students may share in common, the benefits more specific to graduate students typically include:

- Enhanced research skills,
- Expanded research networks,
- Access to specialized equipment and expertise, and
- Enhanced "science diplomacy" skills (in science and engineering).[2]

At the undergraduate level, international collaborations may be created with the primary purpose of enriching students' lives with a rewarding intercultural educational experience. At the graduate level, while such enrichment may be a perceived benefit, the initial motivation often springs from faculty research interests. As discussed in Chapter Four, a better understanding of the benefits to students and all stakeholders through improved assessment of the outcomes of such collaborations is important.

Benefits to institutions and faculty
International collaborations are widely perceived to benefit the institution and participating graduate programs in a variety of ways. The most commonly cited benefits to institutions and their faculty researchers include:

- The increased prestige that may result from an institution's reputation as a global university,
- Increased international student recruitment and tuition dollars,
- The sharing of world-class equipment and resources, and
- An enhanced educational climate that results from the diverse cultural experiences that international students bring to the US and that US students bring back after their study abroad.

Because the funding of international collaborations can prove challenging, especially at the start, and institutions always assume some degree of risk in pursuing them, a solid understanding of the expected benefits and subsequent efforts to measure outcomes once they are in place is an important part of any graduate internationalization strategy.

Public benefits

Beyond the benefits to individual students and faculty, and their institutions, international collaborations may also yield broader public benefits. These can be more difficult to measure, but include:

- **Economic benefits**, such as the creation of jobs, revenue, and patents developed through enhanced student mobility and research productivity;
- **Social benefits,** including quality of life improvements and the amelioration of social and environmental problems; as well as
- **Socio-political benefits** achieved through science and cultural diplomacy.

Regional and national economies benefit from international students studying in the US at both the graduate and undergraduate levels. It is estimated, for example, that international students contributed approximately $15.54 billion to the US economy between 2007 and 2008, and $17.6 billion between 2008 and 2009.[3] Economic benefits may also accrue in more far-reaching ways. For example, the number of international patents developed within a country is a strong indicator of that country's capacity for innovation, which is enhanced when skills and resources are drawn from outside its borders.[4]

Further public benefits arise from the research advances that result from successful international collaborations. For example, partnerships may emerge around issues such as water conservation or sustainable agriculture that affect the local regions of both partner institutions.[5] Indeed, some now argue that progress is not possible on big, global-scale topics such as climate, energy, disease, and hunger without more international research collaboration and more coordination of researchers and policymakers across national borders. Collaborations may directly benefit the local and regional populations of both partnering institutions, or they may benefit some partnering institutions' countries and regions more indirectly, where the consequences of failing to address problems with long time horizons can be detrimental to national and local interests.[6]

The broader public benefits of international collaborations are frequently cited, but can be difficult to measure. Similarly, the long-term economic benefits that may result from student mobility, international networks, and the fruits of these collaborations can be difficult to quantify. One of the metrics commonly used as a proxy for these broader benefits is student mobility.

Student mobility has not been seen uniformly as a positive phenomenon. Where students perceive their career opportunities to be greatest in the country where they pursue their graduate degrees, sending countries have sometimes been justifiably concerned about the long-term loss of their top domestic talent. Such concerns about "brain drain" have been common to both developed and developing countries. Recently, however, rapid economic development in some parts of the developing world has challenged the assumption behind the view that students who travel to the US for graduate education will remain there to pursue their subsequent careers unless there are strong incentives to return (or disincentives to stay in the US). Traditional conceptions of a "developed core" economy and economically "developing peripheries" that might have once supported this view may no longer be adequate to describe employment opportunities for graduates of some international collaborative programs. While such a model might once have described the distribution of career opportunities between partnering countries and lent credence to conceptions of "brain drain" and "brain gain," some researchers now argue that new models are needed to more accurately describe a "flattening" world where developed countries face the prospect of slower growth and emerging economies are host to some of the strongest growth in a knowledge sector workforce.[7]

International collaborations can be developed, and student mobility within those collaborations structured, in such a way as to maximize benefits to all partnering countries. Future success in a global knowledge workforce may well be achieved by countries that can best prepare their researchers to develop international networks and work efficiently and comfortably across national and cultural borders. In both non-academic and academic sectors, the global employment opportunities created out of international research collaborations can yield social and economic benefits to local regions and national populations of both partner institutions.

International collaborations are arguably vital both to the advancement of science and to the realization of its public benefits. Arden Bement, NSF Director from 2004-2010, has made this point on many occasions.[8] Cora Marrett, Acting Deputy Director of NSF, reiterated the message at a workshop co-hosted by CGS and NSF in April 2009, stating that in the new era of extreme globalization, "we must collaborate globally to prosper and thrive individually." Dr. Marrett articulated three ways that global collaborations and engagement enrich the enterprise of science: (1) by "mak[ing] for more vibrant lives and careers for our scientists and engineers"; (2) by "advancing science through intellectual and social networks"; and (3) "by enabling and cultivating *science diplomacy*, the idea that through collaborations in science and engineering, we can enrich relations among nations."[9]

The importance to the economy, to society, and to national security of creating and sustaining successful international graduate collaborations between the US and other countries is recognized by those outside the federal science funding bodies as well. Leaders in the US political and public service communities have joined those in the scientific community to affirm their belief that the United States can neither be economically competitive nor secure as a nation until it extends and deepens its commitment to international research and educational collaborations. The position that international collaborations in science and science diplomacy should play a larger role in US foreign policy is conveyed in the "Statement on Science Diplomacy" below. This statement was issued by a bipartisan group of Nobel Prize-winning scientists, national policy advisors, and national leaders including members from the US Congress:

> US national security depends upon our willingness to share the costs and benefits of scientific progress with other nations. Enhanced international scientific cooperation can also lead to greater economic prosperity at home. The US needs new technologies and markets to create jobs, grow new industries and rebuild consumer and investor confidence. Sustainable international partnerships allow us to leverage limited resources and give American companies access to cutting-edge research and expertise around the world.[10]

Every successful international research collaboration or educational exchange has the potential to yield a full range of benefits to students and faculty, their institutions, and their home countries. We can also learn from failures, as unsuccessful collaborations can shed light on the importance of such things as feasibility planning, sufficient resources, and ensuring a match between quality institutions. As senior administrators and faculty work more closely than before with each other and with policymakers to better understand the impact of collaborations, they can better support each others' missions and contribute to broader public goals.

The US Context for International Collaboration

Chapter Three of this publication discusses specific challenges US universities face in developing and sustaining international programs as well as some strategies they have used to overcome such challenges. But these institutions are also situated in the broader national context. Launching and sustaining international collaborations from the US carries its own unique challenges, despite the many opportunities available to American institutions as a result of their global reputation for excellence in graduate education. These broader contextual challenges include:

(1) Patterns of student mobility that result in underrepresentation of US domestic students in collaborative programs; and

(2) An "ad hoc" national approach to collaborations that reflects the decentralized nature of graduate education in the US and respects the autonomy of institutions, but which may prove to be insufficient as other countries and regions move forward on more concerted strategic investments in international collaborations.

The student mobility challenge

One of the main motivations behind the internationalization of higher education is a desire to increase student mobility. According to the Institute of International Education (IIE), student mobility has increased by 57% since 1999, with 2.9 million students currently pursuing higher education opportunities outside their home countries.[11] Globally, student mobility is projected to grow to include 7.2 million students traveling outside their home countries by 2025.[12] Overall, the number of US students who studied abroad in 2007/2008 (243,360) and of those international students who studied in the US (241,791) is about even.[13] The vast majority of US students studying abroad, however, are undergraduates.[14] Undergraduate student mobility can take a variety of forms: educational and cultural exchanges of even a short duration; participation in a joint or dual degree program that requires a significant period of time in another country; or a full course of undergraduate study at a college or university abroad.

At the graduate level, the picture is somewhat different. On the one hand, international students make up a substantial part of the US graduate education enterprise. IIE reports that 44% of all the international students in the US are studying at the graduate level, and that the ratio of international to domestic students at the graduate level is nearly ten times greater than that seen at the undergraduate level.[15] International students comprise 16% of the total graduate enrollment in the US, but the percentage is much higher in STEM fields, where international students make up approximately 50% of the graduate enrollment in US engineering programs.[16] International students are highly valued by US graduate programs as they bring depth of content knowledge and fresh perspectives to classrooms, seminars, and labs. Collaborative degree programs can be an important part of an institution's strategy to attract international students and strengthen research. As survey data discussed in Chapter Three show, however, US domestic students have not taken advantage of these collaborative research and educational opportunities to travel abroad in the same proportion as international students who have participated in them in the US.

One important argument for the value of international collaborations in STEM fields at the graduate level is that, by studying and practicing research in a foreign country, students can expand their international networks and broaden their understanding of how research is conducted in different settings. According to IIE, US graduate students are much less likely to study abroad than many of their international counterparts.[17] There is no definitive data on the number of US graduate students who study abroad at some point during their graduate program. Estimates suggest, however, that the percentage is very small.[18] US citizens and permanent residents in US graduate programs make up just 11% of the total of all US students studying abroad. Even when joint and dual degree graduate programs or special grants programs have been established to create international opportunities for US domestic students, those programs have typically been characterized by an influx of international students, rather than a balanced, two-way flow between partnering institutions.

Judging by the diverse national origins of the students enrolled in US graduate programs, American graduate education is already a highly internationalized enterprise. International students studying in US graduate programs are not only being prepared as researchers in their chosen discipline, they are also learning skills to conduct research and collaborate with colleagues across national borders. These skills will serve them well in the global knowledge economy. US graduate programs must also seek, however, to prepare domestic students with the skills to succeed in a global research enterprise. The development of incentives for US graduate students to take advantage of opportunities to conduct research in international settings is an important goal that the US has not yet fully achieved, despite the existence of valuable programs sponsored by the National Science Foundation and the US Department of Education. As other countries continue to build capacity in R&D and higher education, employers both inside and outside academia are likely to require researchers with access to international networks and greater understanding of differences in the cultural and national policy contexts for research.

The imbalance between international students and US domestic students in joint and dual degree programs may be the result of a variety of factors, such as: foreign language ability (many US students lack fluency in a foreign language), differential costs (many European students are not required to pay tuition), and cultural issues. The imbalance could also reflect a perception that the benefits of such programs disproportionately accrue to students from partner countries and regions. On the other hand, some partner country institutions have expressed disappointment when a program designed to exchange equal numbers of US and partner country students does not live up to its stated goals, because both partners perceive the value of an equal exchange of high quality students.

Another issue that partnering institutions may encounter concerns the employment opportunities for students after graduation. In some collaborations, especially when one of the partnering institutions is located in a developing country, the potential exists for highly skilled graduates from such programs with advanced training in a discipline to be attracted by job opportunities (and attractive to employers) in the US. More attention to ensuring greater equity between the number of US students studying abroad and international students attending US institutions may benefit the partnership and may also better address a broader national need to prepare US graduate students for success as global researchers and scholars.

"Ad hoc" vs. strategic national approaches
Given the scale of the recent economic crisis that began in 2007, and the serious financial and sustainability challenges that many universities face as a result, it is conceivable that some of the international collaborations planned before the recession will be stalled, scaled back, or dissolved altogether. Lacking good, reliable outcomes measures for demonstrating the success and return on investment of such collaborations, neither the real benefits of continued pursuit nor the consequences of retreat can be well estimated. (The need for better definition and documentation of measurable outcomes is addressed in Chapter Four of this publication.) The consequences of not keeping pace with other countries in the internationalization of graduate education may potentially be experienced, however, in a range of areas. For example, it could result in the loss of "market share" of much of world's best talent to other universities outside the US; in an inability of US domestic graduate students to compete for employment in a global research job market; or even in comparative declines in research productivity. It is arguably all the more important in a constrained fiscal environment for both the US and for individual institutions to balance short-term opportunities, budget realities, and risks with long term needs and strategic priorities.

The number of recent empirical studies on international collaboration that have been conducted in Europe (described in Chapter Two) reflects the fact that in the past decade, European countries have taken a strategic approach to the mobility of talent and to higher education partnerships. By contrast, the US approach has been much more decentralized and piecemeal. In part, perhaps, this difference can be explained by the decentralized system of graduate education in the US and the comparative advantage US graduate programs have long maintained in attracting top students from around the globe. As other countries have struggled to recruit that top talent, many have been driven to innovate, to forge institutional partnerships and alliances, and to create incentives to internationalize their graduate programs. Meanwhile, US graduate programs that have easily attracted talented students from around the world with only minimal active recruiting may have encountered relatively less pressure to pursue institutional collaborations with international partners for reasons other than strengthening research. For many institutions, this situation changed after steep declines in international student applications to US graduate programs following the attacks of September 11, 2001. The declines suggested to observers that historical trends of positive growth in international student admissions could no longer be taken for granted and arguably sparked a new interest in international collaboration as a student recruitment strategy.[19] The broader pattern of international student applications to US programs suggests more global competition and a declining market share for US graduate programs of global PhD degree production. As these trends continue, international collaborations are likely to play an even larger part in the strategic positioning of US universities.

The Role of Strategic Leadership in Advancing International Collaboration

The question for many US institutions, then, is no longer whether to internationalize graduate education, but rather how to do so in a way that (a) is strategic, proactive, and efficient, and (b) benefits students, institutions, and researchers. In answering this question, graduate deans and other senior administrators play an important role. Even where an existing relationship between two institutions' faculty members and students or existing programs provide the foundations of a given graduate international collaboration, a senior administrator's role can range from administrative support and networking assistance to a shaping, driving force.

An institution's context and mission may strongly influence the forms of collaboration under consideration. Some forms, such as joint or dual degree programs, can involve large numbers of graduate students and faculty and require significant institutional commitment. Others, such as research collaborations and exchanges, typically involve fewer faculty members and students and comparatively little administrative burden. Regardless of scale, almost all international collaborations involving graduate students benefit from the input of senior administrators such as graduate deans, who typically provide guidance and assistance in coordinating campus units in support of a range of collaborative endeavors. On a daily basis, graduate deans must help decide about what is appropriate for advancing faculty research, improving the graduate student experience, and enhancing the institution's reputation.

Senior administrators and faculty may review together specific opportunities for international collaboration from multiple perspectives, including whether: partnering institutions are comparable in quality and/ or complementary in research strengths and resources; the programs are sustainable, or should be, prior to start-up; all provisions for student safety and support, including financial support, have been accounted for; and intellectual property concerns have been addressed. Additionally, graduate deans may help to decide where their institutions' policies can be flexible, and where they must remain firm, with respect to admissions, curricular requirements and structure. Different US institutions may answer these questions in different ways, depending on their educational and research missions and their long-term strategic plan.[20] Because the US graduate education system is so decentralized and provides so much institutional autonomy, the responsibilities of senior administrators such as graduate deans may therefore be greater to ensure that important questions are being adequately answered at all stages. Even in cases where there is a permanent office or administrator to oversee international collaborations, graduate deans can provide essential input on issues ranging from negotiating a memorandum of understanding (MOU) through periodic review. At the same time, current trends suggest that regional accreditors and policymakers may well subject international collaborations to greater scrutiny in the near future, and graduate deans must also be kept abreast of such trends and apprised of assessment outcomes and accountability efforts.

As researchers and senior administrators work together to identify appropriate partners and forms of collaboration, they must also consider larger questions pertaining to institutional mission, risk management, and global responsibility. Graduate deans, for example, may be called upon to ask questions on behalf of their institution such as:

- How large a role should internationalization play in our institution's mission?

- How can graduate education best support that mission: through the establishment of campuses abroad, structured joint or dual degree programs, certificate programs, or less formal research and educational exchanges?
- What are the tangible benefits of collaboration?
- Is all the talk about internationalization hype or fad? Do growth trends in the internationalization of graduate education signal a "gold rush" for revenue or a shift in direction that is necessary to support faculty and student success and generate valuable scholarly and scientific progress?
- How do institutions ensure that they are doing the right thing as responsible institutional world citizens, pursuing their own interests while at the same time acting responsibly to ensure equitable benefits to all partners?

The ability to answer these questions in a way that positions institutions and programs for the future requires strategic leadership. The major finding from this project (as reflected in the input of survey, focus group, and technical workshop participants) is that strategic leadership in support of advancing international collaboration is more important today than it has been in the past. As a result, many graduate deans are discovering the need for greater personal familiarity with the issues, characteristics, and structures common to graduate international collaborations. Given the speed and complexity of growth in international collaborations, researchers and senior administrators together must consider issues related to institutional mission, even as they concern themselves with getting the operational details right in any given collaborative program or exchange. The following chapters do not provide answers to the broad questions listed above, which will vary depending upon an institution's mission and context. Rather, they provide graduate deans and faculty with important background information, criteria they should consider when answering these questions for their own institutions, and policies and practices that many institutions with experience in the area of international collaboration have found successful. This information should be useful to all stakeholders as they seek to answer these broader questions in ways that best serve their students, faculty, and institutions.

II. What Do We Know About International Graduate Degree Collaborations? A Review of Recent Studies

International degree collaborations are common in Europe at the graduate level, and several recent studies have emerged to track characteristics, growth trends, and challenges faced in their implementation and acceptance.[21] Because the majority of international joint and dual degree collaborations among US universities include partnerships with European universities, these recent studies are valuable as background to US institutions seeking to enhance their collaborative strategies. The summaries below represent overall findings from six major recent studies.

The EUA Joint Master's Projects (2002, 2004)
With programs such as SOCRATES and Erasmus Mundus, the European Commission has exercised a major influence on the growth of international collaborations between and among European universities starting in the 1990s.[22] The European University Association (EUA) commissioned a study on joint master's degrees with support from the European Commission's SOCRATES program.[23] In 2002, the EUA surveyed the central university contact person for European higher education policy implementation or mobility programs. Thirty-one higher education systems are represented in the study.

The study found international joint master's degrees to be most common in business, engineering, law and management and more common in Europe at the master's and doctoral level than at the undergraduate level. It also found that degrees awarded jointly with international partner institutions tended to be more expensive than national degrees, and typically the result of inter-institutional rather than intergovernmental agreements. In addition to financial barriers to the growth of joint degrees, the chief European barriers identified in the study were legal: "The award of a single degree in the name of several institutions is still legally difficult [in Europe]. Joint degrees are therefore usually awarded either as double degrees (two separate national qualifications) or as one national qualification with reference to the fact that it results from a joint program."[24] The authors acknowledged concerns, however, about the data received due to "lack of a clear and generally agreed definition of the joint degree; and…very little information regarding the development of joint degrees at the central level" at European universities.[25]

In 2002-2004, the EUA launched the "EUA Joint Master's Project," a multi-year initiative that documented experiences, challenges, and lessons learned from 11 international collaborative programs involving over 100 universities.[26] The project report includes qualitative research findings on institutional issues and policy needs in areas such as quality assurance and degree recognition; student experience and mobility; and curriculum integration and sustainability.

The 2004 EUA report on this project identified the following **benefits** of joint degree programs to three groups:

- *Students*
  - o "A range of social, linguistic and inter-cultural management skills" demanded by academic and non-academic employers;
  - o Expanded networks of research contacts; and
  - o Greater exposure to a range of teaching and learning methods.
- *Institutions*
  - o Enhanced global competitiveness through greater mutual awareness of policies and practices in other European institutions and countries;
  - o The ability to gain from complementary institutional strengths;
  - o Enhanced international reputation and attractiveness to prospective students.
- *Europe*
  - o Facilitated adoption of comparable degree structures, degree recognition and credit transfer policies;
  - o Mutual benefit from shared quality assessment approaches;
  - o Greater student retention;
  - o Enhanced ability to attract overseas students;
  - o The establishment of Europe as a global exemplar in discussions of higher education quality.[27]

The EUA Joint Master's Project report also identified **barriers** to creating successful joint programs. The key barriers include the uneven recognition of joint degrees, quality assurance in collaborative programs, and funding. The EUA project noted the great variety of program models and structures that fall under the term "joint master's," and recommended that efforts be made to address serious difficulties in national, legal recognition of these degrees as well the need for common definitions.[28]

German Academic Exchange Service (DAAD) and the German Rector's Conference (HRK), (2006)

Subsequent European studies reported on a variety of joint and dual degrees by documenting national differences in the structuring of these degree programs. A 2006 study of "double, multiple, or joint degrees" commissioned by the German Academic Exchange Service (DAAD) and the German Rector's Conference (HRK) reported on results from a survey of 24 European countries selected from among the then 45 Bologna signatory countries.[29] Results from 303 surveys reflected predominantly German programs (40%), with programs from France, Belgium and Poland each representing about 8%. Most common partner university countries included France (40%), Germany (26%), Spain (17%), the UK (17%), Italy (16%), the Netherlands (11%), Sweden (8%), Poland (7%), and Belgium (7%); the US was identified as a partner by 6% of the respondents. In the study, master's degrees were most prevalent (66%), followed by bachelor's (21%), and bachelor's + master's combined (10%); only 2% of the survey responses reflected doctoral programs. The report noted, however, that while in Europe international collaborative degrees are more common at the graduate level, outside Europe, undergraduate collaborative programs are more common.

Findings in the DAAD/HRK study are reported separately for EU and non-EU participants, though they are not reported by degree level. More than two thirds of the programs described in the study were developed with external funds from either national or regional governments, the European Union or the Erasmus Mundus program; the majority of non-EU countries, however, reported receiving no external financial support.[30] The study found that double or dual degrees, in which students received two or more national diplomas (sometimes accompanied by a joint certification from all partners) comprised 71% of programs represented and were thus much more common than joint degrees, where diplomas were signed by both partner universities, which comprised 16%. A small number conferred only a single national degree, either accompanied by joint certification from partner universities or not.[31] Legislative restrictions, employability concerns, and administrative difficulties were the most frequently cited barriers to the establishment of joint degrees.

The DAAD/HRK study also found that:

- Fields in which collaborations were most common included: engineering and technology, management sciences, and social sciences.

- The average time spent abroad during the course of study was 12 months.

- Nearly two thirds of the programs were accredited by national or international bodies or both.

- Most programs were taught in the languages of both partnering institutions.

Institute of International Education (IIE)/Freie Universität Berlin (FUB), (2009)

The largest study on international degree collaborations to date was conducted by the Freie Universität Berlin (FUB) and the Institute of International Education (IIE), with funding from the EU-US Atlantis Program of the US Department of Education's Fund for the Improvement of Postsecondary Education (FIPSE) and the European Union Commission's Directorate General for Education and Culture. The 2009 report includes findings from a survey conducted between March and June, 2008.[32] Results represent 180 higher education institutions in the US and the European Union, including undergraduate and graduate programs (master's, doctoral, and other). The findings represent 805 EU country programs + 291 US programs (including 125 graduate programs).

The FUB/IIE study found double degrees to be much more common than joint degrees, "and European institutions are about twice as likely to offer at least one joint degree as US institutions and offer about twice as many such degrees as US institutions."[33] European partners are more common for both US and European institutions than partners from any other region. Top partner countries for EU institutions are the US (N=39); France (N=32); Spain (N=32); Germany (N=29); and the U.K (25); top partner countries for US respondents are: Germany (N=17), China (N=16), France (N=12), Mexico (N=10), South Korea (N=8), and Spain (N=8). Among the 805 programs reported by EU institutions, a much higher percentage (84%) were master's, while undergraduate and doctoral degrees each comprised 16%. Among the

291 programs reported by US institutions, 51% were undergraduate programs; 40% master's; 3% doctoral; and 6% fell into the *"other"* category].

Findings from the FUB/IIE report include:

• The most popular fields for international collaborative programs are: business, management, and engineering.
• US students are less likely to participate in collaborative degree programs than European students.
• The most common language of instruction is English (at 39%).
• A large majority indicate future plans to develop international joint and dual degree programs.

The biggest challenges identified in the study are securing institutional support for programs and securing funding.

Council of Graduate Schools, Member Surveys (2007, 2008)
The only recent studies that have focused exclusively on collaborative degree programs at the graduate level prior to the Graduate International Collaborations Project were the 2007 and 2008 CGS studies on the scope of international joint and dual degree programs at US universities. Those surveys were designed to better understand:

• The prevalence of formal joint and dual degree collaborations between US institutions and international partner institutions at the graduate level;
• The number of these programs by type and by discipline;
• The definitions used to describe these programs;
• The geographical distribution by country and region of the partner institutions; and
• Potential growth in this area as evident by reported plans to develop these degrees within the next two years.

In 2007, a survey was sent to 473 CGS member colleges and universities. CGS received 160 usable responses, with an overall response rate of 34%, although response rates among universities in the top 50 with respect to international student enrollment were twice as high (68%), and those in the top 25 and 10 categories of international student enrollment were higher yet.[34] Analysis of the 2007 survey results found that, overall, dual (or double) degrees were more prevalent than joint degrees, and that these formal degree collaborations were most prevalent at universities with higher concentrations of international students. Overall, 14% of all respondents reported having established dual degrees, while 10% reported having joint degrees: 11% of all respondents reported that they had established one or more dual (or double) degree programs only; 7% had initiated one or more joint degree programs only; and about 3% of all respondents reported having established one or more programs of both types of degrees.[35] Among the institutions in the largest 50 with respect to the size of international student enrollment, the preference for dual degrees was even more pronounced, with 41% of respondents in that category reporting the establishment of one or more dual degrees, and 12% reporting joint degrees; and among the largest 10 universities in international student enrollment, 44% reported dual degrees, while none reported joint degrees.[36] In 2007, 24% of US graduate schools among the respondents planned to establish new international collaborative degree programs in the next two years, and the percentage is even higher for the institutions with the largest number of international students [33% of the 10 largest and 39% of the 50 largest – which enroll 41% of all international graduate students in the US – indicated that they planned to establish new collaborative degree programs].[37]

In 2008, a survey was sent to 484 CGS member colleges and universities. CGS received 177 usable responses, with an overall response rate of 37%. The combined results of the 2007 and 2008 surveys shown in Table 1 indicate noticeable one-year growth in dual degrees across all groupings of institutions with respect to the size of international graduate student enrollment (overall, top 10, 25, and 50, and all others). Universities reported little growth in joint degrees at US institutions during that time. While strict comparisons are not possible due to the refinement of definitions in 2008, the 2007 and 2008 surveys suggested that the real growth degree in US international graduate collaborations was the dual degree. Over half of the institutions (51%) in the largest 50 with respect to international graduate student enrollment reported existing dual degree programs with international partner institutions, up from 41% in 2007. And in all of the three groupings in the top 50 and higher (top 10, top 25, and top 50), 60% or more institutions report having one or more existing international collaborative programs (dual degree, joint degree, or certificate program).[38]

Table 1. Percentage of US Graduate Schools That Have Established International Collaborative Graduate Programs With Non-US Universities, 2007 and 2008, by International Graduate Student Enrollment Size[39]

	Dual/Double Degree		Joint Degree		Certificate or Other		One or More Programs	
	2007	**2008**	2007	**2008**	2007	**2008**	2007	**2008**
Total	14%	**21%**	10%	**10%**	8%	**8%**	29%	**38%**

International Graduate Student Enrollment Size

Largest 10	44%	**60%**	0%	**10%**	11%	**20%**	56%	**60%**
Largest 25	38%	**48%**	10%	**14%**	5%	**19%**	48%	**62%**
Largest 50	41%	**51%**	12%	**14%**	12%	**17%**	56%	**60%**
All Others	7%	**14%**	9%	**9%**	7%	**7%**	22%	**33%**

Sources: 2007 CGS International Graduate Admissions Survey II: Final Applications and Initial Offers of Admission, August 2007; and 2008 CGS International Graduate Admissions Survey II: Final Applications and Initial Offers of Admission, August 2008.

Prevalence by Degree Level, Discipline, and Country/Region
Overall, as reported in 2008, collaborations with international partner institutions are by far more prevalent at the master's level than at the doctorate level in the fields of business and engineering, followed by the physical sciences and social sciences (see Table 2). At the doctoral level, collaborative degrees and certificate programs are most common in the physical sciences (at 19%), followed by engineering (at 11%) (see Table 2). At the master's level, collaborations are most common with partner institutions in Europe (36%), followed by China (18%), India (14%), South Korea (12%), Taiwan, Mexico and Singapore (each 8%) and the Middle East (5%). At the doctoral level, 17% of those reporting existing degree collaborations reported doctoral collaborations with Europe, 5% with South Korea, and 3% with China. No doctoral collaborations reported were by respondents with partner institutions in India, Taiwan, or the Middle East. At the doctoral level, 8% of the collaborations were reported with other regions, including Mexico, Turkey, and Russia.[40]

Table 2. Fields of Study in Which US Graduate Schools Offered Collaborative Degree, Certificate, or Other Programs With International Higher Education Institutions in 2008

	Master's	Doctoral
Business	39%	0%
Engineering	26%	11%
Physical Sciences	15%	19%
Social Sciences	15%	5%
Humanities & Arts	8%	8%
Life Sciences	8%	8%
Education	6%	0%
Other	9%	5%

Source: 2008 CGS International Graduate Admissions Survey II: Final Applications and Initial Offers of Admission, August 2008.

Note: Percentages are based on respondents who indicated that their institutions had established at least one dual/ double, joint, or other collaborative degree program with an international (non-US) college or university. Responses are not mutually exclusive (some graduate schools may have established more than one collaborative program.)

The Council of Graduate Schools' 2007 and 2008 international surveys identified joint and dual degrees, and dual degrees especially, as growth areas. While this growth was most pronounced at institutions with the highest concentrations of international students, it was not exclusive to those institutions. Internationalization of graduate education in the form of growth in joint and dual degrees as well as certificate and other non-degree collaborations is a phenomenon that is likely to continue to spread, as suggested by CGS member universities' reported plans to continue developing these degrees and to build on the successes and lessons learned from existing collaborations.

Summary

Table 3 compiles information about survey samples and key findings from all of the recent studies summarized above. Several general trends stand out. [We note that these studies yielded information about the scope of collaborative degree programs, but did not provide data that could support "best practice" guidelines.] While their samples represented different proportions of European nations engaging in intra-European and transatlantic degree collaborations, the most common fields for joint and dual degree programs, overall, are engineering, business, and the social sciences; collaborations at the master's level are more common than at the doctoral level; and dual (or double) degrees are more common in Europe, in part due to the legislative barriers to joint degrees in place at the time these studies were conducted. Though international collaborations are more common in Europe at the graduate level than at the undergraduate level, the reverse is true in the United States. Several studies noted that a lack of common definitions poses challenges for study and recognition of collaborative degrees, and that more research is needed on best practices in developing and sustaining international collaborative degree programs.

Table 3. Recent Studies on Joint and Dual Degree Programs, Scope and Key Findings

Study (Source)	Survey Population: respondents	Number of Programs Represented by Level (US/EU)	Number of Programs Reported by Degree Type (US/EU)	Key Findings
EUA (2002)	26 countries	Data on number of programs not collected.	Joint and Dual (all Europe)	* There is no common definition of "joint degree," which is used to describe a variety of program structures. * Collaborations are most common at doctoral and master's than undergraduate degree levels in Europe. * The absence of legislation does not prevent joint programs from being established, but may create problems for the awarding and recognition of degrees. In some countries, legislation hinders joint programs. * Double degree awards or single national qualification are most common (even when recognizing joint programs), due to legal difficulties surrounding the awarding of one degree in the name of two institutions.
EUA (2004)	73 institutions (11 joint master's programs) *supported and studied by EUA*	All Master's (0/11)	Joint (0/11)	* Most common at doctoral and master's than undergraduate degree levels.
DAAD/HRK (2006)	303 surveys from 24 European (Bologna signatory) countries	Bachelor (63) Master's (197) Bachelor + Master's (30) Doctoral (6)* * *Based on reported percentages.*	Dual (-/212) Joint (-/48)* * *Based on reported percentages. (Joint degrees more common among Erasmus Mundus participants.)*	* Most common in engineering, management, and social sciences. * Legislative restrictions, employability concerns, and administrative difficulties cited as barriers to joint degree. * More than 2/3 developed with external funds. * 64% accredited by national or international bodies or both. * Majority offer classes taught in both national language and language of partner institution country.
Freie/IIE (2008-09)	180 institutions (92 EU; 81 US; 7 non-EU European)	Undergraduate (149/126) Graduate/master's (115/548) Doctoral (10/127) Other (17/4)	Joint (38/50) Double (240/613) Planned (110/172)	*Double degrees much more common than joint degrees * In US, more common at undergraduate level. * Most common in business, management, and engineering. * US students less likely than European Students to participate. * Large majority in US & EU plan to develop more joint and dual degrees. * Biggest challenges for US: funding, sustainability, and institutional support.
CGS (2007)	160 institutions (US only)	*Data on number of programs not collected.*	*Data on number of programs not collected.*	* Most common in business, engineering, social sciences (master's); and in engineering and physical sciences (doctoral). * Partnerships most common with Europe, China, India, Korea, Middle East, Other (Mexico and Singapore).
CGS (2008)	177 institutions (US only)	*Data on number of programs not collected.*	*Data on number of programs not collected.*	* 31% of graduate schools planned to establish new international collaborative degree programs within 2 years (up from 24% in 2007). * 60% of the 10 institutions with largest international student enrollment had one or more such programs.

III. INTERNATIONAL COLLABORATIONS AT THE GRADUATE LEVEL: PERSPECTIVES OF GRADUATE DEANS AND GRADUATE RESEARCH FACULTY

Characteristics of US Joint and Dual Degree Programs

One of the major activities of the Graduate International Collaborations Project was to design and conduct a survey on formal international degree collaborations and non-degree research collaborations. This survey was developed to gain a deeper understanding of the motivations, challenges, requirements and structural characteristics of formal joint and dual degree collaborations. Eighty-four institutions were surveyed. The sample was composed of 47 institutions that had reported in prior 2007 and 2008 CGS surveys having existing programs and 37 that reported planning to develop programs within the next two years. Forty-three universities provided valid responses, resulting in an overall response rate of 51%. [For more information about survey methodology, see Appendix C.]

Definitions

In answering the survey questions, respondents were asked to consider the following common definitions (further refined from the definition used in the 2008 survey described in the previous chapter):

DUAL (OR DOUBLE) DEGREE PROGRAM: Students study at two or more institutions and upon completion of the program receive a separate diploma from each of the participating institutions.

JOINT DEGREE PROGRAM: Students study at two or more institutions and upon completion of the program receive a single diploma representing work completed at two or more institutions. (This diploma may be "double-sealed" or "double-badged," containing names and official seals of all institutions in the international collaborative arrangement, or may be issued by the home institution, with that institution's seal only and accompanied by a transcript, certificate, or other document indicating the student's participation in the international collaborative program.)

A. Institutional motivation

International graduate degree collaborations typically require support from multiple people and units within a university all of whom may have slightly different, though ideally complementary, motives for institutionalizing a partnership. The survey first asked: *What are the primary motivations for your institution to partner with an international institution on joint and dual degree programs?* The most frequently cited motivations in order of frequency (N=43) are listed below (respondents were asked to check all that apply):

- Attract international students (86%)
- Faculty Interest (84%)
- Administrative Interest in Internationalization the Institution (81%)
- Strengthen Academic Research Quality (79%)
- Increase Prestige (53%)
- Increase Revenue (47%)
- Employer/Industry Demand (35%)
- Other (12%)
- Provide International Experience for Students (5%)
- International Relations/Outreach (5%)

The institutional motivations reported reflect a full range of interests and missions supported by graduate school administration. Overall, the institutional motivations for international collaboration at the graduate level tend to cluster around issues related to research and program quality. Less than half of the respondents indicated that revenue or prestige was a primary motivation for partnering on joint or dual degrees; [data below from subsequent questions on challenges further suggest that joint and dual degrees in the sciences are not typically revenue generators]. Of course, the options are not mutually exclusive. One means of increasing revenue is by recruiting international students who may pay their own tuition, and the "faculty interest" that institutions seek to support may include strengthening the quality of academic research in their particular areas. Although the provision of an international experience for students (a common motivation reported for institutional support of undergraduate students) was not an option on the survey, two respondents (5%) provided this as an "other" institutional motivation for pursuing joint and dual degree partnerships. The survey also asked respondents to rank order these motivations in terms of importance. Interestingly, "Strengthen[ing] academic research quality" was listed as most important by the higher percentage (42%) of respondents, with 73% listing it as the first or second most important. "Attracting international students" and "Faculty interest" were ranked as most important by approximately a third of respondents (33% and 31%, respectively). An "Administrative interest in internationalizing the institution" was ranked as such by a quarter (24%).

B. Partner institution selection

Collaborative degree programs at the undergraduate level that focus on students' educational and cultural opportunities may be initiated in a variety of ways: at the instigation of senior university administrators, by the availability of resources that foreign governments have committed to promote exchange, and by faculty and international offices that support particular programs.

To gain a better understanding of how institutions perceived the primary reason for initiating such programs at the graduate level, the second question asked: *How are Partner Institutions typically chosen in your joint or dual degree programs?*

Figure 1. Partner Institution Selection (N = 43)

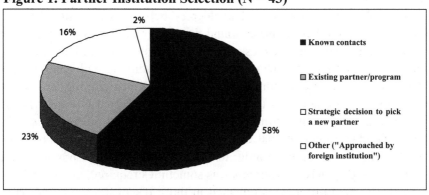

Source: CGS Graduate International Collaborations Survey, 2009

Notably, at a time when some US institutions are receiving multiple requests for formal collaboration from institutions abroad, only one institution indicated that its degree collaboration was initiated by a foreign institution. As with the responses provided for the question on institutional motivation, responses here are not necessarily mutually exclusive, and in fact collaborations may develop as a result of more than one of the above factors. (An existing partnership may, for example, result in, or emerge from, the deepening of faculty contacts that are required for a proposed program to succeed.) The distribution of responses, however, indicates that the primary criterion in selecting a partner institution for graduate international collaboration for the vast majority of respondents was an interest in expanding a relationship already in place, whether it was based on known faculty contacts or existing collaborative programs. Such criteria are often described as the "bottom up" (i.e., faculty- and program-initiated) rather than "top down" (e.g., senior administration-initiated) origins typical of graduate collaborations. Only 7 of the 43 respondents (16%) reporting that partner selection was a "strategic decision."

While graduate deans describe themselves as providing leadership in various aspects of joint and dual degree development, as discussed later in this chapter, partner selection at the graduate level usually originates not from contacts between senior administrators (or governments) but between faculty researchers. All collaborations, however, require careful assessment of whether the partnering institutions are compatible and of comparable quality to merit a formal, degree partnership, as opposed to a more informal research exchange involving graduate students.

C. Field distribution

As noted in Chapter Two, earlier CGS survey research on the scope and field distribution of joint and dual degrees between US institutions and institutions from other countries found that the greatest proportion of such collaborations were in business and engineering, followed by physical and social sciences, with less than 10% of institutions with international master's or doctoral collaborations reporting such degree programs in the humanities or life sciences (see above, Table 2). Prior CGS surveys did not request data on the number of programs. In this more recent survey for the Graduate International Collaborations Project, universities reported on 168 programs overall. In order to interpret subsequent responses where mental averaging across programs was sometimes required, and to account for possible field differences reflected in those responses, we asked: *How many collaborative degree programs of each type [does your institution] have with an international partner institution?* CGS later followed up with a second, short questionnaire to respondents that requested additional data on those collaborative degree programs reported by degree level (doctoral versus master's). The distribution of programs is indicated in Table 4. [The response rate for the follow up survey was 100%].

Table 4. Numbers of Programs by Field and Level (N = 43 institutions responding on 168 programs)

	Business	Engineering	Other Research Degree	Other non-Research (Professional) Degree	*Total # of Programs*
Joint Master's Degrees	18	8	4	2	32
Dual Master's Degrees	48	32	27	2	109
Joint Doctoral Degrees	0	3	4	0	7
Dual Doctoral Degrees	2	9	8	1	20
TOTAL	*68*	*52*	*43*	*5*	N=168

Source: CGS Graduate International Collaborations Survey, 2009

Overall, approximately a third (31%) of the 168 programs are in engineering; 40% are in business; and another quarter (26%) are in "other research" disciplines.[41] Aside from business, where US international graduate degree collaborations are most prevalent, only four master's and one doctoral program were in non-research (professional) fields. Among the "other research degrees" represented in the survey findings, eight are reported as joint degrees and 35 are reported as dual degrees. [42] The dual master's was the most common type of collaborative degree, with 109 programs reported by survey respondents.

D. Accreditation and approval

One of the most frequently cited challenges identified in the focus group was accreditation, which is discussed in greater detail in the next section. In the focus group, as in prior CGS member discussions in summer workshop and annual meeting sessions, it was suggested that joint degrees were subject to much greater scrutiny than dual degrees in these processes. The survey therefore asked: *Who has been involved in accreditation or external approval?*

Table 5. Accreditation and Approval Required by Degree Type (N=43)

	Joint Degrees	Dual Degrees
Regional accreditors	26%	26%
State board(s)	9%	14%
International accrediting bodies	7%	2%
Professional accrediting bodies	19%	12%
Other	9%	5%
None (N/A)	9%	33%

Source: CGS Graduate International Collaborations Survey, 2009

Equal percentages of respondents indicated that regional accreditors were involved in both joint and dual degrees. While this parity might suggest that the two types of degrees require equal degrees of external approval, the overall difference between the percentage who reported no approval required for joint degrees (less than 10%) and those who reported this for dual degrees (one third of respondents) confirm anecdotal reports that the administrative burden for joint degrees is much higher. This may contribute to the higher growth rates of joint degrees. Specific issues that may arise in accreditation approval and review, such as double credit concerns, institutional comparability, and transfer credit, are discussed in greater detail below.

Accreditation, approval, and national recognition have been documented to be among the main challenges facing European institutions as they develop joint or dual degree programs with international partners. In the US, while national legislative barriers to such programs are not an issue, regional accreditation and approval by other bodies (such as state boards and professional bodies) must be considered as institutions seek to develop successful programs and choose between different structural possibilities.

E. Sources of funding
Among the greatest challenges in developing and sustaining international degree collaborations identified in our focus group and in this survey is funding. We asked institutions to *describe the source of funding for joint*

and/or dual degree programs currently in place or being planned? Results are shown in Figure 2 below.

Figure 2. Sources of Funding for Joint and/or Dual Degree Programs (n=43)

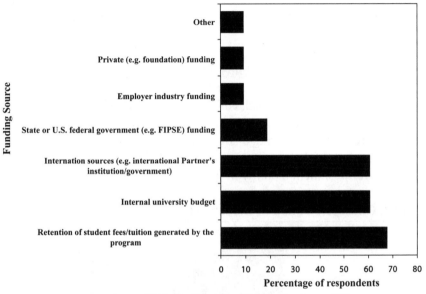

Source: CGS Graduate International Collaborations Survey, 2009

Overall, the biggest source of funding for international collaborative degrees for a typical US institution was the retention of student fees/tuition generated by the program, followed by internal university budget funds and international sources. As shown in Figure 2, fewer than a fifth of respondents reported external support from state or US federal government sources. [By contrast, recall that over two-thirds of the 303 European programs included in the DAAD/HRK study discussed in Chapter Two reported receiving external government support.] While we recognized that a question requiring respondents to mentally average different programs may pose difficulty, we also asked respondents to estimate the percentage of funding from each source for joint and/or dual degrees at their institution. Notably, 23% reported that the retention of student fees provided 100% of program funding, and 62% estimated that this source provided 50% or more of program funding. By comparison, the next most cited sources, "Internal university budget" and "International sources," were reported as providing 100% of funding by only 4% and 9% of respondents, respectively, and as providing 50% or more by less than a quarter (24%) and less than half (45%), respectively. There are some limitations to these percentage estimates, and there are likely to be differences by discipline that are masked by the aggregated field data and the inclusion of doctoral and master's degrees. The results, however, strongly suggest that the majority of joint and dual degree programs are (and/or should be) self-funded rather than reliant upon external sources of funding.

F. Student and faculty mobility

The challenges of student mobility in graduate international programs are well documented. As discussed in the introductory chapter, domestic students tend to travel less in such collaborations than students from abroad, resulting in asymmetries that can sometimes be frustrating to program champions from both partnering institutions. This asymmetry was confirmed by responses to the following survey question: *Which of the following best describes overall student mobility in your programs?*

Figure 3. Characterization of Student Mobility.

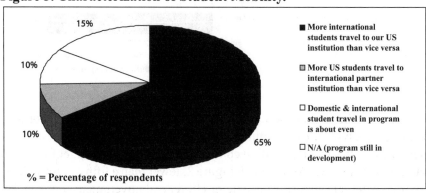

Source: CGS Graduate International Collaborations Survey, 2009

The pattern illustrated in Figure 3, with 65% of respondents reporting that more international students travel to the US institution than vice versa (versus only 10% reporting that more US students travel to partner institutions or that the proportions are about even) suggests a huge challenge for US institutions seeking to build international partnerships. This pattern also suggests a number of subsidiary challenges for preparing students to succeed in a global research community. Parity in numbers of students traveling to each partner institution is often a metric of success defined for the program at the outset. This metric may be built into an MOU, and it may be one of the motivating principles behind enthusiasm for a formal, degree partnership. More information is needed to better understand why the asymmetry exists. Possible reasons include: student funding; language preparation; degree recognition and employability; and concerns, especially at the doctoral level, about supervision and timely progress. Institutions seeking to develop international collaborations should be cognizant of the student mobility challenges and make provisions, where appropriate, to incentivize the participation of domestic students.

Focus group discussions described in the next section identified the importance of faculty travel for ensuring a smooth administrative start to collaborative degree programs. In the survey, we were curious to learn how prevalent faculty travel was for research purposes (as opposed to administrative purposes) in these collaborations. We therefore asked, *Do your joint or dual degree programs involve faculty travel between institutions for the purpose of teaching and/or research?*

Figure 4. Characterization of US Program Faculty Mobility (N = 43).

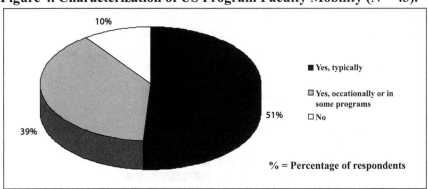

Source: CGS Graduate International Collaborations Survey, 2009

As Figure 4 shows, about half of respondents indicated that faculty travel in their joint or dual degree programs for teaching and research purposes, apart from purely administrative purposes. The relatively high levels of faculty travel may suggest that a lack of faculty support for student travel in such collaborations may be less of a disincentive to US student travel in international collaborative programs than other factors (such as language ability and financial issues). Faculty travel can help to address some of typical concerns when research students travel abroad such as ensuring that there are mechanisms for adequate student supervision and advising on theses or dissertations.

G. Challenges by degree type

International degree collaborations present challenges. Some of these must be overcome in any degree collaboration between two institutions, some are unique to international collaborations but common to both joint and dual degrees, and some are relatively specific to the particular structure of degree collaboration (e.g., joint vs. dual). Figures 5 and 6 show the extent to which various factors were perceived as "very challenging" or "somewhat challenging" in setting up dual degrees and joint degrees, respectively. Overall, the idea that joint ideas pose greater administrative challenges than dual degrees, suggested by growth patterns reported in prior CGS surveys (discussed above in Chapter Two), is given further support here. Eleven factors were reported by 50% or more respondents with international joint degrees as very or somewhat challenging (Figure 6), as compared to only six factors reported by 50% or more among those with dual degrees (Figure 5). [Note that the numbers of institutions reporting on the various degree structures differ: N=23 institutions responding on dual degree programs; N=12 institutions responding on joint degrees.]

Figure 5. Extent to Which Factors Were "Very/Somewhat Challenging" in Setting up Dual Degree Programs (n=23)

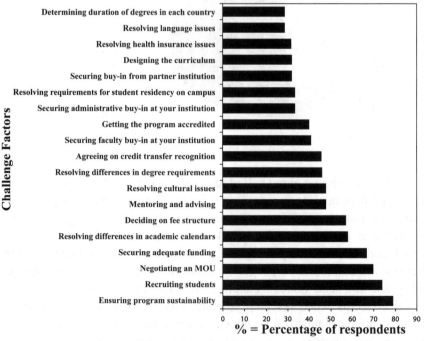

Source: CGS Graduate International Collaborations Survey, 2009

Figure 6. Extent to Which Factors Were "Very" or "Somewhat Challenging" in Setting up Joint Degree Programs (n=12)

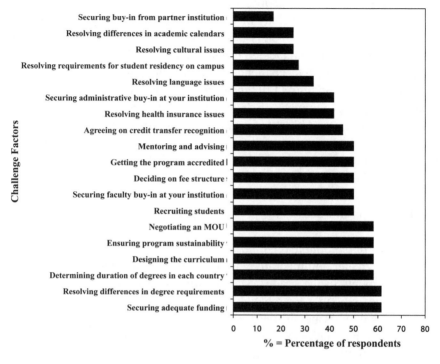

Source: CGS Graduate International Collaborations Survey, 2009

Results shown in Figures 5 and 6 suggest the factors that pose **common challenges** across the two degree types (identified by 50% or more respondents in both questions) include:

- ensuring program sustainability,
- securing adequate funding,
- recruiting students,
- negotiating an MOU, and
- deciding on fee structure.

Factors that appear to pose **greater challenges for joint degrees** than for dual degrees include: determining the duration of degrees in each country, designing the curriculum, and resolving differences in degree requirements (which, along with securing adequate funding, was the number-one challenge reported for joint degrees). Factors that appear to pose **greater challenges for dual degrees** include: resolving differences in academic calendars and resolving cultural issues. (Many of these challenges are discussed in detail in the section below, "Common Issues and Success Strategies in Developing Sustainable Joint and Dual Degree Programs.")

Three of the top five challenges common to joint and dual degrees relate to issues of funding. Differences between the availability of external support for the development of such programs in Europe and the scarcity of such support in the US may prove to be a significant factor in the long-term sustainability of some of these US collaborations with international partners. Funding issues were also identified, however, in the European studies and the IIE/FUB study discussed above in Chapter Two, suggesting that even where external start-up funds are available, funding for long-term sustainability is an issue.

H. Concerns about double credit for a single body of work
Despite the greater administrative burden that joint degrees pose, there are strong arguments in the graduate community for the value of a true joint degree, especially in research fields where a thesis is required. One of the least resolved issues in the acceptance of dual degrees as a structure for graduate international collaboration is the argument that the dual degree potentially rewards students with double credit for a single body of work. When asked, *Were concerns about students receiving "double credit" for a single body of work (e.g., thesis or coursework) an issue in the implementation of your international collaborative degree programs?*, responses were almost equally divided: 51% said that this was a concern, and 49% reported that this was not a concern. Explanations and solutions ranged widely, including: firm institutional decisions "not to explore dual degrees" ("we will only use single-diploma model") to "[asking] students to sign a form acknowledging that they would be receiving dual degrees for a single curriculum and dissertation."

One university reported that its "Graduate Council has established a policy that a single research project can be used to earn only one degree," thereby discouraging dual degrees as an appropriate structure for graduate research collaborations. Several universities noted that existing policies for intra-university interdisciplinary work or institutional collaborations between their own institutions and other domestic institutions have helped to guide university policy on this issue. Existing policies may accommodate or prevent approval of dual degrees as appropriate structures for graduate degree collaborations. One respondent replied that while the existing Graduate College policy was upheld to address course credit transfer, that policy would not allow theses or dissertations completed elsewhere to be counted towards a degree at that institution. Another institution resolved the double credit issue differently by distinguishing between coursework and thesis requirements and turned to existing policies regarding interdisciplinary research degrees to accommodate a dual degree structure: "Having only [one] thesis for 2 degrees continues to be an issue, but has been partially resolved by using an existing internal process for interdisciplinary degree programs as a model for dual degrees." One respondent discussed the importance of the work being deemed appropriate to doctoral-level research as evaluated by experts "not associated with either institution" and meeting requirements of each institutions resolving the issue.

There is no consensus on how institutions should address concerns about the potential for double degrees to confer double credit for a single body of work. Graduate deans, graduate councils, and graduate colleges use a variety of policies depending upon whether they perceive the priority issues to be related to the nature of a doctoral degree and dissertation, the protection of institutional identity, or the integrity of individual students in appropriately identifying their graduate dual degree credentials to prospective employers. The rich variety of responses to the survey's question about this issue points toward the important role that graduate schools and strategic institutional leaders play in the development of international collaborations.

I. The role of the graduate dean and graduate school in overcoming challenges
Graduate deans and graduate schools describe themselves as providing "technical support," "follow up" and sources of institutional "good will." In addition, graduate deans indicate that they support collaborations by providing templates, administrative resources, and sustainability strategies. As expressed in one response, "So many times some of these proposals could have been derailed by a well-meaning office on campus and the graduate dean would have to call directly and resolve the issue so that the faculty could move forward." Other survey responses indicate that international collaborations are evolving from mainly faculty-instigated programs to strategic institutional partnerships where faculty and graduate school leaders are working in collaboration. When asked how universities had overcome some of the main challenges they faced, several open-ended responses indicate that what once began on their campuses as faculty-directed efforts in which the graduate

school administration served a primarily supportive role have developed into more strategic institutional partnerships in which graduate deans and faculty work together; the latter model has helped to address some of the sustainability, funding, and administrative start-up issues. One response captures this:

> Our programs have been in place for several years. Initially, it was a matter of identifying faculty linkages with colleagues overseas and then matching curricula for the degree program. These partnerships were initially based on personalism. We have worked to involve new faculty in the process through orientation, information at the opening convocation and by bringing highly qualified students from abroad to study on our campus. Exposure to exceptional students in graduate courses does a lot to convince faculty of their potential as researchers and industry leaders. Faculty begin to gravitate toward and encourage the international exchange programs.

Multiple responses also describe the importance of identifying models that can be used and replicated for future collaborative programs. While faculty interest and collaboration provide the foundation for success in most international graduate research programs, graduate schools often play a vital role in overseeing the coordination of units that all need to be in communication in the development and sustainability of successful programs. As described in several open-ended responses to the question about strategies for overcoming typical challenges, multiple stakeholders may include: senior graduate administrators (graduate deans and senior research administrators), division or college deans, institutional CFO's, departments, governance bodies and faculty, and the office of international education, not to mention relevant stakeholders from the partner institution.

Common Issues and Success Strategies in Developing Sustainable Joint and Dual Degree Programs

A key element of the Graduate International Collaborations project was a focus group that explored the experiences of graduate deans who had played a role in creating, implementing, or maintaining collaborations. The focus group was designed to gather first-hand accounts of the challenges involved in overseeing joint and dual degree programs, although CGS also collected information about other, less formal collaborations, such as research exchanges. The discussion format presented a number of advantages: it allowed participants to give specific reasons behind decisions made by their universities regarding joint and dual degree programs, to provide context for their observations, and to explain the dynamic relationship between the various institutional and regional factors that affect these degree collaborations. Focused principally on the US context, the focus group included ten graduate deans at US institutions and one graduate dean at a Canadian university. For a discussion of the focus group methodology, please see Appendix C.

The protocol for the focus group included questions covering the following general topics, which are discussed in detail in the following sections:

- The role of the graduate dean in facilitating collaborations
- Benefits of collaboration
- Forces behind joint and dual degree programs
- Advantages/disadvantages of joint versus dual degrees
- Factors promoting program success
- Challenges encountered, and strategies for overcoming them
- Program sustainability
- Areas where future research and coordinated effort are needed

Why pursue a joint or dual degree program?

Forces driving international curricular degree collaborations
As presented in the introduction, a number of recent studies have surveyed the motivations behind international collaborations and outlined several important institutional drivers.[43] Many of the motivations cited in the focus group fell within general categories of motivation, such as the desire to expand curricular options or to increase the enrollment of foreign students. At the same time, the focus group also uncovered some of the particular reasons motivating international joint and dual degree programs at the graduate level. More specifically, respondents placed the greatest amount of importance on expanding and enhancing research capabilities and resources, a motive explored in greater depth in the upcoming section ("Selecting a Partner").

When asked a general, open-ended question about the forces motivating universities, programs, or departments to pursue international degree collaborations, a number of participants divided drivers into the categories of "bottom up" (faculty-driven) and "top-down" (administration-driven). In describing "top-down" drivers, participants identified a range of university leaders as key actors, including the President or Chancellor, Provost, the Director of the International Center, and the Graduate Dean. An additional administrative driver was a comprehensive institutional agenda or strategic plan to foster internationalization or degree collaboration. International institutional partners were also cited as driving forces, but only in cases where there was reciprocal motivation from faculty and administrators at the home institution.

It is important to emphasize, however, that participants in the focus group tended to describe these forces as working simultaneously. Among the eleven participants, seven listed *both* faculty and administrators as initiators of collaborations, and several presented the interests of different stakeholders as overlapping or shared. As one dean put it,

> At [my university,] there is a bottom-up motivation, but there is also a broader [institutional] philosophy with multiple dimensions. Collaboration is seen as a public good. It also satisfies strategic concerns by adding value to degrees. It supports research between faculty and different institutions. Collaboration is also pragmatic for students who want training from different institutions. It also fits the agenda for creating formal international links.

Of course, this comment describes an institution where there is generalized support for international collaborations. At some institutions, a greater degree of motivation may come from faculty, and in these cases, the graduate dean may need to work more actively to harmonize the priorities of faculty and administration.

Benefits of international collaboration
Participants cited four main areas in which international collaborations provide benefits to institutions and suggested that multiple groups benefited in some areas.

Table 6. Benefits of International Collaborations for Graduate Students, Faculty, and Institutions

What is the benefit?	Who benefits?	How?
Development of research activities	Students	More training and research opportunities.
	Faculty	Broader research networks and access to new knowledge, skills, and resources.
	Institutions	Broadened research capacities: a collaboration can "bring together two sets of expertise."
Increases in student mobility	Students	Cultural perspective and skills required for international research projects.
	Institutions	Ability to attract international students and "go global at home."
Support for Institutional Plans	Institutions	Adaptation to international mission and a "new global model in graduate education."
		Support for strategic efforts to develop a certain area of academic study and research.
		Support for efforts to develop ties with certain regions and countries.
Financial benefits	Institutions	Increase in revenues in cases where a degree program is profitable.
		Ability to meet new demands for international degrees or degrees with "added value."

Source: CGS Focus Group on International Joint and Dual Degrees, 2008

The role of the graduate dean

The focus group shed light on the variety of roles played by graduate deans in facilitating joint and dual degree programs and on the range of forces that shape their work. When asked to describe their roles in creating or managing international partnerships, for example, participants described their activities in relation to a number of different institutional regulatory bodies: the Graduate Council, the Provost's Office, and Executive Committees within the Dean's Office or Graduate School, some or all of which were involved in the process of approving new degree programs. As explained in a later section, "The Challenges of Implementation," the rules of these various bodies, along with state laws, may also shape a graduate dean's choice to pursue a joint versus a dual degree program.

As the university leaders who typically provide an institution-wide perspective on all graduate programs, graduate deans may consider the advantages of partnering with a foreign institution in the context of the university's long-term plans and priorities. This role can be more difficult in the relatively unfamiliar territory of international partnerships. When describing their approaches to collaboration, participants generally expressed a need for openness balanced by careful attention to the unique needs of the institution. Focus group comments suggested that research on a potential partner may often lead to promising possibilities. For example, one dean reported that he had been approached by an institution that had already approved a collaboration with his university before seeking its approval and input. In spite of his initial skepticism, he found that sharing the proposal was worthwhile because this led to significant faculty interest. Another dean described her position as one of selective encouragement of new possibilities: "We would be open to [programs] that emerge, but we are not going to actively encourage [programs] that fall outside of our areas of focus." Different institutional contexts may allow for various degrees of flexibility about the number and kinds of collaborations that can be pursued and encouraged.

A number of the graduate deans in the focus group also reported that they played a role in reconciling the commitments of their institutions to domestic students with the plan to internationalize their campuses. This role was more difficult for deans at state institutions with policies that restricted many services and funds to in-state students or to programs designed specifically to serve in-state students. While some deans reported that the goals of internationalization and service to domestic students were sometimes presented as conflicting goals in state-level discussions of higher education policies affecting internationalization, they also noted that international collaborations may support, rather than compete with, broader institutional missions that benefit all students. As the table above shows, ("support for institutional plans,") some deans may strategically choose collaborations that broaden resources in those academic fields the university is seeking to develop.

The Challenges of Start-Up

Selecting a partner
The process of gathering information about international partners is a time-consuming but necessary step in the process of creating (or choosing not to

create) a collaborative degree program. Sometimes institutions will already have well-established relationships with their potential partners when the degree program is first proposed; at other times, they must conduct extensive research on an institution about which they have very little information and no prior relationship.

When asked about the process of selecting and approving partners, focus group participants gave particular attention to strategies used in cases where the proposed collaboration had been initiated by faculty members. A number of the deans described the process by which faculty at their institutions submit to their offices Memoranda of Understanding (MOU). MOUs are designed to ensure that both partnering institutions meet certain criteria before they invest the time and resources needed to go forward. Subsequent activities, such as conducting additional research on a potential partner's affiliations and credentials, are typically necessary before an actual partnership is approved. Some participants indicated that they also use less official documents and procedures to shape the process, including guidelines for faculty members who propose international degree programs. Such guidelines, they noted, can help faculty to better understand the institutional procedures involved in creating a new degree program and limit the number of proposals that are not consistent with broader university standards and goals. Several deans at large research institutions reported that well-established procedures introduced at an early stage help them to save the time of both faculty and administrators involved in the process.

Participants gave less attention to "top down" approaches to the selection process. A number of deans indicated that their role was to guide selection by providing a framework through which faculty-driven collaborations could be chosen. They reported a range of criteria used at their institutions for selecting and approving a partner:

- Evidence of research cooperation between the involved institutions
- Evidence of faculty interest
- The overall quality of the partner institution and its faculty
- The partner's experience creating international collaborative programs
- Satisfaction of strategic interests
- Availability of adequate funding
- Certainty about the partner's investments of time and funding

Focus group participants gave special emphasis to the importance of ensuring the presence and quality of collaborative research projects between their universities and potential partners. A number of participants emphasized two-directional research relationships: some of the phrases used to characterize such relationships included "exchanges in both directions," "mutual collaboration," "research cooperation," and "mutually beneficial research." These responses suggest that many deans are looking for an institutional relationship that is "collaborative" in the real sense of the term, involving the commitments, resources, and strengths of both universities involved. Deans also cited such a relationship as a key criterion for deciding whether or not to scale up an existing exchange program or research collaboration. For example, one dean explained that research collaborations may arise out of more personal or accidental relationships among faculty, as when faculty who are alumni of the same institution maintain or create ongoing research relationships. In these cases, it is important to ensure that the collaboration makes sense not only for the researchers, but for their institutions as well.

Participants also stressed the importance of ensuring faculty interest. Some suggested that the success of a program can depend on the presence of faculty willing to invest time and energy in creating and developing it. At the same time, faculty interest and motivation can be a byproduct of other factors. For example, one dean posited a relationship between the quality of the partner institution and the motivation of his own institutions' faculty to make the program a success: if the program is well-sustained on the partner's end, and if the faculty from the partner institution make other significant contributions to the collaboration, then faculty at the home institution are more likely to sustain an interest in the program. A program that demands an unequal amount of time and energy from the faculty at the home institution may lead to the overtaxing of faculty and dwindling interest in the collaboration. These comments suggest that even when faculty initiate the selection of a partner institution, it may be important to ensure that this interest can be sufficiently sustained.

The Challenges of Implementation

Determining structure: the pros and cons of "dual" vs. "joint" structures
The benefits of a joint versus a dual degree program depend heavily on restrictions imposed by national and state laws and institutional guidelines that are often influenced by these regulations. As reported in the survey

results, joint degrees tend to require layers of approval and accreditation that dual degrees do not, and the focus group confirmed this result: the majority of deans stated that dual degrees were preferred at their institutions because this degree type requires significantly fewer administrative burdens than joint degrees. Of the five deans who addressed this question, only one indicated that neither type of degree posed more administrative barriers than the other, while the other four indicated that dual degrees were easier to implement. One dean indicated that the administrative efficiency associated with dual degrees is directly tied to the fact that there is a longer "tradition" of degrees of this type. This observation raised an important question: to what extent are dual degrees preferred at US institutions because they are more familiar and accepted, and to what extent do they present other, substantive advantages over joint degrees?

According to participants, one reason that dual degrees are preferred is that they present certain financial advantages. More specifically, dual degrees may offer greater financial flexibility, as they may be easier to dissolve when shifts occur in core faculty or student interest. In a dual program, an institution does not need to maintain a reciprocal commitment to the other institution and its students. In the case of joint degrees, on the other hand, institutions may need to make a strong early commitment to work with the partner institution to maintain a "pipeline" of students. For this reason joints may require closer attention to sustainability.

A second reason given in the focus group for preferring dual degrees is that graduates earning this type of degree may be more employable. There is also some secondary material suggesting that the value of each separate degree may be more portable, or easily recognized in the country of the awarding institution.[44] One dean supported this idea with anecdotal evidence of students who had found it easier to find jobs once they returned to their own countries.

As discussed previously, however, dual degrees also raise questions about whether they confer "double" recognition for what amounts to a single body of work. The focus group presented a range of different views on this issue. While one dean stated that he found dual degrees to exaggerate a student's accomplishments, he also expressed hope that potential employers would not recognize dual degrees as two separate degrees. Complicating this view, another dean presented the perspective that a dual degree does, in fact, represent greater value than a joint degree since it requires a greater volume of student work and the satisfaction of different sets of requirements. The next section outlines some of the concrete issues that focus group participants considered when considering the two degree structures.

Structuring coursework and credit

Deciding how to give credit for work completed at a foreign institution is one of the first challenges that universities face when designing the structure of a collaborative degree program. In the focus group, two basic strategies emerged for dealing with the task of counting credits: 1) creating, in conversation with a partner university, a system of equivalence; 2) using the pre-existing transfer credit policy at one's home institution to credit coursework completed at a partner university (to cite the example offered by one dean, counting no more than one-half of the graded course hours). The viability of the second option will vary, however, according to each institution's policies about transfer credits. For example, one dean noted that if the hours are counted at a different institution, then they cannot be counted at his home institution. Some deans raised the question of whether a cap should be placed on double-counting, the practice at some institutions.

As reported in the survey, theses and dissertations raise special questions about conferring credit.[45] The focus group allowed us to explore some of the specific approaches and rationales used for crediting a capstone project and to identify two basic models:

1. **The thesis or dissertation is viewed as a single piece of work and represents the same value/amount of work as a thesis completed at a single institution.** According to this model, additional administrative requirements related to completing the thesis at two different institutions do not augment the amount of work represented by the document or the value of the culminating degree. For example, a dean describing this model indicated that the requirement of producing the thesis in two different languages does <u>not</u> imply that the document represents two separate bodies of work or a more valuable body of work.

2. **The thesis or dissertation is viewed as a single piece of work, but one that represents more value than a thesis completed at a single institution.** In this case, a student must serve twice as many advisors, or in some cases, two committees that hold separate thesis defenses, requirements that are considered to add value to the document. As one dean put it, referring to a master's degree program in which students are assigned

two faculty advisors from each institution, "Essentially, [students] do the work of two theses, even if there is a joint committee." The same dean indicated that this view of the thesis also held for dissertations completed in an international doctoral degree program.

It is important to emphasize that these models do not correspond to established criteria for program or research content. The focus group discussion shed light on the fact that university administrators are called on to interpret the value of the thesis and to make these interpretations in relation to a wide variety of factors. Is the student required to satisfy a significant number of additional institutional requirements at the partner institution? Produce work that is more complex because it involves the integration of different research experiences, (i.e. work completed within different laboratories, or two sets of fieldwork)? Satisfy the requirements of a larger number of total advisors (more than the number required in a non-collaborative degree program at the home institution)? Successfully defend the degree at both of the partnering institutions? Deans may consider these and other questions when deciding how the thesis should be understood at their own institutions.

Addressing cultural factors in the training of international students
When joint and dual degree programs require the mobility of students and faculty, universities often must anticipate the cultural differences that may arise in the context of research, education, and mentoring. Focus group participants directly raised this issue and gave specific attention to the importance of cultural sensitivity among mentors of international students. For example, one participant in the focus group cited the importance of preparing faculty mentors to understand different cultural expectations about class attendance, noting that attendance may be optional at European universities, while at his own university, it is a requirement. Mentors must be prepared to help students understand these differences.

A second, related topic that emerged in the discussion was research ethics training in the context of international collaboration. Secondary research on this topic confirms that many institutions are concerned about the way cultural differences can lead to confusion about responsible research practice. Three of the twelve deans in the focus group independently raised this issue as one of significant concern at their institutions: one dean stated that different standards in human subjects research were a challenge for creating partnerships between programs; a second dean stated that cultural differences raise larger questions about the definition of scholarship and research; and two of the three cited cases where cultural differences had led to cases of plagiarism at their universities. The focus group's observations about RCR and mentoring issues suggest that university leaders could benefit from more information about how best to prepare faculty and students for the specific cultural challenges they may face within various collaborative programs.

A number of deans indicated that a need existed for more collaboration among American and Canadian universities in negotiating difficult cultural differences that arise with partners outside of their home countries. More general information is needed about avoiding cultural conflicts, including "best practices" research that would help universities minimize the possibility of serious cultural misunderstandings.

Administrative challenges

In addition to the challenges presented above, focus group participants noted a number of practical issues related to the mobility of students. The following challenges were specifically mentioned:

- Factoring in the amount of time and fees required to process papers and visas required for student travel
- Encouraging research advisors to support student travel
- Understanding the way visa status affects the status of students within the institution
- Ensuring that collaborative programs do not excessively affect times-to-degree
- Ensuring that students are not overcharged for tuition when they are not present at the billing institution
- Providing support to the administrators who may be burdened with complex and ongoing paperwork issues related to student mobility

A more general issue raised in this context, one that relates to all of the above, concerns the way in which partner universities approve the mobility of students and formalize their status at each university. This process can pose additional challenges if there is uncertainty about the authority and responsibility of administrators at the partner institutions. As one dean suggested, it can be helpful to clarify responsibilities of key leaders, especially in cases where the job titles and responsibilities of leaders at the partner institutions are not parallel.

Evaluating Programs

Program assessment and review

In addition to asking the focus group to reflect on their criteria for selecting good partners, the facilitators asked participants to discuss their institutions' measures for evaluating a program's success. Naturally, many areas of program review corresponded with the benefits reported both here and in the survey report: a program's success was measured by its ability to deliver the potential benefits outlined by the institution developing it. The following is a random-order list of short and long-term metrics for program success provided by focus group participants:

1. **Enrollment numbers**. As one dean put it, "Are people voting with their feet?" While it may take years for a program to attract the number of applicants needed to ensure long-term sustainability, enrollment can be used as one of the clearest signs that a program is working.

2. **An international perspective**. In line with the start-up goals mentioned earlier, one measure of success is that participating students are developing an international perspective on relevant research topics. One dean compared the value of crossing national educational borders to the value of participating in interdisciplinary programs or diverse university communities. The opportunity to cross traditional or social borders—between disciplines, national cultures and social backgrounds—has the potential to broaden students' views.

3. **Development of institutional reputation**. While it is difficult to measure the enhancement of institutional reputation, focus group participants cited the following as possible metrics: the number of international partnerships that the university can claim to hold, the strategic importance of partnerships held in a particular region of the world, the capacity of a university to project an international image to outside visitors, and the ability of students to demonstrate an international perspective on research-related topics.

4. **Development of program reputation**. One dean cited the example of a master's degree program that allowed her institution to draw the enrollment necessary to sustain a PhD program, and, eventually, to build an independent PhD program.

5. **Development of the research collaboration**. The value of a deeper research collaboration can be measured both materially, through access to new resources or equipment not available at the home institution, as well as through the output of scholars participating on international projects.

It is important to note that the successes of international collaborations may be measured differently from those of domestic collaborations, which are often less complex. One dean indicated that because of the experimental nature of some degree programs, universities may choose to set conservative goals with respect to numbers of graduating students and program finances. For information to consider when developing processes of program review, see Appendix A, *An MOU Checklist for International Collaborations.*

Sustainability issues
While revenue may be an important factor in a dean's decision to support or continue a joint or dual degree program, economic rewards may shift over the life of a degree program. For example, one dean reported that profit may be considered a priority consideration at the outset, but become less important as the program gains strength and offers other significant advantages.

In spite of such fluctuations, most universities would not pursue a collaborative degree program unless there is evidence that the program can be maintained for a minimum number of years. Further discussion in the focus group indicated that a range of different approaches may be taken to determine program duration. In cases where a university wishes to ensure that a program will have maximum sustainability, deans may choose to create a Sustainability Plan. One dean noted that he avoids including sunset clauses in such plans, and this allows programs to be more competitive with international programs that do impose clear ending-points. At the same time, a number of deans indicated that there are good reasons to accept the impermanence of programs, as when the demand for a certain degree program diminishes over time. These changes need not be seen as failures. For example, one participant pointed out that a decrease in demand for a certain program may be taken as good news for some universities, citing the case of a joint PhD degree program that had strengthened a department to the point that it became large enough to start its own, independent PhD program. "In that sense," she commented, "the end of a joint degree is the ultimate mark of its success."

Conclusions

One of the most important ideas to emerge from the focus group discussion is that there is no single approach to creating and implementing international collaborative degree programs, and that approaches may need to be tailored to the specific needs of universities. Deans and other university leaders will have different ways of weighing the relative importance of different concerns at their own institutions. As international collaboration becomes more widespread, it may become easier for universities with similar needs to compare practical strategies for starting new programs, and for more general best practices to be established. In the meantime, there is a need for greater coordination among graduate institutions in the US and Canada and for general guidelines provided by "best practice" research.

The focus group on joint and dual degrees highlights what a number of experienced deans deem promising practices, or at least practices that have seen positive results at their own institutions. Further research is needed to give stronger empirical support to the efficacy of these practices; to demonstrate which of these practices are best suited for institutions with strong programs in the STEM fields; and to determine which of the policies and practices outlined can serve as general "best practices" for all institutions seeking to build and maintain all international research collaborations

Strategies for Fostering Research-Intensive Collaborations in STEM Fields

While graduate institutions generally view joint and dual degree programs as ventures involving significant and long-term institutional commitments of time and resources, a different view may hold for research collaborations that do not include formal degree programs. Research collaborations are easier to formalize because they do not require approval from a state legislature, or a university senate or governing board, and graduate schools typically do not need to justify long-term investments or develop sustainability plans. In STEM fields, opportunities for external funding also may not encounter common challenges of joint and dual degree programs, such as identifying sources of institutional funding, aligning programs with a strategic plan, or defending programs to other senior administrators. For example, many institutions compete for grants from prestigious NSF programs, such as the Integrative Graduate Education and Research Traineeship (IGERT) program and the Graduate STEM Fellows in K-12 Education (GK-12) program, both of which may have international components, and the Partnerships for International Research and Education (PIRE) program.[46]

Research-intensive collaborations in STEM also merit further close attention because they involve a distinct set of issues related to the preparation of graduate students and faculty. Some may feel that it is the role of faculty to determine the material conditions and intellectual content of international research projects involving graduate students. However, data from the focus group and technical workshops suggest that graduate deans are playing a stronger role in these areas since they directly involve institutional standards and in some cases, funding sources. How will US students be prepared for professional norms that may differ in a foreign lab, for example, and for different ethical and legal standards that may apply there? How will institutions ensure that faculty from each partner institution are prepared to supervise students from the partner institution, and that culture-specific expectations for mentoring are addressed? How will the impacts of participating in a research collaboration be measured, both through short-term tangible outcomes, such as publications, and through long-term effects on a graduate student's or faculty member's career path in the fields of science and engineering?

To pursue these and other questions, we conducted two technical workshops that focused on the major challenges experienced and lessons learned by participants in NSF-funded grants with an international component, which included both principal investigators for PIRE and IGERT grants and graduate deans at institutions where PIRE and IGERT projects had been conducted. This focus allowed a pragmatic, hands-on approach to discussing structural practices at NSF and universities, as well as policy recommendations for improving graduate collaborations in STEM.

The questions explored with participants at these technical workshops addressed the following general topics, with a focus on the specific administrative needs and strategies used in facilitating research collaborations.

- Benefits of international collaboration to students, institutions, and faculty research
- Challenges of institutional coordination
- Measuring the success of international collaborations
- Legal issues in the development of MOUs
- Financial challenges
- Cultural differences (related to administration, pedagogy, and research cultures)

- Governmental issues that affect collaboration
- Strategies for overcoming barriers
- Recommendations for improving the process and making projects more successful

For a more extensive discussion of the methodology used, see Appendix C.

The three major topics that emerged in these workshops were: 1) the changing role of senior administrators in facilitating research collaborations in STEM fields; 2) the administrative challenges that arise in these partnerships, and some solutions that have proved effective in some contexts; and 3) the need for effective metrics for assessing the impact of research-intensive collaborations in STEM. In the following pages of this section, we discuss each of these areas and provide two brief "problem-solving scenarios" designed to capture the complex processes involved in these types of collaborations.

The Role of Senior Administrators in Facilitating Research Collaborations in STEM Fields

When describing the role of senior administrators in facilitating international research collaborations, participants in the technical workshop discussions reiterated two of the central points that emerged from the focus group on joint and dual degrees. First, participants indicated that it is best for faculty to initiate research collaborations because this ensures that the project will be in line with the research interests of the PI (principal investigator). At the same time, deans must work to harmonize faculty research needs with the university's administrative structure and priorities, an approach that requires flexibility and creative problem-solving.

One dean indicated that her job is to find ways to support faculty research interests whenever possible, and in cases where this was difficult, to propose solutions that are aligned with both the interests of faculty and institutional requirements:

> Faculty members will come to me first with an idea and I try to figure out what we can do within our current structure. If they can't do it within our current structure, I figure out what they would need to do to do something really different. I then might convene a committee that includes our contracts officer, who writes up the [memorandum of agreement], and the head of our international programs office. I feel like

> I'm kind of the translator between the PI (faculty person), contracts person, and the International Officer and we try to come up with something that meets the needs of the PI.

Comments in the technical workshops also indicated that graduate deans overseeing an NSF-funded international grant may exercise somewhat different forms of leadership and allocate their time differently than they would in helping to develop a joint or dual degree program. Since in most cases, deans will not need to justify the use of institutional funding to other senior university personnel or, in the case of state universities, to bodies governing the use of funding within their university, they devote most of their time to maximizing research opportunities through a number of practical measures. Some of the practices cited included:

- Making faculty aware of research opportunities, sometimes in formal presentations, such as informational sessions on the PIRE and IGERT programs
- Providing support services for proposal writing
- Overseeing the total pool of proposals from their institution to ensure that faculty are aware of opportunities to collaborate on proposals

In addition, deans discussed a number of practices that would be more widely applicable to a variety of international collaborations.

- Setting up program infrastructure and assessment
- Working as an "interpreter" or "conduit" between faculty and other offices
- Overseeing risk management issues
- Providing support services for writing MOUs
- Reporting program outcomes

The discussion of roles brought to light the increasingly key role played by senior international officers and international offices in developing international collaborations. In one of the technical workshops this emerged as a major topic of discussion, and seven of eight participants specifically mentioned that their institutions had a senior administrator assigned to international projects. Both graduate deans and PIs reported that these individuals can be very helpful in some of the technical aspects of designing and implementing the collaboration in areas such as: administrative strategy and risk management; program development and, in cases where the research collaboration also involves a formal educational component, course development; faculty development initiatives; implementing tools for program assessment; and administrative support.

Administrative Challenges and Emerging Solutions

In spite of the relative ease of developing research collaborations, participants in the technical workshops reported some of the challenges typically encountered in developing joint and dual degree programs: problems of efficiency and communication surrounding the MOU process, and administrative burdens on faculty. The technical workshops allowed us to explore these topics in detail and to draw out some proposed and proven solutions. Some of these solutions may be easier to implement if a research-intensive collaboration is supported with external funding. Some universities may find that the provision of administrative support to assist with research collaborations may save time and resources over the long term, while other universities that lack the staff or resources to help faculty depend on PIs being as fully informed as possible about possible challenges and solutions.

The technical workshops provided many rich stories about the complex process steps involved in overseeing research collaborations. From these stories we have drawn a number of important lessons: that it is crucial to consider the particular goals and needs of one's institution when making administrative decisions; that collaborations may require both long-term strategies as well as creative, short-term solutions; and that graduate deans often play a crucial role in ensuring that the conditions for collaboration remain strong even while specific collaborations present uncertain variables. To illustrate these lessons, we have provided two problem-solving scenarios that are drawn from various examples described in the focus group and technical workshops.

Problem-Solving Scenario #1: Avoiding Miscommunication in the MOU Process

The graduate dean at a large state research university received an MOU for a research collaboration between her own institution's doctoral program in engineering and a doctoral program at a Chinese university. While she had discussed plans for the partnership with the lead faculty member at her own institution, she had received no communications from him since the previous semester, and was surprised to receive the MOU. She had assumed that discussions of program content were still under negotiation with the partner institution. Upon examining the document, an MOU signed by the partner institution, she realized that the faculty member had promised eight Chinese graduate students tuition and health insurance for one full semester; without knowledge of this promise, the Graduate School had made no allocations for this expense in its budget.

When the dean contacted the faculty member, he explained that he had drafted the MOU using a sample provided by a colleague in a different department, and that the tuition waiver and health insurance was offered to meet a reciprocal promise from the Chinese university. He also explained that drafting a new MOU document would likely make it impossible to proceed with the collaboration by delaying the exchange for at least one semester and taking a very tight research timeline, which was tied to external funding requirements, off track. It might also lead the Chinese university to pull out of the agreement.

The graduate dean weighed a number of options. The surprise MOU was the third of its kind in the past several years, and although previous MOUs had not required changes to her budget, she did not want to set a precedent for giving a program funding and access to resources when the MOU had not been approved through the regular channels. Such decisions were particularly problematic at a state university, where it was often difficult to secure tuition waivers for in-state students. At the same time, she suspected that the pattern of misdirected MOUs indicated that the current policy needed better management. She also knew that the research collaboration would draw resources from a highly competitive external grant and present graduate students and faculty with significant training and research opportunities.

To resolve the problem, the dean implemented a number of short-term and long-term solutions. First, she explained the situation to the VP for Finance, and asked the faculty member to submit a justification for the expense directly to his office. Signing of the MOU was delayed by several weeks, pending this approval, but the MOU was finally approved by her own university.

To prevent future MOUs from missing crucial steps in the approvals process, she arranged for the following changes to be made, in cooperation with the VP Finance's Office and the International Programs Office:

1. **A more explicit policy**. At the next meeting of the Graduate Council, the dean asked the group to develop a more explicit policy for the routing and approvals of MOUs. The current policy stated only that the MOU needed to be reviewed and approved by the Graduate Dean before it

was sent to the partner university, but it did not give faculty information about how long these approvals would take and information about whom to contact with specific types of questions. Without these changes, it was possible for some faculty to believe that the review process was simply a formality.

2. **A better communication strategy with faculty.** The dean ensured that the new description of the process for approving MOUs was provided on the faculty website as well as on the website of the International Office. The new web resource provided a clearly articulated procedure for the routing of the MOU, including a timeline that enabled PIs to understand how much time was needed for approval and make plans that would fit with the requirements of any external sponsors. It also included contact information for the individuals who could answer questions: the graduate dean and the director of the international office. In addition, the dean asked a staff member in the International Office and a member of her own staff to create a new section of the faculty website that provided sample MOUs and an MOU checklist. These helped faculty to anticipate concerns and questions that they might not have considered before, and demonstrated that MOUs are not "one size fits all."

Problem-Solving Scenario #2: Maximizing Administrative Efficacy after Program Implementation.

A medium-sized private university drafted a new strategic plan that made internationalization a priority, with specific emphasis on international collaborations that developed research capacities and provided graduate students with research experiences abroad. In the past, administrative support for those programs had been provided by the graduate dean, faculty members involved in the collaboration, and assistants in both the offices of departments involved in collaborative activities and in the Graduate School office, but this arrangement was highly time-consuming and inconvenient. After the new strategic plan was implemented, the Graduate School office created a more central source of administrative support for graduate-level collaborations in the international office, which in the past had only handled undergraduate exchange programs.

Two graduate departments began to work with the Director of the International Office to handle various aspects of their existing programs. A biochemistry program that had recently scaled up a highly-successful research collaboration into a dual degree program asked the administrator to help develop an assessment tool for this program; meanwhile, the School of Public Health, which had a dual master's degree program that brought international students to campus for one year of study, began to route questions from international students through the International Office. In both cases, the Director of the International Office provided suggestions that had worked with undergraduate students and programs, but often to the dissatisfaction of graduate faculty, who found that graduate programs and students had different needs.

The graduate dean became aware of the problem when a faculty member called to say that she was spending increasing amounts of time doing administrative work for the project, and that the time was a significant drain away from her research and advising responsibilities for graduate students involved in the partnerships. She added that the Director of the International Office felt that he was in a similar position; she too was working beyond the amount of time that had been allocated for her work on graduate programs.

The graduate dean realized that the originally proposed administrative solution was not working, and he began to discuss various short and long-term solutions.

1. **Long-term planning for administrative training and support**. The Graduate School began to develop a full-time position devoted to administrative support of graduate international collaborations. Recently, a faculty member had written a successful proposal for an external grant and included in his budget a half-time position for an administrative assistant, and the dean saw this as an opportunity to train a staff member in the International Office to gain experience administering graduate-level collaborations. The dean worked with the International Office to create a new position for an existing staff member: half of this person's salary would by paid by the grant, and the other half would be paid out of the Graduate Dean's budget. This arrangement allowed the staff member to spend part of her time supporting the development of other graduate international collaborations overseen by the dean's office. By the end of the two-year grant, the assistant was in a position to provide helpful information to faculty in the other existing programs and to provide guidance to both faculty and the dean on the development of future programs. Based on the success of this arrangement, the university was finally able to justify paying a full-time salary to this staff member. She implemented a number of informational sessions for faculty involved in graduate-level partnerships with foreign institutions, and developed a number of resources that made programs more efficient

and made international collaborations more appealing to graduate faculty. As the university's programs developed over time, it was able to create a more senior position for international programs that was housed within the Graduate School. The strategic plan helped the Graduate School justify a number of long-term investments in the development of their collaborative graduate programs, including web development and professional development opportunities for other administrative staff.

2. **Pooling of resources among departments with current and developing collaborations.** As programs grew and developed at the university, involved faculty members were asked to share developing resources with the graduate school and the international office. The program assessment tool eventually developed by the biochemistry program became a model for other programs, and the administrator in charge of graduate collaborations developed a list of "Frequently Asked Questions" specifically tailored to the needs of international graduate students across a wide variety of programs.

IV. NEXT STEPS: POLICY, RESEARCH, AND BEST PRACTICES

Formal degree collaborations with international partner institutions are likely to play a major role in shaping the global future of graduate education. As discussed in this book's introductory chapter, Europe has exhibited a much more strategic approach than the US to fostering international collaborations. European policymakers have targeted international degree collaborations as a means of advancing the goals of the Bologna Process for establishing a European Higher Education Research Area with internationally comparable degrees and qualifications. With a growing number of programs in Europe being offered in English, and the availability of financial support from foreign governments to cover some portion of the costs, opportunities for US institutions to partner with European institutions are growing.[47]

There are some factors, however, that may limit the growth of international collaborations between US institutions and international partners. While there are no national legal barriers in the US to the establishment of joint degree programs, as there have been until recently in some European countries, state boards and regional accrediting organizations in the US may discourage some structures preferred by partnering institutions seeking to establish formal, degree partnerships.[48] (For example, some accrediting bodies may require that the majority of credits earned toward a joint degrees are from the US-accredited institution, though thesis degrees with international collaborators can be difficult to quantify in credit hours; approval for joint degree programs in some states can be required at several levels, such as the university president, the state board, and the regional accrediting body.) Costs for transatlantic and transpacific partnerships may be higher than intra-continental international partnerships. And employer recognition of international higher education institutions may not be as great in the US as in other regions.

There are three areas where more work is clearly needed to position US universities and STEM research faculty to take better advantage of current and future opportunities for international collaboration. These areas are:

1. greater definition of outcomes and metrics of success and agreement upon strategies for assessing them;

2. better preparation of students for the ethical issues that arise in international collaborative research; and

3. greater opportunities for the international exchange of best practices in international collaboration.

The Need for Outcomes Assessment
There is a growing body of evidence to suggest that graduate international collaborations provide crucial opportunities to prepare US graduate students to conduct international research. More rigorous studies are needed, however, to demonstrate the actual social and economic benefits to merit the greater investment required to support this research. In the focus group and technical workshops, many deans and PIs on international research projects reported that the challenges surrounding collaboration could be addressed through the development of more powerful tools for assessing both the short- and long-term outcomes of collaboration. While institutions may have different goals for their internationalization efforts, greater coordination on improved assessment tools might help universities and US national funding agencies make stronger projections about the potential benefits and risks of different types of collaborative activities.

Participants in this study reported two main reasons for improving the assessment of outcomes in international collaborations. The first was a need to deepen our understanding of the potential benefits and risks of collaboration. The following are the main areas of potential analysis discussed by participants in the discussion groups:

*   **Effects of international collaboration experience on individual careers**, in addition to concrete outcomes such as publications and theses. As one dean explained, "The premise of IGERT is broad-based thinking and the international experience is right there [...] If the argument is that the 21st century is going to be more global and interconnected, I think it is safe to say that there has to be a strong, meaningful international experience in [one's] toolbox."

*   **Specific scientific skills** developed through international collaborations. Describing recent methods used by NSF to gather data on international collaborations, one PI and Dean reported, "[...] all of the commonly used methods tended to focus first on the individual and

the cultural understanding that is gained. These experiences may have made a better person, but have we really been able to bridge that gap between being a better scientist? There is a huge area of opportunity there because there aren't good methods for doing that [...]"

- **Impact on US universities.** Deans report significant benefits to their universities in the areas of revenue generation, reputation, competitiveness for research funding, visibility to potential partners and investors abroad, the capacity to build bridges with other institutions, and improved graduate student recruitment.

- **Benefits to the public in terms of economic strength and resources.** A more strategic effort might be made to assess what many deans and PIs considered measures of program success: the impact of the collaboration in local communities, the impact of the research finding, and the acquired workforce competencies gained by those involved in or affected by the collaboration. In the case of workforce skills, one PI indicated that it would be helpful to measure the benefit to US researchers of understanding foreign markets during the technological transfer process.

- **Impact of the collaboration on the perspectives of non-US collaborators.** While many universities measure the impact of the collaboration to their own community, it was suggested that it would be helpful to better understand how other countries perceive programs and their participants.

Improved data on outcomes assessment would also, of course, support more strategic action on the part of university leaders and their funders by illuminating the potential returns on investment that can be garnered through collaborations. As reported in section III, many deans find it difficult to justify the value of collaboration in general, or the value of one collaboration over another, without the capacity to martial a larger body of evidence. One dean observed that there is a strong need for assessments that demonstrate the value of collaboration to groups and individuals outside funding agencies: university leaders and state legislatures. Another dean added, "I firmly believe that doctoral students in science and engineering should get international experience, but it's a hard argument to make."

CGS has begun to pursue further the problems and questions surrounding outcomes assessment identified in the 2009 Strategic Leaders Global Summit, in which summit delegates resolved to pursue common strategies for measuring outcomes (see "International Best Practices Exchange" below). At the 2010 Summit in Brisbane [September 13-15, 2010,] a panel will be held to specifically address the Quality of International Educational and Research Programs. Topics will include the development of metrics for program success, the ability of programs to prepare scholars to lead and conduct research in a global environment, and the use of data to improve existing collaborations. In addition to these activities, CGS will continue to solicit the input of graduate deans on outcomes assessment in workshops devoted to International Collaboration at the 2010 CGS Summer Workshop and Annual Meetings, and will seek the guidance of NSF program officers on helping graduate institutions develop their capacity to measure and analyze the effects of STEM collaborations.

Research Ethics and the Responsible Conduct of Research (RCR)
While US universities have engaged in both graduate international collaborations and in the development of research ethics education and RCR training, there has been little curricular or institution-level attention to the ethical issues students and researchers face when participating in international collaborative research and educational programs. Heightened attention has been given to issues of research integrity and the responsible conduct of research in the United States and across Europe and Asia through influential reports from the National Academies of Science (2002) and the European Science Foundation ("Stewards of Integrity," 2008), the establishment of the UK Research Integrity Office in 2006, and two large-scale conferences on research integrity held in 2007: the OECD Global Science Forum Tokyo conference and the first World Conference on Research Integrity (co-sponsored by ESF and ORI) held in Lisbon, Portugal with a second World Conference to be held in Singapore in July 2010. The primary focus of the global conferences, however, has been the important but daunting issue of coordinating international policy. Given the lack of standard regulatory frameworks, common codes of conduct, and even common definitions, researchers collaborating across national borders inevitably face challenges in interpreting policy that can ultimately compromise both research and collaborative relationships.[49]

In 2008, in recognition of the need for greater dialogue and coordination between institutions on best practices in educational programming in this area, CGS convened thirty-five leaders representing graduate education in Australia, Botswana, Canada, China, England, Hong Kong, Italy, Germany, and the United States to share national and comparative perspectives on research ethics in a global context and identify possible areas for future collaboration.[50] The 2008 Strategic Leaders Summit was the first of its kind, focusing on the capacity of university leaders to improve the institutional climate and graduate curricula for advancing scholarly integrity and ethical and responsible research conduct. Topics addressed included: national policy frameworks and definitional differences; institutional approaches to creating a culture for scholarly integrity; global issues shaping education and training; and emerging best practices in areas such as research mentoring, conflicts of interest and commitment, emergent technologies, curricular and assessment strategies, and the ethical and psychological implications for researchers working with human subjects on sensitive topics.

Participants identified three needs and five specific action items for strengthening scholarly integrity:

1. A common frame of reference that addresses the continuum of educational and training objectives from scholarly integrity to compliance;

2. Leadership at all levels to prepare future scholars, researchers, and professionals to demonstrate integrity in all aspects of their careers as scholars; and

3. Exchange of best practices and resources (including codes of conduct, regulatory frameworks, curricular materials, and instruments for assessment and evaluation).

The specific action items for organizations and institutions that all agreed upon included activities such as: building scholarly integrity into existing structures that prepare future faculty and future professionals; developing and maintaining an open source, online website for facilitating resource and best practice exchange; identifying mechanisms that explicitly address universal and global issues in scholarly integrity, and ethical issues that may arise from the mobility of scholars (including priority areas of digital publishing and plagiarism in an international environment); developing collaborative mechanisms for addressing plagiarism in an international context; and utilizing international joint degree, dual degree, and other collaborative program structures for integrating educational activities to advance scholarly integrity.

Graduate international collaborations provide optimal settings for addressing some of the broader national needs to prepare a workforce for success in the global research enterprise. Graduate student researchers and scholars, especially in STEM fields, should be prepared for professional practice in the context of international collaborative research, education, and scholarship. For example, young researchers should understand the regulatory, legal, and cultural differences of countries or regions where partnering institutions are located as well as the ethical issues that arise when conducting research in international settings or collaborations. Also, students in US STEM graduate programs from international and intercultural backgrounds should be provided with orientation, preparation, and training in the responsible and ethical conduct of research. All STEM students studying in US graduate programs should understand the expectations for RCR in the US context, including regulations of funding bodies relevant to their respective fields, the ethical issues that scientists and scholars typically face that go beyond national compliance regulations, as well as professional standards of their discipline. In the development of such education programs, US institutions should also recognize differences in students' background preparation and in professional standards and expectations while at the same time providing all students with access to professional socialization in the nationally recognized standards of the disciplines. Finally, differences in education and training between partnering institutions should be recognized and addressed in formal collaborative degree programs and graduate educational exchanges, since these programs and exchanges provide concrete opportunities for students and faculty to address issues that arise in international collaborative research.

International Best Practice Exchange
More international dialogue is needed to identify "best practices" in developing and sustaining graduate international research collaborations. This dialogue is needed among research faculty and among university leaders, as well as between both groups. As discussed in Chapter Three, most successful international collaborations at the graduate level either originate in existing faculty research contacts or build upon existing programs. Through the Graduate International Collaborations Project, however, we have learned that senior administrative leaders are playing a larger role in the subsequent development and expansion of these collaborations. The roles they play range from providing administrative assistance in campus coordination to ensuring that considerations of the institution's mission are included at key points in the decision making process, for example, in MOU approval and partner selection for degree programs. If they have overall responsibility for the quality of graduate education across the disciplines,

senior administrators can also provide valuable perspectives on the educational aspects of international research collaborations. In the United States, these senior administrative leaders are typically graduate deans. In other countries, where there may be no clear administrative equivalent to the graduate school, senior administrators at other levels of the university may provide such input. Engaged and informed senior leaders can be crucial when needs arise for things such as: additional or restructured financial support; coordination of different campus units across a university and between universities; assistance in addressing legal issues that may differ by country or in working with international and external stakeholders where structures of collaboration do not conform easily to existing university models or regulations or accrediting body standards. Being informed means knowing what practices seem most promising not only in one's own institution and at other institutions in one's own country, but also at prospective partner institutions in other countries; it also means being familiar with broader international trends that may influence future strategizing.

As discussed in Chapter One, graduate international collaborations take place in a broader policy area and can intersect with issues of national security, diplomacy, and public welfare, as well as with social and economic policy goals for nations and regions. Here too, greater dialogue between institutional leaders who are well-positioned to communicate with their faculty and administrative support units as well as with external stakeholders could help those institutions to better pursue their missions and engage public awareness of the benefits of the resulting research. In such an international best practice forum, graduate deans may be called upon to represent both their particular institutions as well as their countries.

There are some opportunities (for example, NSF-sponsored PI meetings or disciplinary society meetings) for faculty to exchange best practice ideas on international collaborations, and several annual conferences for international office directors to do so (e.g., NAFSA meetings). There are few opportunities, however, for senior leaders of graduate education to exchange their ideas on best practices and lessons learned in ways that might benefit their respective institutions and the broader research community. One such opportunity is the annual Strategic Leaders Global Summit on Graduate Education series, which was explicitly created to provide senior university leaders with a forum for exchanging ideas on best practices in graduate education.

The first, 2006 meeting convened such leaders for a transatlantic dialogue on the pressing issues facing graduate education in Europe and North America. In 2007, the first official Strategic Leaders Global Summit on Graduate

Education took place in Banff, Canada, in cooperation with the Ministry of Alberta, an expanded meeting which resulted in the development of a set of principles for graduate international collaboration that are now widely cited as the "Banff Principles"; the second Global Summit in 2008, as mentioned in the previous section, convened in Florence, Italy and focused on the topics of research ethics and scholarly integrity. While not funded by the NSF grant for the Graduate International Collaborations project, the 2009 Global Summit, themed "International Collaborations: How to Build and Sustain Them," which met in San Francisco, California, provided an opportunity for 32 senior leaders from 9 countries to exchange information about the context, structures, and challenges of international collaborations in their countries, to exchange best practices, and to discuss the emerging outcomes of the NSF-funded CGS Graduate International Collaborations Project.[51]

Whether on specific topics, such as the responsible conduct of research, professional development of graduate students, or quality assessment, or on general issues such as the coordination of policies and practices for developing formal degree and informal research collaborations, further international dialogue among strategic leaders is essential. CGS looks forward to working with its member universities and graduate education leaders from around the globe as we continue to expand the global conversation and opportunities for best practice exchange.

CONCLUSION

ormal international degree collaborations may not be appropriate for every institution, and some universities have more faculty members engaged in internationally collaborative research than others. Nevertheless, there is a strong argument to be made that to be a university in the twenty-first century is to be internationally engaged. In nearly every discipline, discoveries and advancements are being made on an international scale. In such an environment, students in all research fields will benefit from opportunities that prepare them to communicate their findings beyond their immediate context, to participate in international conversations about their discipline or interdisciplinary research, and to seek out opportunities for fruitful collaboration that may one day benefit their field and their own students.

Recent studies and continuing dialogue about graduate international collaborations are contributing to better mutual understanding among partnering institutions of the characteristic challenges faced in each region or country. Such understanding is a necessary first step in ultimately identifying best practices that can help to ensure the aspirations of each partner for their collaborative activities have the best chance to be realized. More information is now available about European collaborations as a result of the numerous studies described in Chapter Two. As a complement to these studies, the CGS Graduate Collaborations Project has contributed to our understanding of the constraints and opportunities for North American institutions.

This project has also identified a number of specific needs and areas where greater clarification is required. These needs and areas for future work include:

- a compendium of "best practice" case studies that could help institutions navigate common administrative challenges in ways that are appropriate to their mission and context;[52]

- a database of international joint and dual degree master's and doctorates that would enhance the ability of senior administrators and other stakeholders to network with each other and consult each other on issues specific to international degree collaborations;

- more national resources to help identify, define, and measure outcomes appropriate to graduate-level research and skills development;

- national and international models for addressing the ethical issues that arise in international collaborative research; and

- greater dialogue on models for coordinating quality assessment and quality assurance efforts, which vary by nation and region.

It is not clear whether or how fluctuations in national and regional economies will affect the future of specific graduate international collaborations. Nor it is clear what future patterns of student mobility may look like or how new trends may inhibit or contribute to the growth of formal, degree partnerships. Given the sustainability, funding, and student recruiting challenges to international collaborations expressed by participants in this project, continued study of both of these issues will be important.

An additional issue where future investigation is needed is the employability of graduates from international collaborative degree programs or programs of study where international research exchange has been a key component. Such an inquiry might look at pathways not only to academic institutions but also to and through other sectors, as more companies transition to "multinational" corporations and as inter-sector partnerships between universities and non-academic partners in industry and government become more important. Another factor that could affect the growth of international joint and dual degree collaborations at the graduate level is increased scrutiny given to these degree types by accrediting bodies and policymakers. In order to ensure a secure future for successful collaborations, university champions and senior leaders should be in dialogue with both groups to understand their concerns and convey the benefits of such collaborations (including their importance to delivering high quality graduate education, generally) as well as to indicate challenges faced.

Successful international collaborations depend upon the contributions from members of vast teams that may include federal program officers of funded research and directors of initiatives to promote internationalization in participating countries and regions, as well as, at all participating institutions, contributors at different levels of the university such as: senior administrators, faculty, directors and staff of campus international offices, registrars and legal counsel. In the US and Canada, and in partnering countries around the world, these stakeholders will need to continue to work together to ensure that the collaborations to which they lend their vision and support are efficient and successful and that, where appropriate, successes can endure and be replicated elsewhere.

Appendix A:
An MOU Checklist for
International Collaborations

Memoranda of Understanding (MOUs) and Memoranda of Agreement (MOAs) for international collaborations vary considerably, depending on the scope and objectives of the partnership and the national and institutional contexts of the universities involved. The following checklist addresses general programmatic issues that should be considered when developing an MOU or MOA for a formal international partnership. The guidelines described in this checklist have been culled from sample memoranda and MOU checklists provided to CGS by institutions that participated in the discussions and activities sponsored by the CGS Graduate International Collaborations Project. While this checklist is designed to cover a range of collaborations, components specific to international joint and dual degree programs are signaled with a "J/D" below.

In addition to considering the guidelines below, institutions with experience overseeing collaborations recommend providing detailed information to faculty members about the process of submitting an MOU or other agreement for approval. Many institutions elect to include this information in online resources for faculty and/or with planning documents that must precede or accompany the MOU, such as an application to submit with a collaborative exchange proposal. It is recommended that these documents:

A. **Define the types of possible agreements (MOU, Agreement of Friendship and Cooperation, etc.) and the purpose of each.**
B. **Describe the different types of documents that must be completed and approved.** Explain the approvals process for different types of agreements, indicating routing and required signatures.
C. **Provide an estimated timeline for approval** once a proposed MOU and accompanying documentation has been submitted.
D. **Provide names and contact information for senior administrators and staff members** who can offer support and assistance for different types of questions.

MOU Checklist

VALUE

1. **Establish the value of the collaboration** to the university and to any other relevant groups of stakeholders. Refer to any documents that demonstrate the commitment of the institution and institutional leadership to internationalization and collaboration (for example, a vision statement or strategic plan).

2. **Outline the rationale** or objectives motivating the collaboration, outlining benefits to all groups of stakeholders.

3. **Describe the potential for development of the collaboration across other departments, programs or schools.**

4. **Describe the potential of the proposed project to complement existing programs or to enhance areas of priority for the university.**

PLANNING

5. **Articulate concrete outcomes or actions that will result** from the collaboration.

6. **Summarize planning and communication activities that have already taken place between partners.**

7. **Define the program structure,** including:

   a. The title of the program and the title of any degree(s) and certification(s) that will result (J/D)

   b. The duration of the program (with start date and end date, as applicable) and duration of the MOU, including provisions for early termination by mutual or single agreement (e.g., what happens to students who are already in progress at the time of termination)

   c. The accreditation status of the partner institutions and programs, if appropriate (J/D)

   d. If applicable, the process of adding participating institutions

8. **Define terms that may be interpreted differently** between various academic contexts ("academic year," "full-time enrollment," etc.) (J/D)

LEGAL ISSUES

9. **Describe basic legal requirements for student mobility** between the countries where partner institutions are located.

10. **Define legal rights and liabilities of universities in relation to the program and its intellectual and material outcomes.** (Issues to be considered would include, but would not be limited to, intellectual property, equal opportunity law, monetary exchanges or reimbursements between universities as the result of profits generated or expenses incurred.)

11. **Establish which institutional rules and policies apply to students** studying at the host institution, and terms of disciplinary action. (J/D)

ADMISSIONS (J/D)

12. **Establish equivalencies for units of credit awarded by partner institutions**.

13. **Establish academic criteria for student participation** in the program and mechanisms by which eligibility and admission to the program will be determined.

CURRICULUM (J/D)

14. **Describe modes and mechanisms of delivering program content,** including, as appropriate:

    a. The language(s) of instruction

    b. The curriculum, including courses and/or instruction that will be provided by each institution

    c. Requirements for the thesis, dissertation, or capstone project, and mechanisms of supervision and defense of the project

15. **Describe graduation requirements and mechanisms for awarding credit and certifying student work,** i.e., transfer credit policy (including the number of credits, if any, that can be double counted at each institution), extenuating circumstances, and transcript release.

RESOURCES AND FINANCING

16. **Outline the funding structure for the collaboration.** Basic categories for funding sources may include: internal university budget; US federal or state funding sources; private US funders;

and international sources (including the partner institution or self-supporting students). Basic categories of expenditures may include: research expenses; facilities for faculty and administrative support staff; tuition/fees; housing; and travel.

17. **Establish terms and resources for student advising and support**, (i.e., visa support services, academic advising, terms of student access to academic, social, and health facilities). (J/D)

18. **Establish student responsibilities and expenses,** (i.e., registration, payment of tuition and living expenses, housing, immigration compliance, health insurance and medical expenses). (J/D)

ASSESSMENT AND REVIEW

19. **Establish benchmarks for program success.** (J/D)

20. **Describe mechanisms and timeline for program evaluation** and if applicable, assessment of learning outcomes. (J/D)

21. **Define period within which the MOU may be renewed or terminated with mutual consent of institutions.**

22. **For agreements of indefinite length, describe university policy on inactive agreements.**

APPENDIX B. RESOURCES

International Collaborations and Joint and Dual Degrees

Global Perspectives on Graduate International Collaborations
Proceedings of the 2009 Strategic Leaders Global Summit. Council of Graduate Schools. 2010

CGS Convenes Strategic Leaders for Global Summit on Graduate International Collaborations.
Council of Graduate Schools. *Communicator* 43(1): Jan. 2010
http://www.cgsnet.org/portals/0/pdf/comm_2010_1.pdf

The Graduate International Collaborations Project: A North American Perspective on Joint and Dual Degree Programs.
Council of Graduate Schools. *Communicator* 42(8): Oct. 2009
http://www.cgsnet.org/portals/0/pdf/comm_2009_10.pdf

Joint and Double Degree Programs: An Emerging Model for Transatlantic Exchange
Obst, D, and Kuder, M. Institute for International Education [IIE]. 2009
http://www.iienetwork.org/page/150347/

Global Perspectives on Research Ethics and Scholarly Integrity. Council of Graduate Schools.
2009. http://www.cgsnet.org/Default.aspx?tabid=348

Global Perspectives on Graduate Education: Proceedings of the Strategic Leaders Global Summit on Graduate Education.
Council of Graduate Schools. 2008. http://www.cgsnet.org/Default.aspx?tabid=348

Student Mobility

Graduate Study in the United States: A Guide for Prospective International Graduate Students
Council of Graduate Schools. 2007. http://www.cgsnet.org/Default.aspx?tabid=348

IIE Open Doors Report on International Educational Exchange (IIE, 2009)
http://opendoors.iienetwork.org/

Comparative Data on Global Higher Education Systems

Education at a Glance 2009: OECD Indicators
Organisation for Economic Co-Operation and Development. 2009
http://www.oecd.org/document/62/0,3343,
en_2649_39263238_43586328_1_1_1_37455,00.html

Meetings and Conferences

Connecting Continents: 21ˢᵗ Annual EAIE Conference
European Association for International Education. Madrid, Spain.
16 – 19 September 2009. http://www.eaie.org/Madrid/

2009 CGS/NSF Workshop: Globalizing Graduate Education and Research
Council of Graduate Schools/ National Science Foundation.
Arlington, Virginia. 20 April 2009. http://www.cgsnet.org/Default.
aspx?tabid=345

CGS 48th Annual Meeting, "Graduate Education in a Global Context"
Council of Graduate Schools. Washington, DC. 3-6 December 2008.
http://www.cgsnet.org/Default.aspx?tabid=345

Strategic Leaders Conference on Graduate Education and Research Ethics
in a Global Context
Council of Graduate Schools. Florence, Italy. August 31 –
September 2, 2008.
http://www.cgsnet.org/Default.aspx?tabid=345

Strategic Leaders Global Summit on Graduate Education
Council of Graduate Schools. Banff, Alberta, Canada. August 31 –
September 1, 2007.
http://www.cgsnet.org/Default.aspx?tabid=345

Transatlantic Dialogue on Doctoral Education
Council of Graduate Schools. Salzburg, Austria. 2–5 September
2006.
http://www.cgsnet.org/Default.aspx?tabid=345

Websites and Newsletters

The Boston College Center for International Higher Education

Information related to research, publication, policy, globalization, and professional development, among other topics. http://www. bc.edu/bc_org/avp/soe/cihe/

GlobalHigherEd
Olds, K, and Robertson, S. Blog. Information on developing links between global higher education and the knowledge economy, including new policy developments and emerging networks. http://globalhighered.wordpress.com/

Universitas 21
Updates on collaborative activities of a consortium of 21 research universities. http://www.universitas21.com/newsletters.html

Recent Presentations

Dual and Joint Graduate Degrees: Conceptual Theory and Administrative Practice
Comrie, A, and Horgan, D. Council of Graduate Schools, 49th Annual Meeting. San Francisco, CA. Dec. 2009. http://www.cgsnet.org/portals/0/pdf/am09_Comrie.pdf

US Perspectives on Graduate International Collaborations
Denecke, D. Council of Graduate Schools, Committee for Science, Technology, and Law National Academies. Washington, DC. 21 Oct. 2009.
http://www.cgsnet.org/portals/0/pdf/NAS_CSTL_2009_Denecke.pdf

Emerging Best Practices in Joint and Dual Degree Programs
Stewart, D. Council of Graduate Schools, EAIE Annual Meeting. Madrid, Spain. 18 Sept. 2009. http://www.cgsnet.org/portals/0/pdf/CGS_EAIE_Madrid_2009.pdf

Dual and Joint Degrees Points of Departure: Graduate Education in a Global Context
Godfrey, JB. Council of Graduate Schools Annual Meeting. Washington, DC. 3 Dec. 2008. http://www.cgsnet.org/portals/0/pdf/mtg_am08Godfrey.pdf

Funding Opportunities

National Science Foundation/Graduate Teaching Fellows in K-12 Education Program
    NSF GK-12 International. http://www.nsfgk12.org/international.php

Office of International Science and Engineering
    National Science Foundation.
    http://www.nsf.gov/div/index.jsp?div=OISE

Partnerships for International Research and Education
    National Science Foundation
    http://www.nsf.gov/funding/pgm_summ.jsp?pims_id=12819

Integrative Graduate Education and Research Traineeship Program
    National Science Foundation
    http://www.nsf.gov/funding/pgm_summ.jsp?pims_id=12759

European Union-United States Atlantis Program
    United States Department of Education. http://www2.ed.gov/
    programs/fipseec/index.html

APPENDIX C.
METHODOLOGY

CGS Survey on Joint and Dual Degrees

Survey Design

CGS worked with a lead researcher on the Freie Universität Berlin/Institute of International Education study to frame questions that would form a basis for comparison with prior European studies and a foundation for further work in identifying best practices in fostering effective collaborations at the graduate level. The survey consisted of 17 questions and took approximately 15 minutes to complete. It was administered electronically to 84 institutions selected on the basis of their response to either the 2007 or the 2008 CGS Phase II International Student Admissions survey, including: 47 institutions that had reported in those prior CGS surveys having existing joint or dual degree programs as well as 37 additional institutions that indicated in 2007 or 2008 plans to develop such programs within the next two years. Forty-three institutions provided valid responses. Not all respondents answered every question; the number of valid responses is indicated for each question. Overall, survey results include data on 168 graduate programs. The response rate was therefore 51% of the total, but significantly higher when calculated for those institutions with known existing joint or dual degree programs.

Survey Limitations

The challenges encountered in designing this survey were similar to those encountered by other organizations conducting similar studies. Because experiences reported anecdotally in the graduate community are so varied across programs that differ by degree type, discipline, and institutional partner institution and region, this survey was designed to capture common challenges and factors across a broad range of issues encountered in collaborating with international partners. The purpose was to provide a more in-depth understanding of issues, including those that facilitate and inhibit collaboration, that would provide the basis for further analysis and follow up. The survey was not designed to capture the structural characteristics of each program by degree type or discipline. The limitations of the survey therefore include aggregation effects:

a) *By discipline:* Questions about "typical" programs required mental averaging across different disciplines that may have different requirements and structures. Alternatively, it would have been possible to request respondents to provide responses based on "one sample program." The potential risk of the latter approach, however, was determined to be the difficulty of ensuring that programs selected would be comparable and representative of the full range of collaborative degree programs. A third approach of requiring institutions to provide separate answers for each existing program was not taken because it was felt to pose too great a survey burden to respondents, thus potentially compromising the response rate.

b) *By degree level:* Because of the small number of collaborations between US and international partner institutions at the PhD level, we did not ask respondents to answer each question separately for master's and PhD programs. While such disaggregation would be important for understanding information about some program characteristics (such as thesis committee structure, for example), we determined that a case study approach will be necessary to describe characteristics and challenges unique to international PhD collaborations. Distribution of degree types by field was determined through a follow-up survey; these data, included in Chapter Three, provide context for understanding the results from the international collaborations survey.

c) For one question on the survey, "How many collaborative master's and PhD programs of each type does your institution currently have with an international partner institution," CGS sent one follow-up question to the 34 institutions that had reporting existing programs on the original survey. Institutions were asked to complete a table in which the main research fields surveyed were broken out by degree level [See Chapter Three, Table 4). Institutions were provided with the original data they had submitted and asked to provide additional data on only those programs that existed at the time they submitted the original survey. The response rate for the second round of surveys was 100%; one survey response was excluded because the institution reporting the data was unable to verify their accuracy.

Some questions invited responses based on research programs only; others invited responses based on the aggregate of programs; and some questions asked respondents to answer the same question separately for joint degrees and for dual degrees, if structural differences in diploma conferral were believed to potentially yield different differences (e.g., on issues of accreditation and approval) based on anecdotal information shared at CGS meeting sessions.

Two initial questions, on the motivation for engaging in international degree collaboration and on partner selection, invited respondents to generalize across all programs regardless of field.

The chief contacts on the CGS survey were graduate deans or other senior administrators with chief academic responsibility for graduate education. While this may possibly reflect some bias in favor of institutional considerations, many of the graduate deans to whom the survey was sent drew on additional appropriate campus informants and expertise when answering these questions in order to provide the fullest information about existing joint and dual degree programs at their institution.

Definitional Issues

There is no clear consensus among US institutions on the definition of either a "joint degree" or a "dual/double degree." CGS summer workshop and annual meeting sessions and the 2007 member survey described above, for example, brought out the fact that these terms are used differently by different institutions (and even by different programs within the same institution) to define a range of program structures.[53] "Joint degree" and "dual degree" are also variously used to describe master's and doctoral programs with different thesis requirements and varying durations spent by students at the home versus partner institutions. Other structural characteristics may also vary by institution within the same degree type, such as: the institution where students start and finish their study, which institutions participate in defining admissions criteria and curricula, et al. Some universities use terms other than joint or dual degree to refer to degree types in ways that emphasize structural characteristics (e.g., "sandwich programs," "cohort programs," or "joint curricular ventures"); others use more general terms such as "collaborative degrees" to describe a wide range of differently structured programs. Several universities have taken a more philosophical approach to defining international collaborative degree types in ways that recognize their similarities to existing non-collaborative degrees.[54]

Recognizing that this definitional variation also exists outside the US, some prior studies have defined the difference between joint and dual degrees in terms of the diploma and transcript mechanisms for conferring recognition of a student's completion of an international collaborative graduate program. For example, "joint" degrees referred to collaborative programs where recognition was conferred jointly (via a dual-branded diploma, or a single diploma with transcript notation and/or certificate from a partnering institution) and "dual" programs referred to collaborative programs where institutions awarded two separate diplomas.[55] Because discussions of policies and good practice in joint and dual degrees in the US have sometimes stalled in confusion over definitions, CGS built on 2007 findings to standardize definitions in the 2008 follow up survey. After studying the feasibility of this approach for collecting data on US graduate programs in 2007, CGS adopted in 2008 the following definitions:

- **Dual (or Double) Degree:** Students take coursework and receive a degree ordiploma from each institution.

- **Joint Degree:** Students take coursework at each institution, but receive one degree or diploma, which may have:
  o The names or "seals" of each institution (i.e. a "double sealed" or "double badged" diploma)

  o The home institution's name, with transcript notation of participation

  o The home institution's name, with certificate signifying participation in collaboration

This approach to definition, as opposed to defining these degree types by their structural characteristics, has the advantage of facilitating comparisons with major European/US studies (such as the IIE/Freie Universität study) and of capturing some of the pivotal issues that have proven to be the biggest challenges in terms of implementation and approval, including: concerns about double branding and about the perception that students are receiving double credit for a single body of work. These definitions were not intended to be normative or prescriptive for universities to use in practice, but were rather agreed upon as reference points for better national understanding of key characteristics and common issues surrounding international collaborations.

Focus Group on Joint and Dual Degree Programs

Focus Group Protocol
The focus group on joint and dual degrees was held on December 6, 2008 in conjunction with the CGS Annual Meeting. Potential participants were chosen by CGS from a pool of institutions that had reported existing or

planned international joint and/or dual degree programs on the 2007 and/ or 2008 CGS International Admissions Surveys. Ten deans from American institutions (both private and public, and of varying size) and one dean from Canada accepted the invitation to participate.

The focus group discussion took place over a two-hour period and was facilitated by a CGS consultant and two CGS staff members. Discussion began with a brief exchange of context information. The facilitators provided participants with the working definitions of "joint degree" and "dual degree" used in this study[56] and asked them to refer to these definitions when making comments. Participants were promised confidentiality before the audio-recorded discussion began.

Technical Workshops on STEM Research Collaborations and Exchanges

Focus Group Protocol
The technical workshops focused on the major challenges experienced and lessons learned by participants in NSF-funded grants with an international component. While some of the topics covered in these workshops overlapped with those addressed in the focus group on joint and dual degrees and in the NSF/DIR workshop, they gave exclusive attention to grant-funded programs in STEM fields. They also involved a more limited set of participants, principal investigators of PIRE and IGERT grants and graduate deans at institutions where PIRE and IGERT projects had been conducted. These highly specific parameters allowed a pragmatic, hands-on approach to discussing structural practices at NSF and universities, as well as policy solutions for improving graduate education.

CGS invited the participation of PIs on PIRE and IGERT grants with the guidance of NSF program officers as well as graduate deans with experience overseeing grants of one or both types. The workshops included 7-8 participants composed of roughly equal numbers of PIs and deans, and each group included individuals who had played both roles (IGERT or PIRE PI and/or Dean or Associate Dean of the Graduate School). The workshops took place on July 13 and July 15, 2009 in conjunction with the CGS Summer Workshop in Quebec City. Each of the two focus groups took place over a 1.5 hour period and was facilitated by two CGS staff and one consultant, who reviewed the IRB protocol prior to the audio recording of the discussion.

Preservation and coding of data for focus groups

The audio-recorded data collected in the three focus groups were transcribed by CGS project staff, and access to both the recordings and transcripts was limited to essential project staff. Data from the focus groups were coded in consultation with the group facilitator and senior consultant. Coding was conducted according to the frequency of responses across and within focus group responses when assigning weight to different comments. CGS, through the analysis of these qualitative data in the present publication, does not presume to capture broad trends in North American or American graduate international collaborations. The focus group format was designed to cull richer information about the experiences of graduate deans and PIs with experience overseeing collaborations that could not be provided in the survey and to give more detail about administrative processes and challenges surrounding various structures of collaboration.

WORKS CITED

Bement, A.L. Jr. (2009). *International Research Facilities and Infrastructure: Advancing Our Common Commitments* [PowerPoint slides]. Retrieved from www.nsf.gov/news/speeches/bement/09/alb090215_aaas.jsp

Bement, A.L. Jr. (2007). *Remarks at a Reception Honoring Opening of Research Councils UK* [PDF Document]. Retrieved from www.rcuk.ac.uk/cmsweb/downloads/rcuk/us/bement.pdf

Bosch, X., & Titus, S. (2009). Cultural Challenges and International Research Integrity. *The Lancet, 373*(9664), 610-612. Retrieved from www.thelancet.com/journals/lancet/article/PIIS0140673609603792/fulltext?rss=yes

Carnevale, A. (2009). *Graduate Education in 2020: What Does the Future Hold?* Council of Graduate Schools, (Ed.). Washington, DC: Council of Graduate Schools.

Centre for Higher Education Development, Center for Higher Education Policy Studies, & Euregio. (2009). *Joint Degrees in European Higher Education: Obstacles and opportunities for transnational programme partnerships based on the example of the German-Dutch EUREGIO.* Nickel, S., Zdebel, T., Westerheijden, D.F. Retrieved from www.jointdegree.eu/uploads/media/Che_Joint_Degrees_in_European_Higher_Education.pdf

Comrie, A. and Horgan, D. Dual and Joint Graduate Degrees: Conceptual Theory and Administrative Practice. Presentation at CGS Annual Meeting 2009, San Francisco. Available at www.cgsnet.org/portals/0/pdf/am09_Comrie.pdf

Council of Graduate Schools (2007). *2007 Graduate Admissions Survey II: Final Applications and Initial Offers of Admissions.* Available at www.cgsnet.org.

Council of Graduate Schools. (2008a). *Global Perspectives on Graduate Education: Proceedings of the Strategic Leaders Global Summit on Graduate Education.* Washington, DC: Council of Graduate Schools.

Council of Graduate Schools. (2008b). *2008 Graduate Admissions Survey II: Final Applications and Initial Offers of Admissions.* Available at www.cgsnet.org.

Council of Graduate Schools. (2009). *Global Perspectives on Research Ethics and Scholarly Integrity: Proceedings of the 2008 Strategic Leaders Global Summit on Graduate Education.* Washington, DC: Council of Graduate Schools.

Council of Graduate Schools. (2010). *Global Perspectives on Graduate International Collaborations: Proceedings of the 2009 Strategic Leaders Global Summit on Graduate Education.* Washington, DC: Council of Graduate Schools.

DAAD (German Academic Exchange Service). (n.d.). Report on a survey of 10 recently-launched DAAD-supported programs in Germany. Retrieved from www.daad.org/file_depot/0-10000000/10000-20000/16426/folder/33804/Survey-Report1.pdf

DAAD (German Academic Exchange Service) & HRK (German Rectors' Conference). (2006). *Results of the Survey on Study Programmes Awarding Joint, Multiple, or Joint Degrees.* Kassel, Germany: Maiworm, F. Retrieved from http://eu.daad.de/imperia/md/content/eu/sokrates/veranstaltungen/jd_report2.pdf

van der Duyn Schouten, F. (n.d.) "Equivalency, Recognition, and Dual Degrees." Retrieved from Netherlands Institute for Higher Education website, www.nihankara.org/web/?lang=3&pageid=180

European University Association. (2002). *Survey on Master's Degrees and Joint Degrees in Europe.* Brussels, Belgium: Tauch, C., and Rauhvargers, A. Retrieved from http://www.eua.be/eua/jsp/en/upload/Survey_Master_Joint_degrees_en.1068806054837.pdf

European University Association. (2002-2004). *Developing Joint Master's Programmes for Europe: Results of the EUA Joint Master's Project.* Brussels, Belgium: EUA. Retrieved from http://www.eua.be/eua/jsp/en/upload/Joint_Masters_report.1087219975578.pdf

Finocchietti, C. and Damiani, M.S. Tr. R. Boyce. (2002). Joint Degrees and Double Degrees: The Italian experience. Retrieved from http://www.cimea.it/files/219_110.pdf

Friedman, T. (2005). *The World is Flat*. New York, NY: Farrar, Straus and Giroux.

Green, M., Luu, D.T. and Burris, B. (2008). *Mapping Internationalization on U.S. Campuses: 2008 Edition*. Retrieved from http://store. acenet.edu/showItem.aspx?product=311770

Institute of International Education. (2009). *Open Doors 2008: Report on International Educational Exchange*. Washington DC: Bhandari, J. and Chow, P.

Institute of International Education and American Institute for Foreign Study. (2009). *Higher Education on the Move: New Developments in Student Mobility*. New York: IIE.

Institute of International Education and Freie Universität Berlin. (2009). *Joint and Double Degree Programs in the Transatlantic Context: A Survey Report*. Berlin, Germany: Kuder, M., and Obst, D. Retrieved from www.iienetwork. org/file_depot/0-10000000/0-10000/1710/folder/80205/ TDP+Report_2009_Final21.pdf

Junor, S. & Usher, A. (2008). *Student Mobility and Credit Transfer: A Global and National Survey*. Retrieved from http://www. educationalpolicy.org/publications/pubpdf/credit.pdf

Knight, J. (2008). Joint and Double Degree Programmes: Vexing Questions and Issues. *The Observatory on Borderless Higher Education*, September 2008. Retrieved from www.eahep.org/web/images/ Malaysia/joint_and_double_degree_programmes_vexing_ questions_and_issues_september_2008.pdf

Leakey, R. (2009). *The Problems for Young Professionals in Developing Countries*. Keynote address delivered at the *CGS/NSF Workshop on Globalizing Graduate Education*. Arlington, VA.

Marrett, C. (2009). *CGS/NSF Workshop: Globalizing Graduate Education and Research* [PDF Document]. Address delivered at the *CGS/ NSF Workshop on Globalizing Graduate Education*. Arlington, VA. Retrieved from http://www.cgsnet.org/portals/0/pdf/ CGSNSF2009_Marrett.pdf

NAFSA: Association of International Educators. (2008). *International Diplomacy: the Neglected Dimension of Public Diplomacy*,

Recommendations for the Next President. Retrieved from www. nafsa.org/uploadedFiles/NAFSA_Home/Resource_Library_Assets/ Public_Policy/public_diplomacy_2008.pdf

NAFSA: Association of International Educators. (2007-2008). *The Economic Benefits of International Education to the United States: A Statistical Analysis, 2007-2008.* Retrieved from http://www. nafsa.org/public_policy.sec/international_education_1/eis_2008/

NAFSA: Association of International Educators. (2008-2009). *The Economic Benefits of International Education to the United States: A Statistical Analysis, 2008-2009.* Retrieved from http://www. nafsa.org/publicpolicy/default.aspx?id=17174

Nerad, M. and Heggelund, M. (Eds.). (2008). *Toward a Global PhD? Forces and Forms in Doctoral Education Worldwide.* Seattle, WA: University of Washington Press.

Organisation for Economic Co-operation and Development. (2009). *International co-operation in research* in *OECD Science, Technology and Industry Scoreboard 2009.* doi: 10.1787/sti_scoreboard-2009-45-en. Retrieved from http:// dx.doi.org/10.1787/sti_scoreboard-2009-45-en

Saxenian, A. (2006). *The New Argonauts: Regional Advantage in a Global Economy.* Cambridge: Harvard UP.

Science Diplomacy is Crucial to US Foreign Policy. (n.d.). Retrieved from *Partnership for a Secure America* website, http://www.psaonline. org/article.php?id=620

Sussex Centre for Migration Research, University of Sussex, and the Centre for Applied Population Research, University of Dundee. (2004). *International Student Mobility.* Retrieved from http:// www.hefce.ac.uk/pubs/hefce/2004/04_30/

NOTES

1. See Junor and Usher, 2008, and Sussex Centre 2004.

2. See, for example, the Partnership for a Secure America, http://www.psaonline. org/article.php?id=620, and the AAAS Center for Science Diplomacy , http:// diplomacy.aaas.org/

3. See NAFSA, 2007-2008 and 2008-09.

4. See OECD 2009, Chapter 4, "International Co-operation in Research," p. 110.

5. CGS Graduate International Collaborations Project, Technical Workshop #2, July 15, 2009. For an extended discussion of the technical workshops, see Chapter 3.C.

6. Leakey 2009.

7. See Saxenian 2006 and Friedman 2005. Thomas Friedman popularized the notion that technology and economic globalization are "flattening" the world.

8. See for example presentations to AAAS (www.nsf.gov/news/speeches/ bement/09/alb090215_aaas.jsp) and the Research Councils UK (www.rcuk. ac.uk/cmsweb/downloads/rcuk/us/bement.pdf).

9. Marrett 2009.

10. Partnership for a Secure America, http://www.psaonline.org/.

11. IIE/AIFS 2009.

12. NAFSA 2008.

13. IIE 2008, p.3, p.18. While the number of American undergraduate students who study abroad is up 50% over the past decade, it is still the case that only a small proportion of graduate students do so.

14. Ibid., pp. 31-34.

15. Ibid., p. 3.

16. CGS 2008b, Table 1.4, p. 8 and Table 1.5, p.10

17. See IIE's 2008 *Open Doors Report,* p. 21.

18. Personal conversation with *Open Doors* author Rajika Bhandari in 2008 and correspondence with co-author Patricia Chow (July 28, 2009).

19. Between 2004 and 2009, application numbers have recovered slowly, but growth has slowed; 2009 data suggest that a turnaround seems evident. CGS surveys since 2004 are available online at: http://www.cgsnet.org/Default.aspx?tabid=172

20. See Carnevale in CGS 2009.

21. See European University Association 2002-2004; DAAD/HRK 2006; IIE/Freie Universität Berlin 2009; Finocchetti, et al. 2002; Green, et al. 2008; CGS 2008a and CGS 2009; Nerad and Heggelund 2008.

22. The Erasmus Mundus program is a program funded by the European Commission "to enhance quality in higher education through scholarships and academic cooperation between Europe and the rest of the world"; the program includes funding of joint master's and doctorates. For more information see http://ec.europa.eu/education/external-relation-programmes/doc72_en.htm

23. EUA 2002.

24. Ibid., p.27.

25. Ibid., p.6.

26. EUA 2004.

27. Ibid., p.12.

28. Ibid.

29. Ibid.

30. As the recent report jointly conducted by the Center for Higher Education Development and Center for Higher Education Policy Studies explains, a chief motivation for this investment in formal collaborative programs was the expectation that they "would have a bottom-up positive effect on the convergence of a European higher education system," p.6. http://www.jointdegree.eu/uploads/media/Che_Joint_Degrees_in_European_Higher_Education.pdf

31. DAAD/HRK 2006, p.16.

32. IIE and FUB, 2009.

33. Idem.

34. Among institutions with large international graduate enrollment, the response rates were as follows: 90% from the ten US universities with the largest international graduate student enrollment, 84% of the largest 25, and 68% of the largest 50 provided usable survey responses.

35. CGS 2007.

36. Ibid.

37. Ibid.

38. Ibid and CGS 2008b.

39. See footnotes 7 and 8 for more information.

40. See the CGS website, http://www.cgsnet.org/portals/0/pdf/R_IntlAdm08_ II.pdf, table 4.

41. Based on results from prior CGS surveys on field distribution, the survey did not ask respondents to report on every discipline, as the numbers were expected to be too small to serve as the basis for further analysis. [See Chapter Two, Table 2].

42. To minimize survey burden and maximize response rate, CGS did not ask respondents to identify the number of degrees for every research field or discipline. Given the structural similarities of financing and accreditation for most research fields, and the documented higher concentrations of international collaborations in engineering and business than in other fields, we elected to ask respondents to report on degrees for these four categories.

43. The 2009 IIE/FUB Report cites the following motivations for creating a joint or double degree program, in order of most to least important: 1. "Advancing internationalization of the campus; 2. "Raising international visibility and prestige of the institution; 3. Broadening the institution's educational offerings; 4. Strengthening academic research collaborations; 5. Increasing foreign student enrollments," p. 13.

44. See Knight 2008 and van der Duyn Schouten, n.d.

45. This issue is typically not encountered in one of the most common types of international collaborative degrees, the MBA, since these degrees often do not require a thesis, and in the focus group, participants did not discuss this type of program.

46. An international component is required of PIRE grant proposals, whereas international collaboration is elective for IGERT grants.

47. See DAAD, n.d.

48. EUA 2002.

49. Bosch and Titus 2009; Sigma Xi 2008.

50. CGS 2008; CGS 2010.

51. CGS published the proceedings of these Summits as: *Global Perspectives on Graduate Education* (2008), *Global Perspectives on Research Ethics and Scholarly Integrity* (2009), and *Global Perspectives on Graduate International Collaborations* (2010).

52. IIE/FUB's 2009 publication provides some important examples and a basis for future work in this area.

53. In order to test whether this approach was appropriate to the US context, CGS invited institutions in 2007 to define their degree structures using the terms "joint" or "dual degree" and, separately, to identify the mechanism for recognizing completion of a degree program. Among 2007 CGS survey respondents that indicated having at least one degree or certificate collaboration, 39% used the term **dual degree** or **double degree** to describe a program in which "students receive a degree or diploma from each university" as opposed to 6% who used the term to describe a program in which "students receive one degree or diploma from the college or university of registration, with the transcript declaring the program." None used the terms "dual" or "double degree" to describe a program in which "students receive one degree or diploma in the names of both colleges or universities."

US institutions use the term **joint degree** to describe programs that confer recognition in a variety of ways, including what would be typically be described by others as "dual degree" programs: 8% used the term "joint degree" to describe a program in which "students receive one degree or diploma in the names of both colleges and universities"; but 10% percent used the term "joint degree" to describe a program in which "students receive one degree or diploma from the college or university of registration, with the transcript declaring the program," and 16% used the term to describe programs in which students receive a "degree or diploma from each university."

54. See Comrie and Horgan 2009.

55. DAAD/HRK and FUB/IIE are examples.

56. **Dual (or Double) degree program:** Students study at two or more institutions and upon completion of the program receive a separate diploma from <u>each</u> of the participating institutions. **Joint degree program:** Students study at two or more institutions and upon completion of the program receive <u>a single</u> diploma representing work completed at two or more institutions.

PLANT-BASED MUSCLE

PLANT-BASED MUSCLE

Our Roadmap to Peak Performance on a Plant-Based Diet

Robert Cheeke
Vanessa Espinoza

Exercises – Workout Programs – Meal Plans

www.veganbodybuilding.com and www.plantbasedmuscles.com

Gaven Press
Los Angeles, CA
ISBN: 978-0-9843916-3-9

Praise for *Plant-Based Muscle*

"*Plant-Based Muscle* provides a wealth of vital information to *help you achieve optimal health and improve your overall fitness, while using a plant-based nutrition plan. In this book, Robert and Vanessa share their enthusiasm and knowledge, by providing practical steps necessary to build and maintain lean muscle mass. I especially like the 'mindset' aspect mentioned throughout the book because as a medical professional, it is well known that mindset shapes positive outcomes and further facilitates success! Plant-Based Muscle is beneficial for a beginner as well as for the experienced athlete."*

— **Harriet Davis, M.D., Board Certified Family Medicine Physician, plant-based IFBB professional bikini athlete, PETA's 2015 Sexiest Vegan Next Door**

"*Plant-Based Muscle* takes the mystery out of building muscle on a plant-based diet like no other book ever has! It's like getting to spend a week with two of the best and most experienced vegan bodybuilders in the world, and having them walk you through their exact, proven routines – in the gym, in the kitchen, and everywhere in between. Whether male or female, beginner or expert, whole-food or high-protein, if you're looking for the motivation, the philosophies, and the step-by-step meal plans and workout routines for building a world-class physique with a diet you can feel great about, you've found it in *Plant-Based Muscle*."

— **Matt Frazier, vegan ultramarathoner, author of *No Meat Athlete* and *The No Meat Athlete Cookbook***

"*Not only are Robert and Vanessa inspiring athletes and human beings, they are extremely intelligent individuals. The knowledge and experience that both Vanessa and Robert have put into Plant-Based Muscle is powerful and will help so many people on their fitness journey. Plant-Based Muscle is thoroughly written and filled with information* that will educate anyone interested in plant-based living and training. I highly recommend anyone, no matter where they may be in their fitness journey or how new to plant-based living they are, to read *Plant-Based Muscle* and learn from these two wonderful and educated souls."

— **Bianca Taylor, personal trainer and fitness model**

"What I love about this book is how Robert and Vanessa's approaches to nutrition & training are vastly different in many ways, yet they have both achieved high-level results by using differing methods. The typical 'one-size-fits-all' model regarding plant-based nutrition & training goes right out the window with this new book. As it really shines light on HOW to figure out what kind of training and nutrition style best fits YOU and your needs. A total game-changer!"

— **Fraser Bayley, founder of Evolving Alpha, vegan nutritionist and bodybuilder**

"*Plant-Based Muscle* is an excellent how-to guide for the beginner and advanced plant-based athlete. Robert and Vanessa have truly laid out the foundation for anyone trying to become the healthiest version of themselves on a plant-based diet. Not only that, but their philosophies on training and mentality can be applied to many other aspects in life."

— **Nimai Delgado, plant-based IFBB professional bodybuilder**

"After igniting the modern vegan bodybuilding movement, Robert has built an incredible worldwide community of world-class plant-based athletes. I've benefitted from his wisdom and expertise in my own fitness training, and I'm absolutely stoked that *Plant-Based Muscle* is finally here! Robert and Vanessa give you the keys to the kingdom of lifelong sustainable fitness, including workout routines, meal plans, mindset hacks, and motivational tips to help you live a strong, compassionate, and purposeful life. This book is a compendium of expert information and will be a trusted resource for newbie fitness fanatics as well as competitive athletes looking to add years to their life and build muscle in a healthy and ethical way."

— **Jason Wrobel, celebrity vegan chef, bestselling author, and host of Cooking Channel's "How to Live to 100"**

"I hold Robert in very high regard as the 'Godfather' of vegan bodybuilding – an early pioneer who helped kickstart the entire movement – which is why I couldn't wait to read his latest book. It did not disappoint. Robert and Vanessa Espinoza make a great duo, and this book is absolutely packed with gems from their wealth of experience. No matter if you're just getting started, or you're an experienced lifter who is curious as to how vegans fuel their workouts, this book is a great resource to help you pack on pure plant-based muscle."

— **Stephen Coote, founder of RiseOfTheVegan.com**

"Plant-Based Muscle is the go-to book for anyone interested in getting lean and building muscle on a plant-based diet. Robert and Vanessa do an incredible job in this book to cover all aspects of nutrition, diet, and ethics. Plant-Based Muscle is great for everyone from the beginner in the gym to the body building pro looking to incorporate a vegan diet. Being a beginner in the weightlifting world, this book has helped me tremendously. I highly recommend it!"

— **High Carb Hannah, YouTuber and author**

"Plant-Based Muscle is an inspiring book that delivers a great sense of knowledge and wisdom that can only come through decades of experience and success in bodybuilding and elite athletics. A real personal look inside the lives of two incredible plant-based athletes! Robert Cheeke and Vanessa Espinoza have magically blended two different styles of eating and training which gives even the seasoned athlete new insights and tips. Loved it!!!!"

— **Jeff Morgan, Certified Personal Trainer, plant-based nutrition certified, and creator of plant-based YouTube channel "Guilt Free TV"**

"Two luminaries in the vegan fitness scene deliver a comprehensive, inspirational, do-it-yourself workshop on building muscle from plants. After all, it's what all the biggest, strongest animals walking the Earth do."

— **Jonathan Balcombe, author of *What a Fish Knows***

"When it comes to first hand, in-the-trenches experience in building muscle on a plant-based diet, you'd be hard pressed to find a better pair than Robert and Vanessa. Robert was virtually the first competitive vegan bodybuilder on the scene and in many ways has propelled the movement on his own shoulders, and Vanessa has over a decade of experience as a trainer and competitive athlete. Plant-Based Muscle brings the knowledge of these two into a text that will serve as a great inspiration and reference for anyone looking to improve their performance, look their best, or optimize their health on a plant-based diet."

— **Derek Tresize, co-founder of Vegan Muscle & Fitness, author, personal trainer, professional athlete**

"I sat down to skim this book with the idea of eventually giving the authors my feedback and possible endorsement, and I accidentally read the whole darn thing in one sitting! I could not put it down! I edit a magazine on this sort of thing all day, but still loved this book that much. This book gives all the details of exactly how Robert and Vanessa train and exactly what they eat — this information is so valuable to anyone who wants to build a more effective physique. While both Robert and Vanessa are quite muscular, and this book definitely tells you how to put on the plant-based muscle, I said 'effective physique' because it also makes a lot of sense for simply getting stronger, and thus more effective in whatever you do in life. If only to prevent injury, strength is vital, but in the quest to excel in any physical endeavor, the information in Plant-Based Muscle will lend a huge boost to performance. Great job providing all these juicy details and for inspiring readers along the way! I cannot wait to read it again."

— **Brenda Carey, founder and editor-in-chief of Vegan Health & Fitness Magazine**

"Robert was one of my earliest inspirations in my vegan journey. From Vegan Bodybuilding and Fitness, to Shred It! and now, Plant-Based Muscle. Honest, inspirational and practical are the three words I would use to describe Robert's style of writing. Along with Vanessa's expertise *as a long-time vegan athlete, this book breaks everything down into its nuts and bolts. From training, to nutrition, to practical tips for everyday life, this is for everyone wanting to live a performance driven plant-based lifestyle. Both legends in their own right, they share their years of experience as athletes with one goal…to help you unleash yours!"*

— Luke Tan, author, vegan bodybuilder, Crossfitter, and co-founder of plantfitsummit.com

"Robert and Vanessa have crafted a book that not only serves as a well-honed guide for building muscle and amping up your fitness level on a plant-based diet, they've created a program that will keep you highly motivated to achieve your goals. Whether you want to simply get fit or increase your athletic performance, Plant-based Muscle is will give you the foundation you need to get there."

— Jason Wyrick, executive chef of The Vegan Taste, author of *Vegan Mexico*, *Vegan Tacos*, and NY Times Bestselling Co-author of *21 Day Weight Loss Kickstart*

"When you put the science into practice, you get Plant-Based Muscle. More than a workout guide, Robert and Vanessa reveal their personal philosophies and insights into building some serious vegan muscle, and how a plant-based lifestyle can unlock your ultimate fitness potential. This ain't no text book. This is real world experience. No matter where you're at on your fitness journey, Plant-Based Muscle is here to deliver you long-term gains, and smash a few stereotypes along the way."

— Tim Moore AKA @veganfatkid, founder of TrainVegan™

"I remember the shock I felt when I stumbled upon Robert on MySpace back in 2005. How had he achieved such a big physique with no animal protein? Years later, I got to know him in person when we were both living in Austin, TX. The book Plant-Based Muscle is a lot like Robert: positive, straightforward, no-nonsense, and it works. There's no hype or grandstanding. Robert and Vanessa lay out the guidelines of what has worked for them and give you the roadmap and the encouragement

you need to achieve it yourself. If you are looking for a guide with the nuts and bolts of getting into the best shape of your life on a healthy plant-based diet, this is it!"

— **Benjamin Benulis, DC, Chiropractor and plant-based athlete**

"Leaving no stone unturned or question unanswered, Robert and Vanessa have packed their new book, Plant-Based Muscle, with all the information you'll need to bulk up and get strong on a plant-based diet. The authors reveal foundational truths that will take you and your body to the next level. Robert and Vanessa have been training hard for decades and are living proof their advice on maintaining a consistent fitness routine truly works! And as Robert says in the book, 'results don't happen without consistent action.'"

— **James Aspey, animal rights activist, touring speaker, vegan athlete**

"All I can say is, 'Wow!' I get so many emails about vegan health and fitness, and I can tell you that Vanessa and Robert answer all of those questions in this book. Plant-Based Muscle covers everything, including eating, workouts, and most importantly, state of mind. I highly recommend this book!"

— **John Lewis, creator of BadAss Vegan & VeganSmart**

DISCLAIMER

The contents of this book have not been approved by the FDA or any other governing body. Though the authors are certified in plant-based nutrition (Robert), and a certified personal trainer (Vanessa), you are advised to consult your physician, nutrition expert, and/or personal trainer before adopting the programs outlined in this book.

The information, including meal plans and exercises, are recommendations to be used as guidelines and models. Consult your doctor, trainer, or nutritionist before embarking on one of the programs described in this book.

The authors, editors, publisher, printer, contributors, and others involved in this publication release themselves from any liability involving injury or loss as a result of applying the recommendations within this book.

Above all else, use reason and common sense when applying principles outlined in *Plant-Based Muscle,* pursue meaningful goals, and aim to be healthy and happy.

There are also a number of products we genuinely recommend, and some of those product mentions and recommendations are associated with affiliate accounts we have with certain products, companies, and brands. Therefore, by ordering a book or product we recommend, we might earn affiliate commission.

WHAT TO EXPECT FROM THIS BOOK

We are writing this book with you in mind. We want this to be an incredibly helpful manual, designed to provide you with the exact tools you need to achieve your health and fitness goals as a plant-based athlete. By athlete, we mean YOU. The inner athlete inside all of us is ready to come out, and this book will give you the confidence to unleash your best plant-based self. From start to finish, this book will provide you with the motivation, instruction, guidance, tips, recommendations, and resources to put you on the path to success. We've got you covered on everything from how to create a workout routine, to how to select quality foods and ingredients to prepare plant-based meals, to what to eat for improved athletic performance, to how to prevent and overcome injuries and setbacks.

Here are some specific things that you can expect to learn from our 35+ years combined experience as plant-based athletes:

- Motivation to get you pumped up to achieve your goals

- Programs for muscle building

- Programs for fat burning

- Programs for fitness conditioning

- Samples of our actual meal plans and workouts

- Grocery shopping lists and tips

- Healthy plant-based meal plans

- Delicious plant-based recipes

- Meal preparation guidelines

- A detailed account of our nutrition and fitness philosophies

- Photo demonstrations of numerous exercises

- Strategies for effective outreach as plant-based athletes

- Techniques to prevent and overcome injuries

DEDICATION

This book is dedicated to everyone who has dreams and the courage to pursue them.

This book is also dedicated to our family, our friends, our dogs, all those who have inspired us, and those we have been fortunate enough to inspire along our journey.

TABLE OF CONTENTS

OUR STORY

Robert

When I first met Vanessa, I was in awe of her physique. It was clear she had been training for a long time, and I felt a little inadequate as a former competitive bodybuilder, just a day away from running a half marathon. I was warming up for my workout on the floor at a gym just outside of Denver when Vanessa approached me. Vanessa introduced herself and said she had been following my career for more than 10 years. I immediately tried to puff up like a rooster to show I still had some muscle, even though the next day would be my fourth half marathon of the year and I had decreased in size dramatically from my bodybuilding days. A compliment about my physique from Vanessa momentarily eased my feelings of inadequacy, and then we made brief small talk and continued on with our workouts.

I was brand new to Colorado. I made the deliberate choice to live in a suburb where I didn't have any friends in order to focus on writing a new book (*Shred It!*). Living in a new state, where I didn't have an established community to interact with was an ideal setting for me to be my best creative-writing self. I was only going to the gym occasionally, as I trained at home and focused on writing, running, and adjusting to a new climate and new environment.

Vanessa and I would bump into each other at the gym again weeks after that initial meeting, and then again and again on a more regular basis. It turned out the gym we both went to was the closest to each of our homes, but we usually went at different times and didn't cross paths all that often. We arranged to work out together, fitting it in among our busy schedules, and eventually became friends and training partners. Fast-forward more than three years and a whole lot more muscle later, we're very good friends, we travel together on tour, hang out outside of the gym, and decided to collaborate on a book to share our experiences as plant-based athletes. I no longer worry about being mistaken for a distance runner, as I was when I first met Vanessa. I gained confidence as a weightlifter for the first time in quite a while after having added 40 pounds of total bulk from more than two years of training with Vanessa.

After initially meeting Vanessa, I learned that she was an all-American basketball player in high school and went on to play for Colorado State University, a top 10 ranked team, and was even drafted into the WNBA. As a major basketball fan myself, I was immediately intrigued. She is also a 3-time Colorado Golden Gloves state boxing champion. These days she is in her 11th year as a personal trainer running her own business, and her 15th year as a plant-based athlete. With our combined experience as plant-based athletes, building plant-based muscle and leading by example, I jumped at the opportunity to have my first co-written book with Vanessa. As the bestselling author of multiple books (*Vegan Bodybuilding & Fitness* and *Shred It!*), I will be narrating the majority of this book, but Vanessa's voice will be heard loud and clear, especially in chapters about workout programs, training techniques, and navigating the ins and outs of creating your own unique training routine, whether you have access to a gym or you workout at home. Vanessa also wrote the majority of the workout plans, and all of the meal plans, so we have a fresh take on both topics in this new book. We will clearly identify who is writing at a given time with our name above our passages.

To put my appreciation of Vanessa's muscle-building knowledge into one specific perspective, when we met in 2014 I weighed about 168 pounds and in 2016, after training together for two years, I peaked at 208 pounds. She helped me rediscover joy and fulfillment in weight training again, and helped me become bigger and stronger than I have ever been. Vanessa's background in basketball, boxing, personal training, and weightlifting, compliments my background of running, bodybuilding, weight training, and writing. We look forward to inspiring readers to apply the tips, suggestions, and knowledge we have to share, and our goal is for you to become the best version of yourself.

Vanessa and I follow similar but also slightly different approaches to both nutrition and training. I follow a supplement-free (aside from the inclusion of Vitamin B12), mostly whole-food, plant-based diet, whereas Vanessa uses some protein powders and a few other sports supplements along with a primarily whole-food, plant-based approach. Both of us are driven by passions for animal rights, health, fitness, and compassion for all beings, human and non-human animals alike. We openly call ourselves *vegan* athletes, but in addition to our ethical pursuit of a more compassionate world, we have learned to connect with a wide audience from a health standpoint and from fitness, weightlifting, and bodybuilding standpoints by identifying as *plant-based* athletes in this book. Therefore, you will often see us refer to ourselves as plant-based athletes to appeal to the plant-based audience curious about the ethical vegan lifestyle, as well as those just discovering a plant-based diet for the first time.

Vanessa and I are both very fortunate because we discovered what we were passionate about fairly early in life, and our behaviors and habits reflected what was truly close to our hearts. We simply pursued our passions and followed our hearts, and those actions took us to where we are now, writing this book together as plant-based athletes determined to teach others how to achieve similar meaningful goals. In late 2016, Vanessa and I both moved from Denver to Phoenix, Arizona, so you will read future references throughout this book to the Arizona climate and environment, and you will view many photos from Arizona mountains, gyms, grocery stores, and vegan restaurants.

Thank you for taking the opportunity to join our conversation about what compels us to work hard in the gym, to achieve the results we crave, and to have the positive impact on the world around us that we strive for. We sincerely wish you all the very best in health and fitness, and we encourage you to focus on what you want *most* rather than what you want *now*, and to create the positive habits that lead you to becoming your personal best. Whatever it is that inspires you, moves you, and drives you, you *can* do it. You have to believe in yourself and connect the dots ahead of time, and when you do, you can write your own future. Now is the time to follow *your* passion and make it happen.

INTRODUCTION TO PLANT-BASED MUSCLE

Robert

How do you define yourself? Are you a vegan, a runner, a mom, a dad, a weekend warrior, a dreamer, a realist, a plant-based athlete or striving to become one? Who are you? Regardless of who you are, we want to show you how to become a healthy, happy, and fit plant-based athlete. All of us have muscles and therefore all of us have potential to become athletes – active individuals, pursuing some form of exercise for pleasure, sport, or for health benefits.

I recently learned the NBA's Denver Nuggets' leading scorer (at the time of this writing), Wilson Chandler, adopted a vegan lifestyle in the summer of 2016. He subsequently experienced a breakout year in the 2016/2017 season, statistically the best ever of his 10-year career. For perspective, most NBA stars have their best seasons anywhere from 3-5 years into their careers, not a decade after it started (with the exceptions of LeBron James, and Kevin Durant, perhaps). This news is very exciting and inspiring for plant-based athletes to witness a 10-year NBA veteran having his best season ever after switching over to a plant-based diet. It is, after all, stories like this, and those of NFL players, MMA fighters, soccer players, tennis champions, and other professional athletes in major professional sports, which have the capacity to have a massive influence on a mainstream audience. It is already common to discover elite professional boxers, runners, bodybuilders, and weight lifters who are following a plant-based diet. And through their success, garnering notoriety as champions in more fringe sports, they inspire athletes in the most popular sports in the world, including professional soccer players, and even the plant-based leaning, 4-time Super Bowl Champion, Tom Brady. Needless to say, the future is bright, and momentum appears to be on the side of the compassionate athlete. The fountain of youth resulting from faster recovery, greater energy, and better performance - which are common to experience on a plant-based diet - excites today's athletes, resulting in greater awareness of the power that plant-based, whole foods possess. Vanessa and I happily play the roles that we do in inspiring those around us and those around the world who follow our work – including professional athletes who have learned from our examples.

We can show you what exercises to do to build muscle, and we can tell you what foods will truly support your muscle-building and fat-burning efforts, but what we aim to do most is help you to create a mindset that is poised for success. There are countless fitness books out there, endless fitness programs online, and quick solutions for readers to get shredded, ripped, and have more energy. Many work well, some work great. But most are just programs, not a mindset, not a way of life, not something that speaks to who we are as individuals passionate about being our personal best. Therefore, many of those popular programs won't work unless the people following those quick-results-driven programs are inherently driven themselves. For those who need more support, more guidance, some actual framework and context, help with the often-difficult step of just getting started, and being able to comprehend the mental approach that is necessary for the physical program to produce results, we're here for you.

This book is an inside look into our daily lives, revealing moment to moment what it takes to achieve success in areas of health, fitness, and beyond. We have both figured out what it takes to truly thrive as a plant-based athlete. Though we came to these conclusions individually, more than a decade before we ever met, we continue to learn from each other and inspire one another. We are excited to share with you decades of lessons learned. Ultimately, we want *you* to succeed in whatever fitness goals you have, providing the action steps for you to follow, ensuring that your success is just around the corner.

By the end of this book you will be equipped with all the tools necessary to fulfill your own health and fitness dreams, and you might even have a new way of defining yourself. We understand that new information can be overwhelming, and that the journey to any destination worth pursuing begins with a single step forward. We invite you to take that step right now, even if it is outside of your usual comfort zone. Change begins when you learn to become comfortable with being uncomfortable. Just as we will walk you through the exercises and workout programs, we will do the same for meal plans, recipes, and even grocery shopping, showing you our actual grocery receipts, removing any guesswork. With this detailed approach we will cover for you every aspect for being your best plant-based-athlete self. The road to success starts with an action plan and a desire to see that plan fulfilled. Look inward to discover *why* you want to become a plant-based athlete, and notice what it *feels* like to set meaningful goals, recognizing your *courage* to pursue them. It's time to build some plant-based muscle. You can do it!

Chapter 1

OUR TRAINING PHILOSOPHIES

TRAINING PHILOSOPHIES

Vanessa

I have been weight training consistently for over 15 years, never taking off more than two weeks at a time. Sometimes I train more than 10 days in a row without a day off. I will only take a day off when I truly need it, and if that means taking two to three days off in a row, I will. I really listen to my body to gauge when I need a break or when I can keep training for days on end. Muscle soreness, fatigue, and other indicators will let me know when to tone it down, just as increased energy and feelings of elevated health and fitness encourage me to keep going. Throughout the years my training has varied, but the two things that haven't changed are my intensity and consistency. I have a certain mindset when I train. I'm a big believer in the idea that every time you step in the gym you are getting better. This means every rep and every set matter. I want to be the best I can be and attack each workout with as much as or more intensity than the last.

People ask me all the time how I get motivated and stay motivated to train day after day. My answer is simple: I love it. I train when I'm happy, when I'm sad, and when I'm tired. Yes, even when I'm tired, especially because I'm tired. It doesn't matter what time of day it is, early morning or late at night, I always feel like training. It always makes me feel better. Some may consider me very extreme when it comes to my training, but that is the approach that has built my physique to where it is today. I focus on working out one muscle group per day, and I train for one to two hours each session. My goal is to blast the muscle and then give it six days of rest. The whole idea is to completely fatigue the muscle and let it repair. In addition to weight training, I also perform cardiovascular training five days a week. I absolutely love doing cardio. My favorite forms of cardio training are sprinting and boxing. I prefer doing cardio outside, so most days I will get out and run sprints. I will do some type of interval running, run hills, or climb stairs. I will run even if it is zero degrees outside and there is a ton of snow on the ground, or if the temperatures are still in the triple digits on an Arizona summer evening. The weather doesn't stop me, and I stay properly hydrated, fueled, and dressed for any particular climate when I'm training outdoors. I also do some sprint work inside on a basketball court. A typical indoor cardio workout will be 10-20 suicide sprints up and down the court. Occasionally I use the Stairmaster before or after a weight training session as well.

The following are my favorite exercises:

CHEST

Barbell and dumbbell flat bench press

Plyometric push-ups

BACK

Deadlifts

Barbell bent-over rows

Wide grip pull-ups

TRX Australian pull-ups

LEGS

Squats

Lunges

BICEPS

Z-bar curls

Dumbbell biceps curls

TRICEPS

Skull crushers

Close-grip bench press

SHOULDERS

Barbell military press

Dumbbell rear flys

HAMSTRINGS

Romanian deadlifts

Good mornings

ABS

Abdominal roller

Kneeling cable crunches

General fitness philosophies:

This is my approach to working out. I have a specific protocol and I follow it essentially every day:

PRE-WORKOUT MEALS

Typical pre-workout meals include Matcha green tea with lemon and one of the following:

- Quinoa with peanut butter, chia, hemp seeds, banana, and cinnamon

- Fruit smoothie

- Powerootz brand protein shake smoothie with almond milk/water and ice

WARM-UP

I perform a quick shoulder routine with lightweight (5-pound) dumbbells, which consists of one set for 10 repetitions of each of the following exercises: side raises, front raises, military presses, rear flys, across the chest flys, rotator cuff rotations, and across the body raises. I combine this upper body routine with 20 minutes on the Stairmaster, or running a dozen suicide sprints on the basketball court to complete my total body warm-up.

WORKOUT

I train one or two muscle groups per day during a single training session.

DURATION OF WORKOUT

My workouts last from 90 minutes to two hours, depending on the muscle groups I am training for a given workout.

COOLDOWN

My cooldown usually consists of foam rolling and stretching out my shoulders, wall snow angels, and snow angels on the foam roller. Occasionally, I use a massage stick to roll over my muscles to break up knots and reduce tightness and stiffness in given muscle groups. I focus on stretching out my shoulders because they are one muscle group that can be especially vulnerable to overuse, since they are engaged in chest, back, and of course, shoulder exercises. I also have a bit of a nagging pain and tightness in my shoulders that flares up from time to time, and to keep my shoulder pain in check, a little bit of extra attention is paid to them when I cool down. Eating anti-inflammatory foods can help, as can a proper warm-up, but since I train so heavy and so hard, a bit of soreness in my shoulders is all but inevitable for me, therefore I work hard to manage it to keep making forward progress. If you have a nagging area of pain, consider giving it the same localized attention with recovery and rehab techniques. Alternating ice and heat therapies on areas of regular soreness is a common practice as well.

POST-WORKOUT MEALS

Following a workout, I typically eat lunch, which usually consists of vegetables, tofu, and a sweet potato, or I'll have a Powerootz brand protein shake.

WORKOUT SCHEDULE AND REST DAYS

As referenced earlier, I will often workout 10 or more days in a row without a day off. Sometimes I will even go 15 or more days of training without a rest day. I only take a day off when my body needs it. I train different muscle groups each day, so I get adequate rest time for each muscle group before training that same muscle group again. I also eat a lot of anti-inflammatory foods, drink plenty of water, stretch during and after workouts, go to bed early, get plenty of overall rest, and my body responds by recovering well and allowing me to train frequently and regularly. I also often train more than once in a day. It is fairly normal for me to train along with at least one of my clients each day, in addition to my own workout I do alone or with Robert or another training partner. My body adapts over time, much like an elite runner who can train seven days a week for weeks on end due to adaptation to exercise and stress. Our bodies are really resilient when we give them an opportunity to show how strong they are. A lot of that has to do with properly fueling our bodies with sound nutrition, properly training, properly warming up and recovering from exercise, and of course, enjoying the process.

TRAINING SOLO VS. TRAINING PARTNER

My workouts vary when I workout with a partner compared to training by myself. When I train with a partner I lift heavier than I would if I were alone. I need a spotter on most free weight lifts and a partner pushes me to do more forced reps with a heavier workload. When I am by myself I still lift heavy but don't max out and go that extreme. I super-set a lot more when I'm alone because I'm not able to put up as much weight, so I really try to focus on volume.

TYPES OF GYMS AND PREFERENCES

I don't really have a preference for a specific type of gym. I can find anything to do in most gyms, even if there isn't a lot of equipment. I love gyms that have Olympic-style equipment to do cleans, hang cleans, deadlifts, and similar compound barbell lifts, but as long as I am training, I am happy with any gym I'm in.

HIGHLIGHTS FROM ALL-TIME BEST WORKOUTS

Every workout is a great workout, so it's hard to pick just one that stands out as my best all-time workout. The two people that I had always dreamed of training with were champion vegan bodybuilders,

Robert Cheeke and Torre Washington. I am so lucky that I get to train with Robert on a regular basis, and I also have had the pleasure of training with Torre a few times.

MINDSET

I'm a big believer in making the most out of every workout. To me, this means going in to the gym with a specific attitude that I am going to work hard, push myself, and give it everything I've got, so I'm better the next time I walk into the gym. Each workout is an opportunity to make forward progress, and I don't take that for granted. I often train each muscle group just once or twice per week, so any given workout might be my only one for that particular muscle group for the whole week, and I'm going to make it count. I love working out, and that makes it easy for me to look forward to each training session and to want to be in the gym. I'd rather be in the gym training than nearly anywhere else, and even when I'm traveling or on vacation, I look for a gym so I can get my workout in. Training has become such a part of who I am that it comes naturally to me, and I embrace and truly love it.

TRAINING PHILOSOPHIES

Robert

When it comes to my current training, I'm a fan of seeking out the best-perceived return on investment (ROI) from a given exercise. What that means to me is that each exercise will give our bodies a response based on the stress we put on it, and depending on our goals at the time, some of those responses are better than others. Resistance weight training will provide an opportunity for muscle-growth stimulation, and clearly some exercises will stimulate more muscle growth than others. I'll share an example a little further down.

My general approach is to train one or two muscle groups per workout, and train five days per week for about an hour to an hour and a half per workout, depending on the muscle group(s) being trained. I tend to have 30-second to one-minute rest periods between sets for smaller muscle groups such as biceps, triceps, forearms, calves, and sometimes shoulders, and I rest for 1-2 minutes in between sets for larger muscle groups such as chest and back, and even up to 3 minutes or more between sets when training legs, especially during very heavy lifts such as leg presses. The heavier I lift, the longer the rest periods, and if I am just doing light weight, high repetition sets for large muscle groups like chest and back, I'll only rest for about a minute between sets because they aren't all that intense or taxing on my body. The same goes for legs when doing leg extensions. I only need a minute between sets since extensions are less strenuous isolated movements just targeting the quadriceps.

I go through periods where I will do essentially no cardiovascular training at all, and then I'll go through phases were I'll use the Stairmaster at least three days per week for weeks on end. My cardiovascular training (or lack of training) largely depends on my goals at the time, my priorities, my schedule, and ultimately my desire to climb copious amounts of stairs, or not. Aside from hiking in the beautiful mountains of the Tonto National Forest behind my house, the Stairmaster is my preferred method of cardiovascular training at the present time.

When I travel I make it a goal to get at least one workout in while I'm away, but I don't always make it happen. If I am unable to make it to a gym, I will often settle for push-ups and bodyweight exercises. I also aim to take the stairs rather than elevators in hotels (once luggage has been dropped off in the room, of course). In essence, I look for ways to incorporate fitness, especially when a gym workout is not practical on a given travel day. Whether that is carrying heavy luggage, taking the stairs, or dropping to the ground to hammer out a bunch of push-ups, or all three, I tend to find a way to stay active regardless of where I am.

I mentioned that I would share a bit more detail about my core philosophy when it comes to my current training, which is to get the best-perceived ROI of a given exercise. This is what I mean by that: There is no question that squats will stimulate more muscle growth than isolated cable leg curls, given the same effort applied to each exercise for the same number of reps, sets, and duration. The former creates much more muscle growth stimulation because it is a multi-joint, compound exercise that calls upon far more muscle fibers to be involved in the exercise. Under the stress of the weight training exercise, micro-tears happen within the muscles and the opportunity for repair and growth is therefore impacting significantly more muscle fibers from doing squats than an isolated exercise relying on a small number of specific muscle fibers. In this example, squats also release more testosterone, and create an opportunity for increased muscle mass gain, strength gain, and adaptation to high physical stress on the body. Squats are also more of a total body exercise, training lower legs, upper legs, glutes, abdominals and the entire core, as well as upper body and stabilizer muscles. That is just one example, but the same could be said for barbell bench press versus cable flys, or dumbbell overhead press versus cable shoulder raises, or numerous other free weight exercises when compared to isolated movements on machines or cables. Though free weights are preferred, there are always pros and cons to any specific exercises, which I'll discuss throughout the book, including the reasons why I tend to use machines and cables more at the time of this writing than I ever have before.

Lastly, I try to make exercise fun, whether I'm in the gym or on the hiking trail. I truly want to enjoy fitness because it will encourage me to engage in it frequently, which puts me in a good position to achieve desirable goals.

My favorite compound, multi-joint exercises:

CHEST

Decline barbell bench press

Incline dumbbell flys

BACK

T-bar rows

High rows

Low rows

LEGS

Plate-loaded squat press

Wall sits

Leg extensions

ARMS

Biceps

Dumbbell biceps curls

Cable biceps curls

Rows of any type (biceps)

TRICEPS

Dumbbell Overhead Extensions (triceps)

Presses of any kind, especially narrow-grip chest press (triceps)

SHOULDERS

Dumbbell overhead press

Dumbbell raises (lateral, forward, rear deltoid)

ABS

Hanging leg or knee raises

Planks

General fitness philosophies:

My approach to fitness is one of purpose, passion, efficiency, enjoyment, and fulfillment. What that means to me is that I make conscious decisions regarding what I eat, how I train, why I'm doing it, what methods I prefer, and what I aim to get out of the experience as far as a desirable feeling, a benefit, or measurable level of fulfillment. Therefore, I eat for the desired impact it will have on my health and fitness, I train with an objective in mind, I have a general passion for achieving high levels of success, I use effective and efficient methods to achieve and attain goals, and I honor and enjoy the meaningful journey.

PRE-WORKOUT MEALS
Fruit is my fuel if I am about to train immediately. My favorite pre-workout meal is eating two or three bananas. If I have some time before my workout, such as an hour or two, then oats, potatoes, beans and rice are all preferred complex carbohydrate energy-rich foods.

WARM-UP
I am a big fan of warming up before exercising. I was injury-free for more than three consecutive years, which might be the longest such period in my athletic career (before a 2016 injury I will address later on), and I credit a lot of that success to my warm-up approach. My style of warm-up is performing about six sets of 25 push-ups and six sets of 50-100 crunches, which takes about 15 minutes. I also do some arm circles, some general movements like swinging my arms across my chest and jumping side to side, to get blood moving for increased circulation as part of a proper warm-up to reduce the risk of injury. When I go through periods of lower back soreness from some ongoing low back disc injuries, I swap out crunches from my warm-up and replace them with arm and leg lifts (bird dog pose) and hip raises from the floor. This not only removes the stress that crunches and sit-ups put on my lower back, but also works to strengthen my low back to prevent future injuries. Those movements are also part

of my low back rehab protocol, so I prioritize them as part of a very important warm-up routine. In general, any combination of my various warm-up approaches typically takes me between 15 and 20 minutes to complete, and I believe this greatly reduces my risk of injury while preparing my muscles for the workload ahead of them.

DURATION OF WORKOUT

My workouts tend to last between 60-90 minutes, typically lasting around 75 minutes, which includes my usual 15-minute warm-up.

STRETCHING

One of the most misunderstood aspects of training is the role of stretching. Some people stretch before a workout, and some don't stretch at all. I am a big believer in stretching once warmed up, and stretching throughout the workout. It is not uncommon for me to stretch between every single set when I am training chest or legs. I also stretch extensively throughout my back and shoulder workouts. I even stretch small muscles like biceps and triceps, and of course, my calves, to dramatically reduce soreness following the workout. Stretching triceps is very common (reaching overhead and grabbing your elbow with your other hand and pulling downward), but not many people stretch their biceps, a muscle group that is fairly easy to injure. Simply extend your arm, palm up, and apply pressure (to your inner wrist) so that full extension can stretch your biceps. It is not only effective, and underperformed by many lifters, but it feels really good during a biceps workout too. I don't believe you should stretch cold muscles, but once warmed up from cardiovascular training, push-ups, light machine, cable, free weight or bodyweight exercises, stretching should be incorporated during and after an exercise session. Stretching helps prevent injuries, reduces soreness (especially for chest and legs, I have found), and assists with increasing flexibility, improved circulation, and overall recovery after exercise. An outstanding place to stretch is in a sauna or steam room if you have access to those, which can typically be found at big box gyms such as 24 Hour Fitness, L.A. Fitness, and Lifetime Fitness. The heat will help your muscles relax, lengthen, and stretch, while also encouraging increased water consumption, which in general helps cell nutrition, recovery, and replenishing muscles following a workout. Otherwise, a mat on the gym floor, on the grass in a park, your own living room floor, or wherever it is you exercise, will work just fine to complete common stretches to help you make forward progress.

COOLDOWN AND RECOVERY

For my cooldown from an intense workout, I typically perform a relatively light cable, machine, or bodyweight exercise following a lot of heavy, free weight exercises that often make up the bulk of my workout. I like to burn out the muscles while developing a nice pump that you get from high repetitions. Examples could include cable chest flys, cable rope pull-downs, machine biceps curls, or machine overhead shoulder press for as many reps as possible with a manageable weight. This develops a great muscle pump and burnout, fatiguing of the muscles, and leaves me with a feeling of satisfaction from a tough workout, while also stretching the muscles out from high repetitions with good range of motion.

In addition to my cooldown, my favorite approach for recovery is to eat some fruit immediately after my workout (or during), and then sit in the sauna or steam room. I don't use heat treatments after every workout, perhaps just a couple of times per week, but I enjoy it when I incorporate them into my recovery program. I stretch and drink a lot of fluids while in the sauna or steam room, and I really believe this helps my overall recovery. Our muscles are made of up 70 percent water, and sitting in intense heat encourages a dramatic increase in water intake while also providing a hot environment for muscles to stretch to help reduce post-workout soreness and expedite recovery. I have been able to consume as much as half a gallon of water while going in and out of the sauna for a 45-minute period, when that is often more water than I consume in a full day when not using heat therapy. I realize not everyone has an extra 45 minutes or more following a long workout, but even just 10 minutes in the sauna before leaving the gym can be a great way to get some effective stretching, rest, fluid intake, and recovery.

As a former professional massage therapist, I am also a big fan of incorporating sports massage therapy into my overall routine. My favorite modalities include deep tissue, Thai massage, trigger point therapy, and sports massage. Massage can aid in overall recovery through increased flexibility, improved circulation, and decreasing stress. It can certainly be a big added expense, but if you're able to incorporate sports massage into your routine every once in a while, it could be something you realize to be beneficial. You can also use massage sticks, massage machines, and forms of self-massage, especially on muscles like legs that are easy to reach, to help your exercise recovery if you don't have access to professional massage therapy. You can also visit large furniture stores and sit in their massage chairs they have on display – a little tip from my experience after moving to Arizona. The high-end ones are surprisingly good, and can no doubt aid in relaxation and recovery. Foam rollers, stretching bands, and, movements such as arm circles, and light static and ballistic stretches are other effective forms of recovery and cooldown, so find what resonates with you and keep it cool.

POST-WORKOUT MEALS

As mentioned, after a workout, it is very common for me to eat fruit as I am walking out of the gym and while driving home. Bananas are my post-workout fruit of choice, but I also eat oranges, tangerines, grapes, apples, and berries. I also drink water or coconut water following a workout. Once I get home, I enjoy eating heavier foods such as brown rice with beans and avocado, or potatoes or yams with salad greens. If I am in a hurry, perhaps a snack bar or two (usually a Lara Bar) containing 200 calories of nuts and fruit in each bar will suffice until I get to a bigger meal. Lately, I have really been enjoying vegetable sushi following a workout. I will eat 10-15 pieces of sushi with rice, seaweed, avocado, cucumber, and carrots in a sitting. I have also been incorporating soups over a bed of brown rice and even peanut butter sandwiches if I want something that is really quick, cheap, and not labor-intensive. In general, my goal is to replenish fluids and electrolytes lost through exercise, replace glycogen stores by consuming carbohydrates, as well as to start the rebuilding process for muscle fibers damaged from exercise (muscle repair and growth). The water and fruit replenish the fluids, electrolytes, and glycogen; and the foods such as rice, beans, lentils, potatoes, yams, vegetables, and salads come into play for the muscle building as they contain large quantities of amino acids, the building blocks of protein. As long as I consume adequate calories in relation to my calorie expenditure, I will continue to make progress.

WORKOUT SCHEDULE AND REST DAYS

My typical workout schedule looks like this:

- Monday – Chest

- Tuesday – Back

- Wednesday – Legs

- Thursday – Rest

- Friday – Shoulders

- Saturday – Arms

- Sunday – Rest

I am often on the road as a touring speaker and avid traveler so I don't always stick to that exact routine. I need my training program to adjust with my travels. This is my current general training approach, focusing on one or two muscle groups per workout and working out five days per week. I strive to follow this outline, but I am transparent about the obstacles that prevent perfection. Life can get in the way for all of us, and I acknowledge that for myself. If I am traveling a lot and find myself in the gym for only three days one week, I will likely combine muscle groups in a single workout, such as training chest, shoulders, and back all in one workout to make up for missed workouts for specific muscle groups.

TRAINING SOLO VS. TRAINING WITH A PARTNER

Throughout my nearly 18 years of weight training, I have hired personal trainers, have trained with regular training partners, and have trained solo. The vast majority of my training over the course of nearly two decades has been on my own. That is the nature of being on tour for some substantial periods of time since 2005 and having an unpredictable schedule. I also train at odd hours and have moved a lot over the past ten years. I haven't lived in any city for more than two years since 2008, which has made it tough to develop routines and regularity, especially with a training partner. I prefer to have a consistent training partner for a whole host of reasons, including the enjoyment aspect of training with a friend, the accountability component of having someone relying on me, and especially for having a spotter to help when lifting heavy weights. For me, lifting really heavy weights – relative to one's own ability and strength – is one of the most fun and rewarding aspects of weight training. There are certain exercises that I absolutely need a spotter for if I am going to be at my personal best, such as the decline barbell bench press. That is my favorite exercise, but for me to lift my heaviest without a spotter I risk having the barbell with more than 300 pounds, lying across my neck in a decline position. That is not something I am interested in. Getting trapped under heavy weight has nearly happened to me a couple of times when a fight-or-flight response kicked in while lifting heavy weight on the decline press on my own. Those were scary moments and I likely won't put myself in that position again. With a spotter, I can press over 315 pounds on that exercise and I aim toward new goals as I continue to get stronger. Without a spotter I typically won't lift over 285 pounds for that same exercise. You can see how having a spotter can make a huge difference in amounts of weight lifted, and with regards to safety, motivation, support, and so on.

The same risk-versus-reward situation lies within heavy dumbbell exercises. If I were to press dumbbells for chest press as heavy as I can go on my own, I risk 120-pound dumbbells in each hand crashing down toward my face. Again, that is not something I am interested in! Having a spotter is a great way to protect me during those heavy lifts. One could argue that I shouldn't even put myself in that position anyway, and lift lighter weights, but with an experienced spotter, like Vanessa, the risk is mitigated and my best-ever lifts are experienced, and the bigger and stronger I get. Of course, I caution others about lifting with maximum effort without an experienced spotter. I only lift to the max on occasion, and only with an experienced spotter to ensure I perform the movements safely and with support. I could probably reach some similar goals lifting lighter weights, but the enjoyment and fulfillment would be missing and that is one of the main reasons I train in the first place. A good spotter can really help you have safer and better workouts. It's not about ego, but about the experience. I am driven by the training process itself, and by the rewards, the fun, and the fulfillment experienced from training hard with heavy weights.

Overall, I prefer to have a regular training partner, but alas, most of my workouts are performed solo at my local gym, in hotel gyms, or in random gyms out on the road somewhere. Now that I am settled in Arizona and Vanessa lives 20 minutes down the road, and champion vegan bodybuilder, Will Tucker is just 10 minutes away, I tend to have a training partner more often, and it has brought a new level of fun (and strength) to my training.

TYPES OF GYMS AND PREFERENCES

I prefer to train in a 24-hour gym because my workouts come at all different times, and I can occasionally be found lifting weights at midnight. Sometimes I am traveling in dramatically different time zones, and having access to a gym open around the clock is preferred. I also prefer gyms that have a decline barbell bench press, and specific equipment such as dumbbells that go up to 100 pounds or more, a T-bar row, a high row machine, and a leg press, inverted leg press, or plate-loaded squat press. I train at the national chains, 24 Hour Fitness and LA Fitness, but I also drop in to YMCAs around the country and iconic gyms like Quads in Chicago and The Mecca, Venice Gold's Gym in southern California. When traveling, especially internationally, I have found that the chain, Anytime Fitness, has been an awesome solution. I sign up for a week or so, get an electronic key to let myself in anytime 24/7, and I get great workouts in major cities and in small towns around the globe.

HIGHLIGHTS OF SOME ALL-TIME BEST WORKOUTS

My favorite and most memorable workouts in recent memory have been with Vanessa. She often out-lifts me and pushes me hard to set new records, reach new heights, and adapt to a new workload.

Most of my record lifts have been while training with Vanessa. Other memorable workouts came at Bonebreaker Barbell, a vegan owned and operated hardcore gym in Austin, Texas. Owner Mike Crockett brought out some of my best strength when we trained together during a year that I lived in Austin. I shoulder-shrugged 540 pounds using free weights in the squat rack, and my best deadlifts were at Bonebreaker Barbell.

My general fitness philosophies change as my experiences change, and I will discuss my approaches in more detail in future chapters dedicated to workout programs and exact routines.

MINDSET

Above all else, I believe in consistency, transparency, and accountability. I like to know what I am actually doing and what I am not doing, so I can make the appropriate changes to get closer to achieving meaningful goals. Skipping workouts and eating poorly is something we all face at one time or another, and I try to recognize behaviors and patterns that lead me astray so I can correct them and take myself down a path that will lead to positive results. One of the steps I take to ensure accountability is documenting my workouts to confirm I am, in fact, training regularly, which is a prerequisite for forward progress. To do this, I use a *Shred It! 13-Week Training Journal* to document my daily workouts. This is a helpful resource that assists in consistency, accountability, and transparency. I use it because it works and I think it can be an outstanding tool, especially for those who struggle with consistency.

In addition to documentation of workouts, I also aim to put forth a good effort when I train. I am actively aware of the times I am just going through the motions, and of the times when I am putting forth a much more deliberate and substantial effort. I look for patterns to reveal why one workout may be much better than another one, and I make necessary changes based on my observations.

At the end of the day, I realize I am very fortunate to get to do what I do as a representative of the plant-based athlete lifestyle, and I truly want to be an effective and positive ambassador for the movement. Therefore, I aim to allow my actions to support my goals, and I work hard to achieve them.

Chapter 2

OUR CURRENT TRAINING PROGRAMS

MY CURRENT TRAINING PROGRAM

Vanessa

My current training program consists of focusing on one muscle group a day. For example, I will train chest on Monday and won't train chest again until six days later. I will spend one to two hours really blasting those muscles, and then give them adequate rest before training them again the next week. If I feel like a muscle group is lacking then I will hit that muscle twice in one week. Lately, I feel like my back needs more work so I have been spending two hard days during the week training back. Just like Robert, I will start my workout with a compound, multi-joint exercise and then focus on isolated movements. During the course of my workout I will go super heavy for 1 to 5 reps, medium weight for 6 to 15 reps, and lighter weight for 25 to 50 reps. However, I focus mostly on the 6- to 15-rep range because my aim is to gain as much muscle mass as possible. I've found though, including a high rep range can also aid hypertrophy (muscle growth). It is important for me to also have muscle endurance, which is why I incorporate a high rep range into my workouts.

Over my years of training, I swear by adding high-repetition training into my everyday routine, and I feel like my strength has increased tremendously as a result. Muscle endurance will increase muscle mass as well. The whole idea behind this is to hit all the muscle fibers, both fast and slow twitch. When I'm training, my goal is to work and recruit as many muscle fibers as possible. Targeting more muscle fibers means greater gains in strength and muscle mass. During my workout I always include a burnout set at the end of an exercise. For example, when training chest, on my last set I will strip the weight to about half of my max and bust out as many reps as possible. Another type of burnout I incorporate is single-arm isolation exercises. One example of this is the dumbbell chest press. In this exercise I will press one arm holding a dumbbell while the other arm is up in the air holding a dumbbell in a static contraction the whole time, then switch arms. I also include negative (eccentric) movements and unilateral movements in my workouts. Negatives refer to resisting the movement of the weight in relation to gravity, such as resisting the weight coming back down when doing chest or shoulder presses. Sometimes I will end a set with negatives or perhaps I will perform my entire workout with this type of training. This puts lots of added stress on the muscle fibers and makes me extremely sore, so I don't do this type of workout everyday.

The last type of technique I add into my workouts is unilateral movement, which means working one arm or one leg at a time. This approach is important because you want to work each arm or leg independently to balance out your strength. When we squat, bench press, or military press, for example, it is common that one arm or leg is always working harder than the other, even though you feel like you're pressing each one evenly. I will add a unilateral movement at the end of each set or will complete a whole workout just doing unilateral movements. It is important that both your right and left arms and legs are equal in strength. An imbalance in strength can cause problems later in life, such as back and knee injuries, pain, imbalances, overuse, compensation, and muscle weakness.

On the days that I don't have a lot of time for exercise, I will do an entire bodyweight workout at home or at the gym. For example, I will do 1,000 push-ups, which usually takes me 45 minutes. I will do many different variations of push-ups to really hit every muscle in my chest, shoulders, and arms. I will do the same when training legs. I will complete 1,000 reps of different types of bodyweight squats and lunges. For back I will do 500 pull-ups of various types. I love to be outdoors so I will go to the local park and do pull-ups and muscle-ups on the monkey bars. You don't need fancy or expensive equipment to get a great workout in. These bodyweight workouts are some of my favorites to do because they are super challenging and I'm completely fatigued when I'm done.

Here is an example of a typical workout for each major muscle group. Every workout usually takes me 90 minutes to complete:

CHEST

Barbell flat bench press

- The bar (45 pounds) x 25 reps
- 135 pounds x 20 reps
- 135 pounds x 20 reps
- 185 pounds x 10 reps
- 205 pounds x 5 reps
- 215 pounds x 3 reps
- 225 pounds x 2 reps
- Max weight x 1 rep
- Burnout: 135 pounds x 25 reps

Dumbbell incline press

- 60 pounds each arm x 12 reps
- 70 pounds each arm x 10 reps
- 80 pounds each arm x 6 reps
- 90 pounds each arm x 3 reps
- Burnout: single arm isolation 40 pounds x 15 reps each arm

Dumbbell chest flys on a flat bench

- 40 pounds each arm x 15 reps
- 50 pounds each arm x 10 reps
- 60 pounds each arm x 8 reps
- 65 pounds each arm x 6 reps
- Burnout: 30 pounds x 25 reps each arm

Hammer Strength (plate-loaded) machine press

- 90 pounds x 15 reps
- 140 pounds x 12 reps
- 190 pounds x 10 reps
- 240 pounds x 8 reps
- Burnout: 140 pounds x 15 reps each arm

Cable chest flys

(High to low)

- 70 pounds x 25 reps
- 80 pounds x 25 reps
- 90 pounds x 25 reps

(Middle)

- 60 pounds x 25 reps
- 70 pounds x 25 reps
- 80 pounds x 25 reps

(Low to high)

- 40 pounds x 25 reps
- 50 pounds x 25 reps
- 60 pounds x 25 reps

Single arm chest cable flys

- 30 pounds x 15 reps each arm
- 40 pounds x 15 reps each arm
- 50 pounds x 15 reps each arm

Push-ups (variations x 250 reps)

Regular push-ups:

- 25 reps
- 25 reps

- 25 reps
- 25 reps

X-fit push-ups:

- 25 reps
- 25 reps
- 25 reps
- 25 reps

Plyometric push-ups:

- 25 reps
- 25 reps

* As you move through the book if there are any exercises that you are unfamiliar with, or unsure how to perform, please refer to Vanessa's YouTube channel (youtube.com/VanessaEspinozaPlantBasedMuscle), where you will find demonstrations and explanations of the exercises she outlines in the workout programs.

Without listing the exact amount of weight used for every ensuing workout, this is the general approach I take to training each additional muscle group:

LEGS	SETS X REPS
Warm-up	Skip rope 10 minutes
Squats	11x25, 20, 25, 10, 10, 6, 4, 2, 1, 1, 1
Barbell sumo squats	4x15
Barbell lunges	3x10 each leg
Step-ups	3x10 each leg
Side lunges	3x10 each leg
Hack squat	3x15
Single leg, leg extension	3x15 each leg
Single leg, leg press	3x10 each leg
Pistol squats	3x6 each leg

BACK	SETS X REPS
Deadlift	9x25, 15, 10, 10, 8, 6, 3, 1, 1
Wide grip pull-ups	4xfailure
Barbell bent-over rows (overhand)	3x15
Barbell bent-over rows (underhand)	3x15
TRX W,Y,&T's	3x7 each way
Neutral grip pull-ups	3xfailure
Australian pull-ups	3x25
Close grip pull-ups	3xfailure
Dumbbell bent-over rows (neutral grip)	3x25
Cardio	10x100 yard sprint

TRICEPS/HAMSTRINGS	SETS X REPS
Skull crushers	5x25,15,10,8,6
Close-grip bench press	4x15,12,10,8
TRX skull crushers	4x15
Reverse grip push-downs	3x20
Dips	4x25
Cable push-downs	3x25
Cable kick-backs	3x15 each arm
Push-ups on medicine ball	4x25

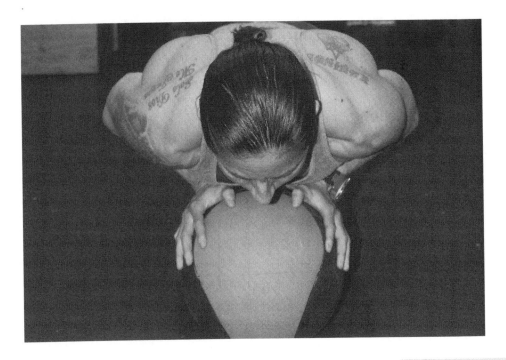

HAMSTRINGS

SETS X REPS

Good mornings	3x10
Romanian deadlifts	3x15
Back extension	3x20
Hamstring curl machine	3x15
Cardio/Boxing	10x1 minute, 10x30 second, 10x20 second and 10x10 second rounds

SHOULDERS

	SETS X REPS
Barbell standing military press	6x25, 15, 10, 10, 6, 3
Side raises	5x15, 10, 10, 8, 6
Rear fly (neutral grip)	3x15
Handstand push-ups	3xfailure
TRX face pull	4x15
Smith machine upright rows	
Super set with rear upright rows and Side upright rows	4x10 of each
Rear fly (overhand and underhand)	3x10 each grip
Cardio	25 hill sprints

BICEPS/ABS	SETS X REPS
Barbell biceps curls	6x25, 15, 10 ,8, 6, 3
Hammers in and out	3x10 each way
Single-arm preacher curl	3x10 each arm
Hammers in front	3x10 each arm
Chin-ups	4xfailure
TRX curls in and out	3x10 each way
Reverse-grip cable curls	3x15
D-handle single arm face curl	3x15 each arm

ABS

	SETS X REPS
Ab roller standing	5x5
Sit-ups	5x15
Ab roller on knees	5x15
Leg lifts	5x15
Kneeling rope crunches	3x15
V-ups	3x15
Cardio	10x100 yard, 10x50 yard sprints

My goal for each workout is to blast the muscle so hard that it needs six days to recover. I focus on keeping my intensity high during the whole workout, resting very little. I will take more rest time when I'm going super heavy on compound lifts such as chest press, deadlifts, and squats. My volume is very high for each workout as well, as I want to hit every part of the muscle to completely fatigue it. Most gains occur when you have "forced" reps. Forced reps are those in which you push beyond your normal level of fatigue when you are about to the put the weights down. If you feel like you are starting to fatigue at eight reps, then you need to pump out five more reps. This type of technique is tough to do by yourself. It is helpful if you have a partner who can help you push out five more forced reps. At the end of my chest workouts I love to finish with 200 or more push-ups to really fatigue and burn out the muscles. I love to challenge myself and push my body beyond its limits. I love the feeling of being completely exhausted, and leaving nothing in the tank. I want to leave the gym feeling accomplished, knowing that I got better today.

MY CURRENT TRAINING PROGRAM

Robert

I am really enjoying my current training program that is designed to build strength and add mass. I came up with my new training approach on my own, somewhat by accident, as I found myself completing my favorite lifts each time I went to the gym, pressing as much weight as I could, even if it meant doing just one exercise for my entire workout. How is it that I would just stumble upon my current training program by accident? I think the way I came up with my approach is very similar to others who have coined their own training systems. I have decades of experience in the gym, and out of a desire for more creativity, more fulfillment, and more fun with exercise I started trying new things. Experimenting with creativity is an innovative way to expand our own exercise foundation, giving ourselves more tools in our tool belt. It by no means suggests that my current approach is the best, most effective approach out there, and there is no guarantee I will stick with it, but it is something I have thoroughly enjoyed and have learned from. We cautiously use the word "current" describing our training programs, because like any interest, technique, or hobby, it is always subject to change.

My current training philosophy looks like this: I select one or two muscle groups to focus on for a given workout, and I choose the exercise that is the most strenuous to perform first. Once I determine what the initial exercise is, I create a pyramid to perform as many as 8-12 *sets* on the beginning exercise. That's right, I might spend a *full hour* just on my starting exercise depending on the muscle group or specific exercise. What's the point of all of this? The way I see it, each exercise provides an estimated return on investment (ROI), and I want to pick the exercise that provides what I determine to be the best ROI first, when I am at my strongest. I warm up with light weights and high repetitions (such as performing push-ups or dumbbell or machine shoulder raises and biceps curls), and then move on to working sets. I pyramid up, increasing weight and decreasing repetitions, and then when I reach the apex of my set, typically a 1-rep max, I pyramid back down. Let's take decline barbell bench press, as an example. My first exercise of a chest workout would look like this:

NUMEROUS SETS OF PUSH-UPS TO WARM UP

Decline barbell bench press

- The bar (45 pounds) x 50 reps (25% effort)
- 135 pounds x 20 reps (50% effort)
- 135 pounds x 20 reps (50% effort)
- 185 pounds x 12 reps (60% effort)
- 205 pounds x 8 reps (70% effort)
- 225 pounds x 6 reps (80% effort)
- 245 pounds x 4 reps (90% effort)
- 275 pounds x 3 reps (100% effort)
- 300 pounds x 1 rep (100% effort)
- 245 pounds x 4-6 reps (90-100% effort)
- 225 pounds x 6-12 reps (90-100% effort)
- 185 pounds x 12-15 reps (90-100% effort)
- 135 pounds x 25 reps or as many as possible (100% effort)

This type of approach allows me to warm up with light weights, which prepares my muscles for a heavy, high-volume workload, giving them some flexibility and good range of motion while stimulating good blood circulation. I then pyramid up in weight on my primary exercise until I hit a 1-rep maximum, and then I pyramid back down to where I started, and I do a burn-out set to failure, performing as many reps as I can on my final set with light weight. Once I have completed a dozen or so sets on this pyramid for my primary exercise, I move on to additional exercises (or in some cases, this *is* the entire workout). For subsequent exercises I only perform about four sets, pyramiding up in weight, and I aim to target the muscle group from different angles (incline and decline, for example, and presses as well as flys). Sticking with this chest workout example, the remaining exercises for my workout might look like this:

Incline barbell bench press

- 135 pounds x 10 reps (70% effort)
- 155 pounds x 6 reps (80% effort)
- 175 pounds x 4 reps (90% effort)
- 185 pounds x 2 reps (100% effort)

Dips*	Dumbbell flys
• 15 reps (70% effort)	• 50s x 12 reps (70% effort)
• 15 reps (80% effort)	• 60s x 8 reps (80% effort)
• 12 reps (90% effort)	• 70s x 6 reps (90% effort)
• 12 reps or as many as possible (100% effort)	• 80s x 4 reps (100% effort)
	(Optional, depending on level of fatigue)

*Even though this is a bodyweight exercise, it gets progressively more challenging with each set as you fatigue, as in the case for pull-ups and other bodyweight exercises.

I often perform four sets of a final exercise such as dips, cable cross-overs, or cable flys at the very end to develop a muscle pump, and to work on range of motion and flexibility, and that would conclude my chest workout. When you train really heavy with low repetitions, you don't always get a good muscle pump, which is a feeling of the muscles filling up with blood, becoming tighter and harder. That pump comes with higher repetitions and from squeezing and holding muscle contractions. I really like the feel of it and that is why I often incorporate some machine, cable, or bodyweight exercises into the end of my heavy chest workout. You can develop this pump feeling with any muscle group, but for me, chest is especially rewarding to get pumped up following a tough workout. Even with all this volume, my chest workouts are usually completed in just a little over an hour, rarely ever exceeding 90 minutes. As you can see, I spend the majority of my time during my chest workout performing the exercise in which I can move the most weight. By using this approach, I ensure that while I am at my strongest, I am lifting the most weight that I can handle. As my energy dwindles throughout the workout (even if I snack throughout the training session, which I often do, drink lots of water, and take long rest periods), I perform the exercises that require smaller amounts of weights, such as dumbbell, bodyweight, cable, and machine exercises.

This is the approach I take for essentially every workout with my current training routine. In addition to the decline barbell bench press for chest, these are some of my favorite initial exercises that I perform 8-12 *sets* of as a way to set the tone for my workouts:

- Back = T-bar rows
- Shoulders = Seated dumbbell overhead press
- Biceps = Dumbbell hammer curls
- Triceps = Dumbbell overhead extensions
- Legs = Plate-loaded squat press
- Abs = Hanging leg raises

Following this style of training for the past couple of years has made me the strongest I've ever been in most exercises. I continue to gain strength in all muscle groups, and sometimes I complete only one or two exercises during an entire hour-long (or longer) workout. Examples include completing an entire workout consisting of just flat bench press, especially when practicing powerlifting techniques, or performing leg presses and plate-loaded squat presses for nearly two hours, and sometimes I will complete a whole workout of just leg extensions if I want to take pressure off of my lower back. An entire workout consisting of pull-ups, like Vanessa sometimes does, would be another example, varying the grips throughout the training session.

When I share this strategy with others, one question that naturally comes up is whether I put myself at risk for injury by lifting heavy for so long during a workout targeting just a single muscle group. This approach of targeting a single muscle group for a whole workout is common practice in powerlifting and Olympic weight lifting, where athletes may spend an entire workout focusing on just deadlifts, or exclusively squats, or some form of overhead press such as clean and jerk. So it's not uncharted territory, and is in fact incredibly familiar territory for some of the strongest lifters on the planet, but, that risk for injury is there, and it's not uncommon for powerlifters, strongmen and strongwomen, and Olympic lifters to experience some form of weightlifting-induced injury. As with anything, there will be a risk-versus-reward scale to evaluate and come to your own conclusions about your desired training style. I weighed out the risks and rewards for myself and found the absolute enjoyment, and muscle-building benefits, of lifting heavy weights to be worthwhile. Becoming the biggest and strongest I have ever been in my life is a reward that compels me to keep this training style commonplace within my entire exercise regimen. Then again, I also spend a fairly significant amount of time hiking and playing basketball these days, cutting into my possible muscle-mass building progress, but again, the rewards of enjoyment and fulfillment outweighs the fact that I am burning excess calories which could potentially suppress some strength or muscle mass gains. As you can see, it's all about what interests you, and what you hope to get out of your exercise programs and experiences.

There is a chance for injury when pressing heavy weights well into the workout with wear and tear of the same muscle over and over. I acknowledge that risk, and some of the ways I mitigate the risk of injury are by warming up properly, eating a snack mid-workout when necessary to boost energy and the consumption of amino acids which help the repairing process after (or even during) exercise, drinking water or electrolytes, stretching throughout the workout, and adapting to this kind of workload over time through consistency. Where it could be a shock at first to spend ten sets on bench press when you're only used to three sets, you will naturally adapt over time if you start with four sets next time, then five sets one week, then six the following week, then seven, and onward until you adapt to the strenuous workout of doing the same exercise for up to a dozen intense sets. I also really only go super heavy in my initial exercise. As you can see in the example above, I will lift very heavy weights when doing decline barbell bench press, but as the workout progresses I will use lighter weights since my energy and strength is diminishing, and because the muscles have been under a lot of stress from lifting heavy weights. I want to lessen the risk of injury and wear and tear by dropping the weights throughout the workout. That usually means I use better form and have greater range of motion using more manageable weights.

I have no interest in getting injured, but in the summer of 2016 I did suffer an injury, though to this day, I don't know the exact cause. It could have been a result of wear and tear over time, but it could have also been from a single, isolated incident. And the injury itself, a torn disc in my low back, was not a new injury. I have aggravated this old injury dating back to the mid-'90s, nearly a dozen times over the past twenty years. I just happened to have another episode of torn disc aggravation when I was at my biggest and best. Even though I saw a doctor a dozen times, and took months off from training during the summer of 2016, I never dropped below 200 pounds body weight, and after months of doing rehabilitation exercises, I was back doing some of my best lifts again as 2017 rolled around. I still train with caution to avoid the pain that comes from pinched nerves and torn discs, and I continue to learn ways to prevent injuries, rehabilitate, and recover from setbacks.

I stumbled upon this way of training out of boredom and desire for change. I was tired of doing the same old exercises, including the ones that weren't all that fun. I realized that I wasn't going to the gym as often as I used to, and certainly not as often as I *thought* I was. I found plenty of other things to do instead, including spending an unconscionable amount of time scrolling through social media websites, rather than doing something far more productive, including writing this book. My level of fitness suffered as well, as you can imagine, when I wasn't putting myself in a position to progress.

Luckily, I met Vanessa at an important time when I was so fully engaged in running that I lost all measurable muscle mass and thought about folding my Vegan Bodybuilding & Fitness business. Vanessa helped me rediscover fun, enjoyment, and passion in my weightlifting fitness pursuits, and I simply changed my approach, and my attitude toward a preference and desire to get stronger and break my own lifting records. It worked for building muscle strength and size, so I've stuck with it for most workouts. I credit Vanessa's influence, coupled with my search for rediscovering enjoyment in the gym to stumbling upon a workout routine that is incredibly rewarding and fulfilling, and productive. Following this low back disc issue, the only adaptations I have made in recent months is that I am taking a break from using heavy dumbbells, and I am not performing shrugs, which I recall causing low back stress just days before my disc suffered another tear. As long as my low back is supported and I don't have to lift individual dumbbells off the ground or off the rack, I feel empowered to get right back to where I was with my strength gains I experienced last year.

At the present time, I am only using barbells for chest presses, and using dumbbells only occasionally for biceps curls and shoulder raises. The foundation of my current effort to build muscle strength and size is comprised of exercises that don't hinder my low back, such as: barbell, machine, and cable presses and flys for chest, high rows and plate-loaded front pull-downs for back, machine and cable curls for biceps, seated machine and cable press-downs for triceps, and machine and cable overhead presses and lateral raises for shoulders. Following the same approach of spending a significant amount of time on the best exercise for each given muscle group, I call upon the best ones to start with, and then incorporate my favorite exercises into the remainder of my workout. This ensures I still get a positive return on investment from the exercises I perform, and that I have fun doing it. I have simply moved from free weight to plate-loaded or machine exercises for my primary starting exercise, and compliment the rest of my workout with machines and cables, and things are moving along quite well. I miss using barbells and dumbbells as the foundation of my training program, but by following the equipment adaptations of incorporating heavy machine and cable exercises while using the same general philosophy, I should continue to rehabilitate my back, recover from the low back injury, and get back to doing the free weight exercises I enjoy in the near future.

What I like best about this approach is that rather than performing a bunch of isolated exercises for a single muscle group on one joint axle, I perform compound, multi-joint lifts that are fun, challenging, and yield the best results when made a priority in my training program. I encourage you to give this approach a try, but ease into it as the volume is high and the overall workload and intensity is also high. There will be an adaptation period, so you have to be patient and increase your workload in small increments to allow your body to adapt and adjust, while also avoiding overtraining or injury.

Here is an example of how to incorporate this kind of training into your routine:

Select your favorite compound free weight exercises for each muscle group to determine what exercise you will start with for each training session. Refer to my sample chest workout above, followed by my list of favorite starting exercises for each muscle group below, for some ideas. In general, consider the ROI of a given exercise when you make your selection for which movements will make up the bulk of your training program. Then, select about three other exercises that compliment and support the primary exercise. If you're training back, and you select pull-ups as your primary exercise to perform a dozen sets, perhaps you'll pick a rowing movement such as bent-over rows, or one-arm dumbbell rows as your next exercise. Then you'll select another exercise to work on width or thickness, perhaps close-grip or reverse-grip lat pull-downs for width, or T-bar or other types or rows for thickness. After those couple of exercises, maybe you will finish with some cable or machine rows to target your mid-back or low back in addition to all the emphasis on lats and the width of your back. The goal is to train a muscle group sufficiently, hitting it from different angles with a variety of techniques and equipment. Written out, perhaps it would look like this:

Pull-ups (as many reps as you can perform until failure)

- 15 reps
- 12 reps
- 10 reps
- 10 reps
- 8 reps
- 6 reps (weighted or with a different grip)
- 6 reps (weighted or with a different grip)
- 6 reps (weighted or with a different grip)
- 8 reps
- 10 reps
- 12 reps
- 12 reps

Bent-over rows

- 135 pounds x 10 reps
- 185 pounds x 8 reps
- 205 pounds x 6 reps
- 225 pounds x 4 reps

High Rows

- 160 pounds x 12 reps
- 180 pounds x 10 reps
- 200 pounds x 8 reps
- 220 pounds x 6 reps

Close-grip pull-downs

- 135 pounds x 15 reps
- 150 pounds x 10 reps
- 160 pounds x 8 reps
- 175 pounds x 6 reps

Seated cable rows

- 135 pounds x 12 reps
- 155 pounds x 8 reps
- 175 pounds x 6 reps
- 195 pounds x 4 reps
  (Optional, depending on level of fatigue)

In this case, we focused on the challenging and muscle- and strength-building exercise of pull-ups to perform first, followed by four sets of another quality exercise, bent-over rows, and then eased up a bit with easier-to-perform machine high rows, close-grip pull-downs, and wrapped up with seated cable rows to exhaust and burn-out the muscles. That looks like a pretty awesome back workout to me!

When you embark on this approach, if you decide to give it a try, be sure to take it easy at first, use a spotter when lifting heavy weights, and take personal assessments to see how you feel with the increased workload. *I repeat again, it is important to ease into this way of training.* If you're not used to pyramiding, or doing low reps with heavy weights, or 1-rep max lifts, you will need to test these out (and have a spotter), and slowly incorporate them into your routine until it becomes normal. Once you have totally adapted to this style of training over the course of four to eight weeks, I think you'll experience some of the same muscle strength and size gains that I did, and hopefully you'll have fun in the process since you will be performing your favorite exercises during every workout. That's really what I enjoy most about this way of training. It's fun, and when things are fun I am more likely to do them, and I look forward to each new challenge.

If I am short on time and have only 45 minutes, I will perform exercises that target multiple muscle groups, especially free weight and bodyweight movements, such as pull-ups, dips, overhead presses, and rowing and pressing movements in general. One recent morning, for example, I was short on time for my hotel workout before catching a flight, so after completing about 150 push-ups and 250 crunches, I went straight to the dumbbell rack to do a few sets of shoulder raises and presses, as well as hammer curls to target my shoulders and arms. I also performed numerous sets of lat pull-downs for my back and biceps, and did a quick cool down of arm circles and stretching, and I was done. Even when short on time, I go for the best ROI I can get out of a given workout. During that brief exercise period, I was able to train chest, shoulders, biceps, triceps, back, and abs, just doing some basic movements at a hotel gym.

If you asked me to only perform one exercise for each muscle group and still build my physique and gain strength, based on my preferences, I would create the following workout routine:

- Decline barbell bench press (chest)
- Dumbbell overhead press (shoulders)
- T-bar rows (back)
- Plate-loaded squat press/leg press (legs)
- Narrow-grip bench press (triceps)
- Reverse-grip pull-ups (biceps)
- Hanging leg raises (abs)

Alternatively, given more limited options or equipment, say, if I just had a single barbell and weight plates, I would perform overhead and chest presses (for shoulders, chest, triceps, and even targeting abs and legs), and rows and shrugs for back, biceps and shoulders, and perhaps some Olympic lifts that my lower back could handle, three or four days a week. That would be another way to impact the entire body doing free weight exercises. Those without lower back problems could easily engage in even more Olympic lifting movements including cleans, hang cleans, power cleans, deadlifts, and snatches. I have followed an Olympic lifting-only approach for months at a time, and my muscle size and strength seemed to increase until it was a little too much for my lower back to handle, and I gave it a rest. Then I moved back to more traditional compound free weight exercises like presses and rows with dumbbells and barbells. One thing I try to always keep in mind is to be open to trying something new. I've tried CrossFit exercises, powerlifting exercises, bodybuilding exercises, endurance exercises, and variations of common weight lifting and bodyweight exercises. I've also taken a number of different approaches from low rep to high rep, low volume to high volume, and I continue to be open to change. For example, after 988 consecutive days performing more than 100 push-ups and crunches per day, ending on a day I suffered from severe food poisoning (April 30, 2016), I decided to take a break from those daily exercises to find something new to pursue in the form of daily health and fitness habits. Hiking on the trails in sunny Arizona has become a new favorite regular activity. I also perform rehabilitation exercises for my low back as a technique to help strengthen my core to prevent future injuries.

Though I have a preferred way of training, as outlined above, focusing on the best exercises, combined with my favorite exercises for a given muscle group, I don't always follow that approach for every workout. Just as I might have a favorite food or favorite meal, it doesn't mean I eat it every single day. As you will see from my sample workouts for each muscle group below, some will clearly focus on my preferred training method, and others will have a different approach, depending on what my goals are on a given day – which could factor in a desired pump, a heavy training session, an abbreviated workout when short on time, or other factors, such as training with a partner and doing exercises I don't normally do on my own. The following are samples from my actual workouts that I extracted from my training journal. Since I have outlined a sample chest and back workout above, I will now share my workouts for other muscle groups.

Here is an example of a typical <u>arm</u> workout. It usually takes me 60 minutes to complete:

WARM-UP:

Hip raises

- 30 reps, 30 reps, 30 reps

Arm and leg lifts (bird dog)

- 15 reps, 15 reps, 15 reps (each side)

Face pulls with rope (warming up shoulder and elbow joints before workout)

- 50 pounds x 25 reps
- 65 pounds x 20 reps
- 75 pounds x 25 reps
- 85 pounds x 20 reps
- 105 pounds x 15 reps

WORKOUT:

Rope extensions

- 75 pounds x 25 reps
- 85 pounds x 20 reps
- 105 pounds x 12 reps
- 115 pounds x 8 reps
- 105 pounds x 12 reps

Cable rope biceps curls

- 65 pounds x 15 reps
- 75 pounds x 15 reps
- 85 pounds x 15 reps
- 85 pounds x 15 reps
- 85 pounds x 15 reps

Machine biceps curls

- 70 pounds x 15 reps
- 80 pounds x 12 reps
- 90 pounds x 11 reps
- 100 pounds x 10 reps
- 110 pounds x 8 reps

Push-ups

- 20 reps
- 22 reps
- 23 reps
- 24 reps
- 25 reps

High position unilateral machine biceps curls

- 50 pounds x 10 reps
- 50 pounds x 12 reps
- 50 pounds x 12 reps
- 60 pounds x 8 reps
- 60 pounds x 10 reps

Machine triceps extensions

- 100 pounds x 10 reps
- 95 pounds x 12 reps
- 95 pounds x 15 reps
- 95 pounds x 11 reps
- 95 pounds x 13 reps

Single-arm cable preacher curls

- 40 pounds x 15 reps
- 45 pounds x 12 reps
- 50 pounds x 8 reps
- 50 pounds x 8 reps
- 45 pounds x 10 reps

Machine press-downs

- 150 pounds x 20 reps
- 170 pounds x 16 reps
- 190 pounds x 17 reps
- 200 pounds x 13 reps
- 205 pounds x 13 reps

*You might have noticed that I don't always complete an even number of reps such as 8, 10, or 12, or even a common number such as 15 reps, for every set. I aim for a specific number, say 12, and adjust the weight accordingly so that I will likely end up with about 12 completed reps, but if I have more strength and energy, I'll keep going. Or sometimes I'll run out of gas and have to stop early. Therefore, for certain muscle groups, especially arms, listed above, and shoulders listed below, you'll see me end up with uncommon rep ranges such as 7, 13, 17, and 22. Those aren't typos. I just got a second wind or ran out of wind during a set when my target was a more common number of reps I was aiming for.

Here is an example of a typical <u>shoulder</u> workout. It usually takes me 75 minutes to complete:

WARM-UP:

Hip raises

- 30 reps, 30 reps, 30 reps

Arm and leg lifts (bird dog)

- 15 reps, 15 reps, 15 reps (each side)

Push-ups

- 20 reps, 20 reps, 20 reps

WORKOUT:

Cable overhead press

- 40 pounds x 25 reps
- 50 pounds x 20 reps
- 60 pounds x 15 reps
- 70 pounds x 15 reps
- 80 pounds x 12 reps

Plate-loaded shoulder press

- 90 pounds x 12 reps
- 140 pounds x 10 reps
- 160 pounds x 8 reps
- 180 pounds x 8 reps
- 160 pounds x 10 reps
- 140 pounds x 14 reps
- 140 pounds x 14 reps

Neutral-grip machine press

- 50 pounds x 13 reps
- 70 pounds x 13 reps
- 90 pounds x 7 reps
- 100 pounds x 5 reps
- 100 pounds x 6 reps

Machine shoulder press

- 80 pounds x 12 reps
- 90 pounds x 8 reps
- 90 pounds x 6 reps
- 100 pounds x 3 reps
- 60 pounds x 17 reps

Dumbbell lateral raises

- 15-pound dumbbells x15 reps
- 22.5-pound dumbbells x 12 reps
- 22.5-pound dumbbells x 12 reps
- 25-pound dumbbells x 6 reps
- 25-pound dumbbells x 7 reps

Dumbbell front raises

- 15-pound dumbbells x 15 reps
- 22.5-pound dumbbells x 12 reps
- 22.5-pound dumbbells x 12 reps
- 25-pound dumbbells x 6 reps
- 25-pound dumbbells x 7 reps

Machine rear deltoid flys

- 75 pounds x 10 reps
- 75 pounds x 10 reps
- 75 pounds x 12 reps
- 85 pounds x 8 reps
- 100 pounds x 6 reps

Here is an example of a typical <u>leg</u> workout. It usually takes me 90 minutes to complete:

WARM-UP:

Hip raises

- 30 reps, 30 reps, 30 reps

Arm and leg lifts (bird dog)

- 15 reps, 15 reps, 15 reps (each side)

Push-ups

- 20 reps, 20 reps, 20 reps

WORKOUT:

Leg extensions

- 50 pounds x 60 reps
- 70 pounds x 60 reps
- 90 pounds x 35 reps
- 110 pounds x 40 reps
- 130 pounds x 30 reps
- 150 pounds x 30 reps
- 170 pounds x 25 reps
- 190 pounds x 30 reps
- 215 pounds x 15 reps
- 230 pounds x 12 reps

Seated machine calf presses

- 130 pounds x 100 reps
- 175 pounds x 75 reps
- 250 pounds x 50 reps
- 280 pounds x 50 reps
- 300 pounds x 35 reps
- 305 pounds x 40 reps
- 305 pounds x 35 reps

Wall sits (static hold for as long as possible for each set)

- 105 seconds for set
- 82 seconds for set
- 123 seconds for set
- 92 seconds for set
- 96 seconds for set

Seated or standing machine calf raises

- 100 pounds x 75 reps
- 110 pounds x 60 reps
- 130 pounds x 45 reps
- 140 pounds x 45 reps
- 150 pounds x 35 reps
- 150 pounds x 30 reps
- 140 pounds x 20 reps
- 130 pounds x 50 reps
- 120 pounds x 50 reps
- 110 pounds x 60 reps

Unilateral leg lifts with hip raise (for hamstrings)

- 12 reps per leg
- 16 reps per leg
- 20 reps per leg
- 20 reps per leg
- 20 reps per leg

Here is an example of a typical <u>abdominal</u> workout. It usually takes me 45 minutes to complete:

WARM-UP:

Hip raises

- 30 reps, 30 reps, 30 reps

Arm and leg lifts (bird dog)

- 15 reps, 15 reps, 15 reps (each side)

Push-ups

- 20 reps, 20 reps, 20 reps

WORKOUT:

Planks (static hold for as long as possible for each set)

- 77 seconds for set
- 104 seconds for set
- 66 seconds for set
- 73 seconds for set
- 64 seconds for set
- 65 seconds for set
- 73 seconds for set
- 106 seconds for set
- 77 seconds for set
- 71 seconds for set

Weighted machine crunches

- 70 pounds x 25 reps
- 70 pounds x 25 reps
- 90 pounds x 20 reps
- 100 pounds x 15 reps
- 100 pounds x 15 reps

Rope cable crunches

- 100 pounds x 25 reps
- 120 pounds x 20 reps
- 130 pounds x 15 reps
- 140 pounds x 12 reps
- 150 pounds x 10 reps

Stationary bear crawl with reach and static hold

- 10 reps each side
- 8 reps each side
- 8 reps each side
- 8 reps each side
- 10 reps each side

This has been a recap of my current training program, and I hope that you discovered some strategies and techniques that resonate with you. Training programs evolve and adapt over time, and trying new things could be an important step in your own pursuit of fitness goals. One of my approaches is to work toward something every day, to chip away at a goal day after day until I achieve it. That is one sure way to make forward progress, to stay motivated, upbeat, and inspired. My wish for you is that you enjoy your fitness journey and learn new things along the way. Stay consistent, accountable, and transparent with your training and you will be well on your way to achieving meaningful levels of success. Use the *Shred It! 13-Week Training Journal* to track your results, log your progress reports, and to stay inspired and motivated. Join our online plant-based athlete communities to connect with others and learn from the experiences that others have to share. I learn from Vanessa and other plant-based athlete colleagues all the time, and even though I am an experienced athlete, there is always so, so much more to learn.

Chapter 3

SELECTING WORKOUT PROGRAMS TO FOLLOW

TRAINING METHODS AND SYSTEMS

Robert

Over the twenty years that I have been an athlete, I have followed numerous weight-training programs. My earliest memories take me back to the high school weight room, but my real formal training would come much later, when I would learn from Bill Phillips' Body-for-LIFE program, and then I hired a top bodybuilder as a personal trainer. From there I would hire another personal trainer, train with other competitive bodybuilders, and hire more trainers. I never try to be so confident that I don't think I can learn from someone else. Though I have been doing this for a long time, I still learn new techniques, methods, approaches, and training styles all the time. In fact, during the writing process of this book, I have learned a lot from Vanessa. Just the other day, while we trained together at the gym, I learned another new technique from Vanessa regarding super sets and grip position when doing upright rows. Learning, and trying new things are key components in growth, mentally and physically.

One of the benefits of trying many different training programs is the opportunity you get to have first-hand experience with a variety of techniques and decide which ones resonate with you the most. Rather than just reading about this or that program, getting your hands dirty, testing them out, is a great approach to take. I have tried programs that consist of high repetitions, low repetitions, 5x5, Olympic lifts, bodybuilding training, powerlifting training, and have been under the guidance of half a dozen personal trainers and coaches to earn my twenty years of training experience. From those experiences, I have taken what I like best and applied those techniques and approaches to my current training. Even after all these years, I still learn from Vanessa nearly every time we train together. Not only does her passion and intensity rub off on me, but her innovation and creativity in exercise does too. I am inspired by particular plant-based athletes I follow online, and many of whom I know personally. Watching lifting videos by Fraser Bayley, Torre Washington, Nimai Delgado, and Giacomo Marchese, to name a few, is encouraging. I've become a fan of many of my peers, including Simone Collins, Derek Tresize, Geoff Palmer, Mindy Collette, Luke Tan, and Frank Medrano, among others. Having the opportunity to train with them, learn from them, and spend time around them enhances my mindset, my knowledge, and my passion for what I do. But nobody inspires me more than Vanessa, and I am truly fortunate to have her as a mentor, training partner, and great friend that I can count on. Though Vanessa and I have a lot to share about exercises and workout programs, from our decades of experience, we're not the end-all, be-all of plant-based fitness. We're constantly learning, remaining open to new ideas, and we are inspired by the successful plant-based athletes mentioned above. We know they, and others, have inherent value to share too, and as we learn from them we continue to grow as individuals. So know that your options for inspiration and information are limitless, even within the niche plant-based-athlete movement.

Though there are many training styles, and really no one-size-fits-all approach, because we are all so different in our backgrounds, abilities, training history, injury history, body mechanics, work ethic, and goals, there are some standard approaches that nearly everyone can benefit from, namely the basics, such as walking, stretching, and movement of any kind. There are some rather comprehensive training styles, often reserved for elite, professional, and Olympic athletes, but aren't necessarily practical, feasible, or even beneficial to the weekend warrior just looking to get in better overall shape. We won't be recommending 6-hour gymnastics sessions, or 3-hour wrestling practices, nor will we suggest ultra-complicated lifting movements that require a basic foundation and knowledge of proper body mechanics to complete the lifts before ever attempting them.

We will, however, share some of the more popular general approaches like high reps and low reps, free weight, machine, cable, and body weight exercises, and some common practices in the gym that tend to yield positive results for most people. We will also touch on, and provide information for, some of our favorite training systems – ones we have experience with and have found to be beneficial. There are training techniques I learned from the Body-for-LIFE program 18 years ago that still influence me today. There are also many lessons learned from mistakes made along the way that have helped shape the approaches we take today. Avoiding injuries by warming up properly, stretching sufficiently, understanding and implementing proper techniques, and knowing what your limits are, all come to mind.

Vanessa's training approach, and my training approach, didn't come from our own minds alone. They came from experiences throughout our entire lives. What we do now is a culmination of the accumulated knowledge from our sports backgrounds. We simply kept the aspects of training programs we liked or found beneficial, and discarded or set aside the rest.

Though Vanessa and I have already gone through our own trial and error, experiencing many of these popular training programs and methods first hand, it doesn't mean that her current approach, or my current approach for that matter, would be the best approach for you. Perhaps you don't have the same goals of putting on as much muscle mass as possible that Vanessa strives for and works incredibly hard at every day. Perhaps you don't share my passion for training for muscle size, strength, functionality, and fun all wrapped up into one approach. Perhaps your career is not based around your exercise schedule or athletic performance and you don't have the time or interest to invest as much energy that we do into our programs. Even if we don't share all the same goals, I have no doubt that our decades of trial and error through personal experiences will be helpful to you, but we want to share a diversity of programs to ensure you find something that resonates with you. We shared some basic information about Olympic lifting and powerlifting, which could be your area of interest, but not something that either Vanessa or I currently pursue, *though at the time of editing this book,*

Vanessa is exploring powerlifting with aims of competing in it for the first time in the near future. We didn't want to omit those options because they are solid training programs for those who have that interest.

How are you supposed to know what is best for you? 5x5? Push/pull? Olympic lifting? You've got to test them out for yourself. We have specific training programs listed in a later chapter that are designed using Vanessa's expertise for muscle building, fat burning, conditioning, and partner exercises, and those could be good starting points for you. Once you establish what your specific goals are, you can start to put together a training approach aimed at achieving your goals. You will no doubt encounter some of the training strategies we shared in this section of the book, and you can include the ones that are most beneficial, and set aside the rest for now. You never know when your interests will change. I didn't know that after a decade as a competitive bodybuilder, that I would go back to endurance running and have my training completely flipped on its head. Therefore, it is beneficial to have some sort of first-hand experience with myriad training styles and approaches so when one training style runs its course and you're ready to try something new, you will at least be a little bit familiar with it. Ask yourself what specific fitness goals you are most interested in pursuing right now. Then, determine which exercise programs most closely match what you aim to achieve. Do you want to build strength? Or muscle? Or burn fat? Improve endurance? Or find something quick and easy to help improve your overall fitness with just 20-30 minutes of activity a day? Are you looking to be part of a group class, community, or a member of a team? There are approaches to all of those goals, and more. The journey starts with taking that initial step forward, by doing something that takes you closer to what you want to achieve. And if all of that sounds intimidating, refer to the fitness guides later on in the book where Vanessa outlines precise exercise programs to get you started in your quest to build muscle, burn fat, or improve your cardiovascular conditioning.

If you are a beginner, just starting out, or coming back from a long layoff due to injury or for some other reason, a practical approach is to start slow, ease into any new program, and allow for adaptation to help you progress over time. For example, if you're recovering from an ankle, knee, or hip injury, you won't immediately go into marathon training, but rather, you'll start by walking for 15-30 minutes a few days per week. You may graduate to 30-45 minute sessions, or to jogging, or to walking or jogging five days per week, but the point is to start slow, even if you have a previous background or experience in athletics. I know what it's like to be a beginner again, even after a decade as a competitive bodybuilder. Injuries can humble you real quickly, and I know that we have to respect the process and start at the appropriate places.

Getting Started

If you are just starting out, your first month of training might look like this:

WEEK 1:

- Walk for 15-30 minutes a day, three days per week

- Do some light stretching after each walk

- Incorporate more whole plant foods into your diet, and reduce processed and refined foods

WEEK 2:

- Walk or jog for 15-30 minutes a day, five days per week

- Do some light stretching after each jog or walk

- Incorporate some bodyweight exercises such as a few air squats or push-ups each day, a few days per week

WEEK 3:

- Walk or jog for 30-45 minutes per day, five days per week

- Do some light stretching after each jog or walk

- Incorporate some new bodyweight exercises such as lunges and planks, and continue to perform squats and push-ups to adapt and progress

WEEK 4:

- Walk or jog for 30-45 minutes per day, five days per week

- Do some light stretching after each jog or walk

- Incorporate some other forms of cardiovascular training such as cycling, rowing, swimming, stair climbing, or other preferred method of burning additional calories and strengthening heart and lungs, for 15 minutes a day, three days per week

- Continue to perform some bodyweight exercises a few days per week to target legs, abs, arms, shoulders, and chest, before graduating to pull-ups for back, and free weights, machines, and cables in the coming weeks

As you ease into some basic weight training after a month or more of walking, jogging, bodyweight exercises, and any additional forms of exercise you do, a general approach is to do some circuit training using machines and cables to train numerous muscle groups per workout as you familiarize yourself with the movements. A sample week, training in the gym three times per week with a rest day between workouts, might look like this:

DAY 1: (EMPHASIS ON CHEST, BACK, AND SHOULDERS)

Rest for about 30 seconds to 1 minute between each set and for 1-2 minutes between exercises:

- Warm up for 10 minutes doing cardiovascular exercise such as walking/jogging

- Machine chest press = 3 sets x 10-15 reps per set

- Machine lat pull-downs = 3 sets x 10-15 reps per set

- Machine rows = 3 sets x 10-15 reps per set

- Machine overhead shoulder press = 3 sets x 10-15 reps per set

- Machine or cable lateral raises = 3 sets x 10-15 reps per set

Totals = 15 sets

DAY 2: (EMPHASIS ON LEGS)

Rest for about 30 seconds to 1 minute between each set and for 1-2 minutes between exercises:

- Warm up for 10 minutes doing cardiovascular exercise such as walking/jogging

- Machine leg extensions = 3 sets x 10-15 reps per set

- Machine leg press = 3 sets x 10-15 reps per set

- Machine leg curls = 3 sets x 10-15 reps per set

- Wall sits = 3 sets x 30-60 seconds per set

- Machine calf raises = 3 sets x 10-15 reps per set

Total = 15 sets

DAY 3: (EMPHASIS ON ARMS AND CORE – ABS AND LOW BACK)

Rest for about 30 seconds to 1 minute between each set and for 1-2 minutes between exercises:

- Warm up for 10 minutes doing cardiovascular exercise such as walking/jogging

- Cable triceps extensions = 3 sets x 10-15 reps per set

- Machine biceps curls = 3 sets x 10-15 reps per set

- Machine abdominal crunches = 3 sets x 10-15 reps per set

- Machine lower back extensions = 3 sets x 10-15 reps per set

- Plank = 3 sets x 30-60 seconds per set

Total = 15 sets

The workouts listed above are examples of easing into exercise by warming up your muscles from walking and jogging, increasing activity to incorporate some bodyweight exercises and aerobic activities, and than transitioning into some gym exercises. After becoming familiar with a number of machine, cable, and bodyweight gym exercises, moving onto free weight exercises would be a natural next step. In Chapter 5 you will see specific workout programs that Vanessa designed for various fitness approaches to achieve desired goals. These will combine bodyweight, free weight, and some cable exercises as well as some additional equipment for some movements. Evaluate the programs, see how they fit into your current lifestyle, determine what equipment you need to follow them, and give them a try if you so desire. There might be some movements you have never tried before, or perhaps some you've never even heard of, but that's what makes learning and trying new things fun. And you're in good hands. Vanessa is an outstanding personal trainer, and she has an extensive weight training background. She also has perhaps pound-for-pound the strongest and most muscular physique of anyone I know, and I know a lot of athletes. She walks her talk and has an incredible ability to inspire, motivate, educate, and help others achieve their goals.

If you only train with one approach now, you may not realize how much you might enjoy some other training modality. You also might find that what you expected to enjoy isn't all that enjoyable after all. And other things will really surprise you and you may discover what you've been missing out on. Have you tried hill sprints? 100-rep lifts? Long-distance running? Calisthenics? Or sports activities like rock climbing or water skiing? Have you ever been part of a team? There is so much variety in the fitness world and so many styles of exercise worth trying.

The point is, you can follow our programs and our approaches and likely get in very good shape and enjoy the process, but the best way to discover what really speaks to you is to try out a little of everything and keep what you like most and put the rest on the back burner for another time.

Here's how to determine what your next training program should look like. Answer the following questions:

1. What are your current fitness goals? Be as specific as you can.

2. What programs have you followed in the past?

3. What program are you currently following?

4. What type of gym/exercise equipment do you have access to?

5. How many days per week do you exercise?

6. Do you have any injuries or limitations?

7. What best describes the most successful program you have followed?

8. Which outcome is most desirable to you – Muscle building? Fat burning? Conditioning?

9. What do you like best about training?

10. What do you like least about training?

11. Have you encountered obstacles in the past? If so, how did you overcome them?

12. How would you rate your current level of fitness?

13. What is holding you back or keeping you from doing what you truly want to do?

14. Are you open to trying something new?

15. Would you be willing to give a new approach a try for 8 weeks?

Add up the accumulation of your answers to determine what you really *want* to do, what has or has not worked in the past, and what excites you about trying something new in pursuit of specific goals. Often I find there is a strong correlation between what you *want* to do and what you *will* do, just as there is a strong relationship between what you *don't* want to do and what you *won't* do. Once you come to some general conclusions, refer to Vanessa's training programs in the upcoming chapters, and start piecing a new program together and give it a shot for eight weeks. Evaluate your progress, continue to answer the 15 questions listed above, and make any necessary changes over time.

Chapter 4

WORKOUT TIPS FROM OUR 35+ YEARS COMBINED EXPERIENCE

WORKOUT TIPS

Vanessa

The reason I can workout two hours everyday, day after day, for more than ten days in a row is because I fuel my body the right way. I take as much pride and passion in what I eat as I do with my training in the gym, and I make nutrition a priority to get the best from my workouts. What you put in your body is the key to a great workout, and a key to longevity with your training and in life. I have such great energy all the time because of what I eat. I consume mostly whole plant-based foods. I wouldn't be able to train as hard and as frequently without proper nutrition. My focus is counting nutrients (micronutrients, including vitamins, minerals, and phytonutrients). I don't worry about macronutrient (protein, carbohydrates, and fats) or calorie quantities, but I always make sure I'm getting enough micronutrients. I prepare my meals at home every week to help me stay on track so that I am always prepared, always ready to fuel myself with the best nutrition. This is something I highly recommend because it helps prevent you from grabbing unhealthy foods. It's all about preparation. It definitely takes more time, but is worth it in the end. Remember, you can't outwork a bad diet.

HERE ARE SOME OF THE FOODS I CONSUME EVERYDAY:

Fruits, vegetables, nuts, seeds, legumes, tofu, quinoa, nutritional yeast, hemp, chia, Matcha green tea with lemon, spirulina, and chlorella

STAY ENERGIZED

One of the main reasons why people skip workouts is because they are too tired. It's easy to workout when you feel great, but in reality most people are exhausted from everyday life, and don't feel like exercising. Every time I feel tired and don't feel like working out, I always remember what my dad used to tell me: "don't let being tired beat you." This has stuck with me, and I think of this every time I'm tired or feeling down. I won't let anything beat me or stop me from achieving my goals. Some of the qualities that I attribute to my success in the gym are that I am prepared, nourished, and energized. When others are skipping workouts from being too tired, I'm in the gym, putting in work, making progress.

WOMEN

For all our female readers, this is for you: Don't be afraid to lift heavy weights. At least once a week I hear from women who say that they are afraid to train heavy because they have a fear of getting "too big" or "looking like a man." This is almost impossible unless you are taking steroids or have crazy genetics that allow for incredible muscle development. First of all, most women don't often achieve this "huge" look simply because of the vastly different levels of testosterone between women and men, and testosterone is a major factor in building muscle more rapidly. And secondly, you have to train super heavy for years on end to gain a good amount of muscle mass. It is, however, possible to gain quality muscle, it just takes a lot of time and dedication. I have trained for more than 15 years consistently, training and eating like a bodybuilder, and have basically dedicated my life to training, and it has taken me years and years to achieve the physique I have built. Women, don't be afraid to push yourselves. Get out of your comfort zone. Achieve the goals you have set for yourself. Work hard, knowing that with the right approach, you can succeed and achieve the health and fitness goals you desire. Don't be afraid to lift heavy weights and work hard in the gym if that is something you are passionate about. You can do it, and you can follow my approaches if you share the same desires of getting muscular and strong. And even if you don't want to get "muscular and strong," realize you can still lift heavy weights to improve muscle tone, burn fat, and improve overall fitness without "looking big."

TRAINING PARTNERS

Finding yourself a great workout partner can really make or break you. If you have a workout partner that isn't consistent, or is always late or lazy, you are likely to pick up those traits as well. However, if you have a partner that is super motivating and as enthusiastic as you are about working out, then you will find yourself one step closer to achieving your goals. Having a workout partner can also can make working out a lot more fun. Some of my best workouts are when I am training with a partner. I have achieved many weight lifting personal records with my workout partner that I would have never been able to do by myself.

MINDSET

Every time I step into the gym I have the mindset that I'm going to be better than I was yesterday. I believe every workout, every set, and every rep matters. If you approach each workout this way, then I promise you will get results. It's all about consistency, but the passion, intensity, and effort you train with make a big difference too. Remember, "DON'T LET BEING TIRED BEAT YOU!"

WORKOUT TIPS
Robert

When you go to the gym, you should enter with focus, ambition, determination, and with a positive attitude. If you treat your workouts like they are a chore, you will be in a hurry to get in, get out, and get on with your day. But that's not how you achieve high levels of fitness. The road to success is paved with hard work and inspired work ethic that drives your performance to be above average. Have a game plan and stick to it. If you wander into the gym without a set action plan, you will likely do the bare minimum, cut corners, and justify inactions because you made it to the gym and that was half the battle. What about the other half – you know, the battle of exercising with purpose? The mental aspect of training is almost as important as the physical aspect. You can go through the motions of lifting things up and putting them down, but if it is not with a certain level of purpose and intensity, it will not provide the positive return on investment you are likely seeking.

I know I can be a bit hard-hitting with my approach focused on accountability and transparency (and admittedly, a bit repetitive, by design), but I'm growing tired of people stating fitness goals they claim to care about but not following through with the actions necessary to achieve them, and then complaining that things just didn't work. Things don't work when you don't work. It may be tough to hear, but you can either take it to heart and resolve to make this year your best ever, or say I'm a little too hard on readers and not follow through, and likely wind up short of your goals. What's it going to be?

When you select exercises to perform, consider the ROI of a given exercise. As discussed previously, this could make all the difference. For me, rather than doing a bunch of different exercises to fill the hour or so that I am at the gym, I often pick just one, two, or three major compound, multi-joint exercises to perform during the bulk or entirety of my workout.

Total-body and bodyweight exercises are also excellent ways to stimulate a lot of muscle growth and develop a good pump. An added benefit is that some of these can be performed anywhere, anytime, such as burpees, jumping jacks, air squats, hand-stand push-ups, pull-ups, dips, lunges, and many variations of push-ups. I suggest selecting one or two bodyweight exercises to do every day, even on days you don't go to the gym, if only for a few sets. You could choose squats, lunges, pull-ups, planks, climbing a few sets of stairs or going for a short jog, or anything else you desire. The idea behind this is not to burn out your muscles or train with lots of intensity, but rather, to be doing something every day that contributes to your health and fitness in a positive way. This also helps develop new behaviors and habits that will in turn create new outcomes as a direct result. I find that often it is the mental and psychological benefits of daily exercise I enjoy most, even more than the physical benefits from actually performing the exercise. Don't be afraid to start your own consecutive day exercise streak out of fear that you'll forget one day or be too busy or too tired. Just start doing something and repeat it every day, and watch how your body and mind adapt to the new stress you put on your body. This could be as simple as going for a walk or a quick run, doing push-ups during commercial breaks while watching TV, doing squats in between doing chores at home, or a morning ritual of planks or push-ups upon waking. How about walking a dog a couple of times a day? Get creative, have fun with it, and very importantly, find something you enjoy, and you'll be more likely to stick with it.

When it comes to getting and staying fit, words such as *purpose, action, drive, enjoyment, consistency, dedication, adaptation, passion, transparency, follow-through,* and *achievement* come to mind, at least for me. That is because results don't happen without consistent actions, either positive or negative ones. Positive consistency (developing habits supportive of goals), such as eating healthy and exercising regularly, usually leads to desirable end results. Negative consistency (developing habits unsupportive of goals), such as eating poorly and being inactive, typically leads to undesirable results. Here are some tips for you to consider as you focus on developing positive habits:

5 STEPS TO GET AND STAY FIT

Step #1 – Write your goals down, tell a few people you trust who can help keep you accountable, and work to develop habits that will support your goals, while detaching yourself from the habits that prevent these goals from being achieved. I find that the more meaningful the reason behind your health or fitness pursuit, the more likely you are to achieve it. Qualify the desire behind your goals and compare it to other priorities, and see where this fits into your life in the big picture.

Step #2 – Understand your starting point. Don't give yourself too much, or not enough credit. Just be honest and accurate. What is your daily caloric expenditure, based on your gender, age, height, weight, and activity level? What is your daily caloric intake? Do you understand the important difference between nutrient-density and calorie-density? Do you apply appropriate principles into your diet/ lifestyle based on these factors? Determine these metrics for yourself so you have a baseline and foundation from which to work. There are easily accessible calculators online to discover these figures for yourself. You can search "BMR calculator" and "Harris-Benedict calculator" online to get started.

Step #3 – Learn from others who have achieved what you desire to achieve. There is often pride and honor associated with paving your own way and carving out your own path (I know, I became a vegan athlete before the Internet came around, back in the mid-'90s so I had to create my own path), but that isn't always the most efficient way to reach your goals. It often brings a pat on the back, but it could cost you a lot of time when you could learn lessons from others who have been down that road. Find role models who have had success in the specific areas of your own pursuit. Study what they did to get where they ended up. There were probably a lot of setbacks, lessons learned, and ups and downs all along the way before they ended up where they are now. Trial and error doesn't have to be yours; it could be learned from others.

Step #4 – Once you have combined steps 1-3, implement what you've learned into a program or approach that you can follow with consistency, developing positive habits. A health or fitness program tailored to your specific interests will put you on a path to success. This generally means you'll ensure your diet (based on caloric intake, not weight or volume) is primarily comprised of plant-based whole foods, and that you will be exercising with regularity, perhaps four to five days a week. You can also establish daily exercise habits, ensuring you do *something* to burn additional calories daily.

Step #5 – Evaluate your progress every few weeks. Is what you're doing working? Is something working exceptionally well, or holding you back? Are there struggles or obstacles that need to be addressed? Have you plateaued, or are you ahead of schedule? This kind of reflection every three to four weeks will help keep you on a path to success. As you achieve goals, it is time to set new ones. Start over at step 1.

I hope these action steps give you the confidence to pursue your own fitness dreams with passion, and the belief that you can achieve your goals. Learn to connect the dots ahead of time and take the actions today that put you on the path for success tomorrow. Do this day after day and success will be yours.

OVERCOMING INJURIES AND SETBACKS

Many of us have suffered small or big physical setbacks in the name of sports. In general, a few ideas to prevent injuries from happening are the following actions to consider:

- Warm-up properly so muscles are loose, supple, and more flexible. They are then less likely to be strained and injured from the stress of athletic movement.

- Stay adequately hydrated to avoid cramping and to ensure proper cell nutrition.

- Prepare your body for the stress it is about to be put through. If you are training legs, be sure to warm-up your legs by walking, jogging, stair climbing, playing basketball, or by some other means. If you are planning a heavy chest workout, be sure to warm up those muscles before engaging in heavy lifting. The same goes for all forms of exercise – prepare your body ahead of time.

- Understand proper techniques whether referring to weight lifting, martial arts, or a technical sport like baseball or golf. Know how to properly maneuver your body to complete the athletic tasks without compromising joints and muscles.

- Following a warm-up, stretch throughout your workout. This will help keep muscles loose and should enhance flexibility throughout your training session.

- Stretch at the end of your workout, especially the muscles that were engaged the most during your training session.

- Replenish nutrients lost through exercise – electrolytes, carbohydrates, and of course, water.

I've been a plant-based athlete for more than 20 years and through it all I have had my share of injuries. That seems to come with the territory. I have cracked a bone in my foot and broken a bone in my wrist while playing soccer. I suffered from shin splints as a runner and strained my back in track and field (all of those were when I was younger, before I became vegan.). I tore a disc in my back and tore a muscle in my chest through weight lifting, and I have suffered a few other weight-training-related injuries, from ongoing back issues to a wrist injury that lasted for many months, to an abdominal strain. My list of injuries is actually fairly short, considering a nearly 30-year athletic career, dating back to my childhood, and in comparison to many other athletes who have suffered far more injuries, including having multiple surgeries (which I have had none). Nevertheless, I have certainly had my share of injuries and setbacks and feel confident speaking to this topic, especially given my background as a former professional sports massage therapist.

As athletes, or active people, we no doubt suffer setbacks every now and then. A twisted ankle here, neck or back soreness there, a week off to recover from an illness, or other obstacles that get in our way and slow us down. During the process of writing this book I suffered a torn disc in my lower back, a setback that I finally just wrote about publicly, after largely keeping it to myself, close friends, and training partners for the past few months. It was frustrating, and came at a time when my enthusiasm was high and my goals were even higher. It left me in a lot of pain daily, and took the wind out of my sails a bit, even slowing, and at times, halting the writing of this book. Sometimes we have to take a break, accept reality, and start over with a fresh new outlook. Though there may be bumps along the road, and the journey isn't always a joy ride, the important thing to remember is to keep moving forward, so when things are going well again, you're already further along.

As far as tangible steps for overcoming injuries are concerned, some of the following modalities may be helpful in your recovery and rehabilitation:

- Chiropractic care

- Physical therapy

- Sports massage therapy

- Acupuncture

- Acupressure

- Natural herbs and anti-inflammatory foods

- Creams, gels, and over-the-counter medications (vegan-friendly, not tested on animals or containing any animal products or by-products)

- Sauna, steam room, hot tub

- Ice and heat treatments

- Yoga and stretching protocols

- Rest

- High water intake

It is always recommended that you see a doctor or other medical professional when you suffer some sort of injury.

Our wish for you is that you stay injury free and that you enjoy whatever athletic endeavors you pursue.

AIM TO BECOME THE BEST VERSION OF YOURSELF

One of my favorite tips to share is simply this: take in all the knowledge you can, apply what makes the most sense to you, and work hard to become the best version of yourself. That's what we're truly striving for, and what compels us to train hard and eat well. We want to look and feel our best, and I believe we can achieve these outcomes if we make becoming our own personal best part of our pursuit. So, the next time you feel like skipping a workout or buying a junk-food meal, ask yourself, "What will this do for me? Will this action help me get closer to achieving my goals?" Ask those questions, take the appropriate actions, and enjoy your workout and delicious post-workout plant-based meal, if that's the direction you go in.

Chapter 5

SAMPLE WORKOUT PROGRAMS FOR MUSCLE BUILDING, FAT BURNING, AND CONDITIONING

MUSCLE BUILDING WORKOUT PROGRAMS BY VANESSA ESPINOZA

1-Week Sample

In this section, each exercise is to be performed for the number of sets and reps outlined, before moving on to the next exercise. In the case of squats, as listed below, you will complete ten sets starting with 25 reps for the first set, and finish with just a single repetition, increasing the weight for each ensuing set from start to finish. Complete all ten sets of squats, then rest for one or two minutes, and move on to the next exercise.

* If there are any exercises listed below that you are unfamiliar with, or unsure how to perform, please refer to Vanessa's YouTube channel (youtube.com/VanessaEspinozaPlantBasedMuscle), where you will find demonstrations and explanations of the exercises she outlines in the workout programs.

MONDAY	SETS X REPS
Legs	
Quads/Hamstrings	
Squats	10x25, 15, 12, 10, 8, 6, 4, 3, 2, 1
Barbell lunges alternate legs	3x10 each leg
Front squats	4x10

Step-ups (Keeping one leg on bench whole time)	3x10 each leg
Sumo squats	4x10
Pistol squats	3x10 each leg
Leg extensions	4x25
Romanian deadlifts	4x10

TUESDAY

SETS X REPS

Chest

Flat barbell bench press	8x25, 15, 12, 10, 8, 6, 3, 1
Incline barbell bench press	6x10, 8, 6, 3, 2, 1
Decline barbell bench press	5x10
Dumbbell flys	4x15

Cable flys

High-to-low pulley	3x15
Medium pulley	3x15
Low-to-high pulley	3x15

WEDNESDAY

SETS X REPS

Back

Deadlift	10x25, 15, 12, 10, 8, 6, 4, 3, 2, 1
Wide-grip pull-ups	4xfailure
Barbell bent-over rows (overhand)	4x15
Barbell bent-over rows (underhand)	4x15

Dumbbell one-arm row	4x10 each arm
Neutral-grip pull-ups	4xfailure
Seated cable rows	4x25

THURSDAY

SETS X REPS

Biceps/Calves

Barbell curl	6x10, 8, 6, 4, 2, 1
Hammer curls	4x10 each way
Single-arm preacher curl	3x10 each arm
Reverse barbell curls	3x10
Rope curls	3x15
Seated cable curls	3x15
Pull-ups	4xfailure
Seated calf raises (feet facing forward, in and out)	4x25 each direction, lighter weight
Standing calf raises	4x10 each direction, heavy weight
Bodyweight calf raises	4x50 each direction

FRIDAY

SETS X REPS

Shoulders

Seated dumbbell military press	9x25, 15, 12, 10, 8, 6, 3, 2, 1
Handstand push-ups or Arnold press	3xfailure
Single-arm leaning dumbbell side raise	4x10 each arm
Single-arm rear fly	4x10 each arm

TRX face pull	4x15
Smith machine rear upright rows (wide)	4x15
Superset with plate upright rows	4x15

SATURDAY

SETS X REPS

Triceps

Close-grip bench press	5x10
Barbell skull crushers	4x10
Weighted dips	4xfailure
Rope push-downs	4x15
Close-grip push-ups	3x15
Reverse-grip cable kickbacks	3x15 each arm

Abs

Ab roller or sit-up	3x10
Hanging leg raises	3x10
Hanging knee raises	3x10
Hanging oblique raises	3x10

Fat Burning Workout Programs by Vanessa Espinoza

1-Week Sample

Perform the following exercises in pairs as they are matched below. For example, in the first exercise, you will complete ten repetitions of the one-arm snatch, immediately followed by a set of 15 push-ups. Treat this as a two-exercise circuit. Therefore, you will not have a rest period until all three sets of each of the paired exercises are completed. Then rest for one or two minutes and move on to the next series of exercises and follow the same model.

* If there are any exercises listed below that you are unfamiliar with, or unsure how to perform, please refer to Vanessa's YouTube channel (youtube.com/VanessaEspinozaPlantBasedMuscle), where you will find demonstrations and explanations of the exercises she outlines in the workout programs.

MONDAY	SETS X REPS
Legs and chest	
One-arm snatch	3x10 each arm
Push-ups	3x15
Sumo squat with one-arm upright row, alternating arms	3x8 each arm
Pause push-ups	3x15
Thrusters	3x10
Romanian deadlifts	3x10
Dumbbell chest press	3x10
Burpees	3x10

| Backward lunge (one leg at a time) | 3x10 each leg |
| Incline chest flys | 3x15 |

TUESDAY

SETS X REPS

Back with cardio

TRX – W,Y,&T's	3x7 each way
Jumping jacks	3x50
Dumbbell bent over row (overhand grip)	3x15
Seal jumping jacks	3x50
Australian pull-ups (neutral)	3x10
Side burpees	3x5 each way
Dumbbell bent over rows (underhand)	3x15
Half burpees	3x15
Dumbbell one-arm row	3x15 each arm
Mountain climbers	3x50
Australian pull-ups (over and underhand)	3x10 each way
Plank jumping jacks (push-up position)	3x50

WEDNESDAY

SETS X REPS

Biceps, triceps, and legs

TRX face curl	3x15
Speed skaters	3x50
TRX skull-crushers	3x15
Hammer curl in and out	3x10 each way
Squat jumps	3x15
Dips	3x10

Rope curls	3x15
Split jumps	3x30
Rope push-downs	3x15
TRX curl to chest	3x15
Sumo jumps	3x15
Reverse close-grip push-ups	3x15
Barbell curls	3x10
Box jumps	3x10
Dumbbell kickbacks (neutral grip)	3x10

THURSDAY   SETS X REPS

Abs and shoulders

Wood-choppers holding a 5-pound dumbbell	3x15 each way
Dumbbell military press	3x15
Bucket throwers holding a 5-pound dumbbell	3x15 each way
Rear flys	3x10
Side-to-side twist holding medicine ball	3x15 each way
Side raises	3x15
Opposite elbow to knee (standing)	3x15 each way
Dumbbell upright row	3x15
Figure 8 holding a 5-pound dumbbell	3x10 each way
Handstand push-up	3x10

FRIDAY

SETS X REPS

Total body workout:

Deadlift	5x15
Power clean	4x5
Sumo squat with side raise	3x15
Ab roller or full crunch	3x10
Step up (alternate legs)	3x10 each leg
Ab roller side-to-side	3x5 each way
Uneven push-up	3x10 each arm
Abs v-ups	3x25 second sprint
Single-leg Romanian deadlift	3x10 each leg
Leg raises	3x15
Walking push-ups	3x15
Windshield wipers on floor	3x10 each way

Conditioning Workout Programs by Vanessa Espinoza

1-Week Sample

Using the workout listed below, in the first series of exercises as an example, you will complete 15 thrusters, then 20 push-ups, then 14 thrusters, then 19 push-ups, and so on, without resting, until you complete all the reps in each exercise. Once you reach the stopping point, in this case getting down to 10 reps of thrusters and 15 reps of push-ups, move on to the next pair of exercises. Rest for one to two minutes between each pair of exercise sequences.

If there are any exercises listed below that you are unfamiliar with, or unsure how to perform, please refer to Vanessa's YouTube channel (youtube.com/VanessaEspinozaPlantBasedMuscle), where you will find demonstrations and explanations of the exercises she outlines in the workout programs.

MONDAY	SETS X REPS
Thrusters	15 reps down to 10 reps
Push-ups*	20 reps down to 15 reps
One-arm snatches	10 reps down to 5 reps
Pause push-ups	15 reps down to 10 reps
Burpee deadlift	15 reps down to 10 reps
Decline push-ups	15 reps down to 10 reps
Sumo squat with side raises	15 reps down to 10 reps
Chest flys	15 reps down to 10 reps

(*example: 15 thrusters, 20 push-ups, 14 thrusters, 19 push-ups, 13 thrusters, 18 push-ups, 12 thrusters, 17 push-ups, 11 thrusters, 16 push-ups, 10 thrusters, 15 push-ups)

TUESDAY

	SETS X REPS
Boxing/kick boxing	10, 1 minute rounds, 10, 30 second rounds, 10, 20 second rounds, 10, 10 second rounds. 1:1 ratio rest.

WEDNESDAY

	SETS X REPS
Ball slams	4x15
Squat jumps	4x15
Sumo oblique crunches (standing)	4x15 each way
Burpees	4x10
Figure 8 holding a 5-pound dumbbell	4x10 each way
Half burpee	4x20
Side-to-side twist	4x15 each way
Split jumps	4x30
Opposite elbow to knee (standing)	4x15 each leg
Jumping jacks	4x50

THURSDAY

One-mile warm-up run	10-100 yard sprints 10-50 yard sprints 10-20 yard sprints

FRIDAY	SETS X REPS
Deadlift	4x10
Skip rope	1 minute
Push-ups	4x25
Skip rope	1 minute
Standing barbell military press	4x10
Skip rope	1 minute
TRX Australian pull-up	4x15
Skip rope	1 minute
Hammer curls	4x15
Skip rope	1 minute
Medicine ball push-ups	4x15
Skip rope	1 minute

Bodyweight Workout Programs by Vanessa Espinoza

1-Week Sample

For the following exercises, use the same formula as used for fat-burning and conditioning. Perform the exercises in pairs, resting once you have completed all the reps and sets for each sequence, and then move on to the next pair of exercises.

* If there are any exercises listed below that you are unfamiliar with, or unsure how to perform, please refer to Vanessa's YouTube channel (youtube.com/VanessaEspinozaPlantBasedMuscle), where you will find demonstrations and explanations of the exercises she outlines in the workout programs.

MONDAY	SETS X REPS
Squat jumps	3x15
Pause push-ups	3x15
Split jumps	3x15
Push-ups	3x15
Sumo squat jumps	3x15
Decline push-ups	3x15
Speed skaters	3x50
3-way push-ups	3x15
Burpees	3x15
Decline medicine ball push-ups	3x10

TUESDAY	SETS X REPS
Jumping jacks	3x50
Abs full crunch	3x15
Tuck jumps	3x15
Abs iron cross	3x15 each side
Oblique climbers	3x30 each side
Abs scissors (up and down)	3x50
Step-ups (alternate legs)	3x10 each leg
Abs knees into chest	3x15
Side step-ups	3x10 each leg
Abs jackknife	3x10 each side

WEDNESDAY	SETS X REPS
Modified handstand push-ups	3xfailure
Abs v-ups	3x15
Squat jumps	3x15
Abs leg raises	3x15
Pause push-ups	3x15
Abs opposite arm/leg	3x10 each side
Split jumps	3x10 each leg
Abs windshield wipers	3x10 each side
Close-grip push-up	3x10
Abs bicycle	3x50

THURSDAY	SETS X REPS
Mountain climbers	3x50
Speed skaters	3x50
Seal jumping jacks	3x50
Half burpee	3x15
Side burpees	3x5 each way
High knees clap under knee	3x50
Lay down/Get back up	3x10 each side
Burpees	3x10

FRIDAY	SETS X REPS
Walking push-ups	3x15
High knees clap under knee	3x50
Abs Russian twist	3x50
Dips	3x15
Squat jumps	3x15
Abs legs up touch toes	3x20
Modified handstand push-ups	3xfailure
Split jumps	3x10 each leg
Abs opposite elbow/knee (standing)	3x15 each side
Decline push-ups	3x15
Mountain climbers	3x15
Abs leg raises	3x15
Close-grip push-ups	3x15
Burpees	3x10
Abs bicycle (side to side)	3x50

Partner Exercise Workout Programs by Vanessa Espinoza
1-Week Sample

Partner exercises are a great way to incorporate fitness into your lifestyle with a friend, partner or member of your family, or anyone else. If you have a regular training partner and you're looking to change things up from the usual weight training exercises, some of these creative partner exercises could be just what you're looking for. As with the other exercise programs, perform the exercises in pairs, resting once you have completed all the reps and sets for each sequence, and then move on to the next pair of exercises.

* If there are any exercises listed below that you are unfamiliar with, or unsure how to perform, please refer to Vanessa's YouTube channel (youtube.com/VanessaEspinozaPlantBasedMuscle), where you will find demonstrations and explanations of the exercises she outlines in the workout programs.

MONDAY	SETS X REPS
Medicine ball toss	3x10 each side
Resistance push-ups	3x15
Jump squat with twist and high five	3x15
Wheelbarrow push-ups	3x15
Jump lunge with high five	3x15 each leg
Medicine ball partner crunches	3x20
Plank hold and jump	3x10
Medicine ball twist	3x10 each way

Partner band squats	3x15
Decline medicine ball push-ups	3x10

TUESDAY | SETS X REPS

Partner shuttle run, tag, and switch	3xeach
Partner band rows (neutral grip)	3x25
Resistance dips	3x15
Partner band rows (underhand grip)	3x25
Triceps push-ups	3x15
Partner band rows (overhand grip)	3x25
Partner band kickbacks	3x15
Partner assisted pull-ups	3xfailure
Partner band triceps extensions	3x15

WEDNESDAY | SETS X REPS

Partner shoulder press	3x15
Partner assisted pull-ups (palms up)	3xfailure
Partner band side raises	3x15
Partner band biceps curls	3x15
Wheelbarrow crawl and plank	3x10
Partner biceps curl to face	3x15
Resistance band rear flys	3x15
Resistance band reverse grip curls	3x15
Plank with high five	3x10 each arm
Plank with side rotation and clap	3x5 each side

THURSDAY	SETS X REPS
Kettlebell toss	3x10 each
Partner shuttle run, tag, and switch	3x
Partner resistance band squats	3x15
Resistance band sprints	3x50 yards
Wheelbarrow push-ups with squat	3x15
Resistance band side shuffle	3x30 yards
Partner band chest press	3x20
Partner shuttle run, tag, and switch	3x

FRIDAY	SETS X REPS
Resistance pull-ups	3xfailure
Resistance push-ups	3x15
Partner band shoulder press	3x15
Squat jump with twist and high five	3x15
Partner band biceps curl	3x15
Partner band triceps extension	3x15
Partner band rows (neutral grip)	3x15
High five push-ups	3x15
Resistance pull-ups (palms up)	3xfailure
Resistance dips	3x15

Chapter 6

OUR PLANT-BASED NUTRITION PHILOSOPHIES

Salad from Graze vegetarian restaurant in Nashville, TN

Robert

Before we launch into our specific nutrition philosophies, it is important to address a few key fundamental differences in our approaches to nutrition. I come from a bodybuilding background that at its core has an extreme focus and emphasis on consuming a high protein diet. I bucked that trend about five years ago when I was influenced by the film, *Forks Over Knives*, and had the incredible opportunity to work for the film, and in some respects, work directly with the doctors who starred in the highly acclaimed documentary. That led to an interest in a lower protein diet, and then getting certified in plant-based nutrition through the online Center For Nutrition Studies course at Cornell University sealed the deal for me. I have been consuming, and emphasizing, a low-protein, mostly whole-food, plant-based diet ever since. Therefore, it shouldn't be hard to notice that I have a deliberate approach to actually avoiding high protein foods in excess, especially high concentrations of isolated proteins, such as in the form of protein powders, which I have abstained from for the past half decade.

By contrast, Vanessa has more of an interest in high protein foods, to the point that she might make a food selection based on its high protein content, over a lower protein counterpart, as she has described in previous sections. This interest, a common approach in bodybuilding and mainstream fitness, has been long associated with increased muscle mass, size, and strength. She has a degree in exercise science, and has built one of the world's best physiques, so the amount of protein she focuses on isn't something I am going to take issue with, just as she doesn't take issue with my abnormal adherence to a protein-reduction approach, even though we both share similar health and fitness goals. It's worth noting that neither of us believes that one approach is substantially better than the other. For us, it truly comes down to personal preferences, behaviors, and habits we have developed over time, and we both remain open to change, as we do in every aspect of nutrition, health, and fitness. It could be that one approach might have slightly superior health implications for overall mortality rates and longevity, and the opposite approach might have some slight benefits to repairing muscle tissue efficiently, leading to slightly accelerated muscle tissue repair and growth. But those differences are, as suggested, slight to the best of our knowledge. Since we are both mindful of our nutrition approaches, we don't have extreme highs or lows when it comes to protein intake, Vanessa just focuses a bit more on it, and I focus a bit less on it, yet we both focus on eating as many whole plant foods as we can, ensuring that is the true foundation of our nutrition program, making up the majority of our daily calorie intake.

It is also not our intention to confuse readers with our differences and robust enthusiasm for our own individual pursuits of health and fitness goals, as they relate to nutrition, but to show that there are variations in human nutrition, however slight or dramatic they may seem, and that there truly is no one-size-fits-all approach that works for everyone perfectly. Having said that, you can evaluate our reasons for why a high- or low-protein approach is a personal preference for us, but more importantly, evaluate the specific foods we consume, the areas where we overlap with glowing enthusiasm and endorsements for specific foods and food groups (such as beans, leafy greens, fruits, and cruciferous vegetables), and from there deduce what applications resonate best with your own nutrition goals, habits, and preferences. Lastly, please understand that even among experts in lots of fields, including in nutrition, there may be passionate disagreements on fundamental approaches (think Dr. McDougall vs. Dr. Fuhrman) or more broadly, plant-based vs. Paleo, or low fat vs. high fat, or the popular low carbohydrate vs. high carbohydrate debate. The same juxtapositions and opposing viewpoints may be present among experts in exercise science, and in all forms of science, so take our slight differences on nutrition with a grain of pink Himalayan salt.

My Current Nutrition Philosophy

Vanessa

I always start my morning with a big cup of Matcha green tea with a whole lemon squeezed in it. I add lemon because it balances pH (keeping the body alkaline), boosts the immune system, flushes out unwanted materials, is great for weight loss, and is a natural energizer. Lemon hydrates and oxygenates the body as well. The reason I drink Matcha tea instead of regular green tea is because one serving has the nutritional equivalent of 10 cups of green tea and has 137 times more antioxidants than regular green tea. Matcha tea also boosts metabolism, helps burn calories, detoxifies the body, and is rich in fiber, chlorophyll, and vitamins.

When it comes to meal planning, I typically eat six to nine times per day. Everyday my morning starts at 4am and my first meal is a few hours after my Matcha green tea lemon water. I eat the same breakfast pretty much everyday: quinoa with peanut butter, banana, chia, hemp, and cinnamon. The reason why I eat quinoa for breakfast is because it is one of the most protein-rich plant foods and has twice as much fiber as other grains. I also add chia and hemp for the same reasons; both are high in protein, fiber, and antioxidants. Adding cinnamon not only makes it taste great, but also offers so many health benefits, such as anticarcinogenic, anti-inflammatory, antifungal, antibacterial, and even antiviral properties. It also helps regulate blood sugar.

I focus on eating mostly whole, plant-based foods, but like many people, I consume some processed foods, and like many athletes, some sports supplements as well. People ask me what I eat all the time, and my answer is, "real food." I don't count macronutrients, and I never have. I count micronutrients. People also frequently ask me where I get my protein. I tell them I get protein from everything I eat. All my food contains amino acids, which are the building blocks of protein. I look at food from this perspective: "Is this meal helping me and giving me energy, or is it hurting me?" My food is my medicine. I meal prep each week so I'm always prepared with good food and I will be less likely to grab something unhealthy. I avoid refined carbohydrates, processed, and fried foods. I hardly ever eat out because I don't know what kind of oil or how much salt is put into my food. When I travel, I pack a ton of healthy snacks so I'm always prepared and never tempted to grab junk food. My staple when I travel is a Powerootz brand protein shake with water. I make sure I have my blender bottle so I can make it anytime. Another great snack I always have with me is trail mix, a mixture of all types of raw nuts, preferably with no oil or salt. I also carry around fruit, Larabar, Rawxie, and Health Warrior brand food bars, and one of my favorite snacks, which is dried peas. Dried peas are a perfect snack to take anywhere because you don't have to refrigerate them; they pack so many nutrients, and have more than 10 grams of protein and fiber in each cup. Every so often I will have a vegan treat of some sort, like a chocolate chip cookie or a donut. If I'm really craving something sweet, which happens in the evenings, I will grab a piece of dark chocolate with at least 70% cacao.

When I meal prep I make large quantities of food, and I typically meal prep once or twice per week. My staple foods are tofu, tempeh, sweet potatoes, quinoa, lentils, beans, fruit, green vegetables, chia, hemp, and nutritional yeast. I make enough of these foods to last me all week. Sometimes during the week I will eat the same thing for lunch and dinner. I also drink one or two Powerootz protein shakes a day because it provides 23 grams of vegan protein, it's 100% organic, and there's not a single artificial ingredient in it. Powerootz also has all my favorite superfoods and herbs all in one shake: raw alfalfa leaf, raw chlorella, goji berry, green papaya, cordycep mushrooms, bladderwrack, pomegranate, raw sea buckthorn, raw ashwagandha, raw maca root, raw amla fruit, raw spirulina, raw acai berries, raw noni fruit, and raw mangosteen. It gives me a ton of energy and helps me recover from my intense workouts.

I eat every two to three hours, usually small meals. My biggest meals are breakfast and lunch with dinner as my smallest. My dinner usually consists of a large salad with a bunch of veggies and lentils on top, or tofu with a ton of veggies. Typically I eat dinner before 4pm because I have to work in the evenings. I don't like to go to bed with a full stomach so I eat lighter in the evenings. I'm not active after dinner and I am not burning off those calories, so I don't want them to accumulate and get stored as fat. I consume most of my carbohydrates earlier in the day, so I try not to have many carbohydrates after 4pm. I feel like this approach keeps me looking leaner. My eating is always very consistent, and I feel so much better with a consistent routine, and having lots of energy for my workouts. I wouldn't be able to get up at 4am everyday, train twice per day, and work all day long, if I didn't fuel my body with the right nutrients.

Before I train, I always fuel up on Matcha green tea and sometimes coffee. I don't like to consume very much food before exercise so I have a Powerootz shake or fruit pre-workout. Post-workout, I eat a meal, usually tofu, sweet potato, and a bunch of veggies. I also take spirulina and chlorella tablets post-workout, which are great forms of amino acids that help with recovery.

I try to keep my nutrition program and philosophy very simple and nutritious, consisting of mostly real, whole, plant-based foods. It doesn't matter how hard you workout, you can't outwork a bad diet.

Powerootz protein drink

My Current Nutrition Philosophy

Robert

If you have read my previous book, *Shred It!*, you know that I emphasize a whole-food, plant-based diet, and have written dedicated chapters to that specific component of a healthy lifestyle in that book. A whole-food, plant-based approach is what I take most of the time, but as I travel more frequently and eat out at more restaurants, processed foods make their way into my nutrition program a little more often these days. I don't beat myself up for it, but I am aware of it and work hard to make conscious decisions when I am traveling in order to stay on track and achieve my health and fitness goals. When I am on the road I aim to eat most of my meals from hot food and salad bars at health food stores, but I also enjoy Mexican, Indian, Thai, Ethiopian, and Japanese cuisine, and I find international restaurants in every major city I visit, and often in small towns too. Additionally, I do a lot of grocery shopping when I travel so I can keep sufficient amounts of fruit on hand at all times. I also pick up prepared foods such as vegetable rice paper rolls, avocado rolls, wraps, sandwiches, and burritos. Vegetables and hummus is another go-to meal when I am traveling. I was recently on tour for nine consecutive weekends all across the country. I was lucky to be in very vegan-friendly cities such as Los Angeles, Austin, Asheville, and Oakland most of those weekends, but I also had a trip to the not-as-vegan-friendly city (though it is growing rapidly) of Beijing, and had trips to Alabama, Tennessee, and a less progressive part of Florida. All provided different levels of plant-based food options, restaurants, stores, and communities. In Asheville I found a vegan-friendly restaurant on seemingly every street, and in Los Angeles I could stumble upon four Whole Foods Market locations within walking distance from one another, but in Talladega, Walmart was probably my best bet. There are late night vegan-friendly eateries abound in Austin, fewer options in honky-tonk bars in Nashville, and the list goes on.

Regardless of where I am, I emphasize consuming high carbohydrate, low protein, and low-fat, whole, plant foods. One easy way to ensure that whole foods make up the majority of calorie consumption is to prepare favorite staple foods in bulk quantities. I do this with potatoes, yams, beans, lentils, brown rice, oats, and other heavy, filling staple foods, thus ensuring that I have a main course meal ready anytime. I simply add salad greens, fruits, vegetables, toppings like avocado, pickles, olives, and peppers, and other additions to these primary staple foods. I can have a different themed lunch or dinner every night of the week, mixing and matching my preferred staple foods with various sides. Broccoli, salad greens, organic tofu, squash, avocado, kidney and chickpeas, sunflower seeds, almonds, and similar filling foods are great to have at home to be used to help create diverse whole, plant-based meals. This approach can even be applied when traveling by air, rail, or water. For my recent flight to China, my fiancée, Karen, prepared sealable, reusable containers of nectarines, apricots, blueberries, raspberries, mangoes, cherries, and Yukon gold potatoes for my flight. As long as they are consumed before touching down and going through customs, they are absolutely allowed on board for international flights, just like domestic flights. I ate them all during my 24-hour long trip, and you bet I used the bathroom the very moment I got to my hotel room in Beijing, before even turning the lights on in the room! I do the same for domestic trips (not the bathroom experience), and preparing whole plant foods for travel is an efficient way of ensuring healthy meals while traveling. Having the reusable containers to use for leftovers at restaurants to keep in a hotel room refrigerator is also an effective practice, reducing resources, saving food, and cutting future meal expenses.

In addition to my enthusiasm for whole plant foods, I am also known for being a fairly outspoken advocate for a sports supplement-free diet/nutrition program for the general population. I don't use powders, isolated nutrients, extractions and other reductionist approaches to eating certain foods for a specific reason – because the foods are high in this or that nutrient. This sports supplement-free approach puts me on a bit of a tight rope I have been walking for some time, namely because I am one of the very few plant-based athletes I know of taking this type of stance. Nearly every plant-based and non-plant-based athlete I know of uses some sort of sports supplement, be it a pre-workout or post-workout powder, branched-chain amino acids, creatine, meal replacements, or something else packaged, bottled, and promoted to have myriad health benefits beyond what nature can provide on its own.

It is rarely ever inherently easy to go against the grain, especially among peers, and among good friends who are in the business of selling the precise products that I deliberately avoid, but I am becoming more and more open to having a general discussion about the role that supplements play in our overall health. For years, I stayed away from all sports supplements, uninterested in even discussing their potential benefits, because, quite frankly, I viewed the usage of sports supplements by non-serious athletes and the general population at large, to be quite silly. I viewed it almost like an inactive desk job worker taking steroids. What do you really have to gain from the perceived competitive edge of sports supplements if you're a weekend warrior, excising on the rare occasion? Is your protein drink really making you that much bigger and stronger? Is it worth it? I now accept the various reasons why even non-serious athletes line up by the millions to spend money on containers of powder, I just find it rather unnecessary, even though I better understand why people have these behaviors and habits they developed over time and got accustomed to. I still fundamentally disagree with the use of *sports* supplementation, on the foundation that I don't believe sports supplements are necessary for increased health or measurable athletic improvements for the average person, or weekend warrior, who is not pursuing Olympic Gold. I can, however, understand why elite, professional, and Olympic athletes would want to find a nutritional competitive edge, which may be achieved through the use of some specific sports supplements. I've been fortunate to spend some time with elite, professional, and Olympic athletes, and I know their mindset, their work ethic, and their craving for anything that will enhance their athletic productivity. So I totally get it. My concern is that the mainstream supplement industry preys on the general public, convincing them that the consumption of their unique concoctions will help improve their lives, and I'm not so sure that it truly does improve lives of the average citizen in the real world. Yet it costs them a lot, not just money, but in some cases, hope, that if they can just use supplements to reach their goals they won't have to work as hard when it comes to exercise.

The topic of sports supplement use is a rather complex issue, one that I am giving a lot of attention to in this section of the book, and one that Vanessa and I are on somewhat opposite ends of the spectrum on. But it's a conversation we have had, and a conversation I have had with other elite and champion athletes who use sports supplements. Because Vanessa is an elite and world-class athlete, I understand and appreciate her approach to getting a nutritional competitive edge through the use of certain sports supplements to aid in muscle recovery and growth, as she has described above. Just as she understands where I am coming from, having become my personal best after getting certified in plant-based nutrition through Cornell, and subsequently ceased all use of sports supplements. We have both attained our top form with somewhat opposite methods regarding sports supplement use. Without trying to sound too repetitive, again, we respect one another's practice in this area of sports performance and for us it really does come down to our own personal preferences. I concede that there may be some benefits to the use of certain sports supplements, but I don't believe that their use is a practical approach for the majority of people who take them in the place of eating real plant-based foods. I also believe that nearly every "benefit" achieved through the use of sports supplements could likely be attained through the consumption of real foods without the extra baggage that comes with packaged, powdered, capsulated, solid or liquid forms of altered nutrition. There also tends to be a psychological placebo effect of taking a sports supplement that boasts a list of benefits one may expect to experience by using it, and often a subsequent addiction to and reliance on said supplement by the user in the pursuit of health claims written on the package.

Though sports supplements are not something I can currently get behind, the work by Dr. Michael Greger, Dr. Joel Fuhrman, Matt Frazier of *No Meat Athlete*, and others, has me thinking a little differently about general health supplements that may be beneficial for those on a pure plant-based diet – namely, Vitamin B12 (which I have been a longtime advocate of using), Vitamin D (specifically vegan forms of D3), and DHA/EPA. For years I have recommended Vitamin B12, and Vitamin D, especially for those who live north of the southern USA states like California, Texas, and Florida, but now I have a deeper interest in the relationship between ALA and DHA/EPA Omega-3 essential fatty acids. It's an interest I continue to explore further with an emphasis on supplementation that may benefit the masses, not just elite athletes seeking a temporary edge, rather than a long-term health pursuit. One of the latest products to come out is called Complement, and it contains only Vitamin B12, Vitamin D, and DHA/EPA Omega 3 essential fatty acids. Perhaps something like this combination is worth looking into for those seeking to boost their intake of those rather hard to find aspects of nutrition. I think this is a rather important topic, and I am happy that Dr. Greger has been so wildly successful with *How Not To Die*, and Dr. Fuhrman with his nationally televised show, to let people know that it is OK to use some helpful supplements like Vitamin D and B12, and that there's nothing wrong with that, and no need to feel that one's plant-based diet is inadequate because of the inclusion of one healthful supplement or another. There is a fundament difference between supplementing with Vitamin B12, which many people on a pure plant-based diet do not get naturally with their food intake – and which a deficiency in has consequences, and consuming protein powders by the bottle, hoping to get bigger muscles, as advertised.

It seems as though sports supplements are unequivocally unnecessary (but clearly preferable for many), though some particular ones could provide short-term benefits for some users, and some sports supplements help with very specific objectives – such as creatine's ability to retain water, or the role that branched-chain amino acids in supplemental form play in repairing muscle tissue. Elevated intake levels of the amino acid, L-leucine, many help retain muscle mass and aid in muscle repair and growth, having anti-catabolic affects. There could be some other benefits such as an increased water intake for those who use a protein powder mixed with water, and a reduction in muscle or joint soreness from the use of anti-inflammatory supplements. It appears that there is a sports supplement for nearly every stage of athletic performance, and one could easily become quite the pharmaceutical connoisseur, even with the best of intentions. Ultimately, the use of sports supplements seems to come down to preference, not necessity, as nearly every sport supplement's benefits can be experienced through the consumption of real food found in nature. Where did the supplement manufacture get their ingredients after all? And as is the case with many things in life, preference, perhaps supported by convenience in some cases, often wins out, even at the literal monetary expense, and at the expense of consuming unnecessary additives, fillers, and by-products that are often a packaged deal with sports supplements. The subsequent reliance many people have on sports supplements for a substantially long time is a concern for not only your wallet, but because they all too often tend to take the place of real food in one's diet. I know, from a decade-long addiction to protein supplements, and an ongoing battle with the reliance on energy drinks.

The risks and benefits of long-term sports supplement use are largely unknown, and at this point in my athletic career, I aim to focus on the key areas that we might want to pay special attention to, such as the consumption of Vitamin B12, Vitamin D, and the conversion and absorption, or lack thereof, of ALA into DHA/EPA Omega-3 essential fatty acids, giving them a higher importance than powdered, processed, packaged, and heavily marketed sports supplements. The reason those *general* health supplements take precedence in the big picture is because they are often devoid in a pure plant-based diet because they are simply harder to come by. That's not to say that a healthy whole-food, plant-based diet is inherently insufficient, but it is accurate to say that many people (vegan and non-vegan alike) find themselves on the short end of Vitamin B12 and D consumption/absorption, and some people may have ineffective ways of converting ALA Omega-3 essential fatty acids into DHA/EPA, and there could be some health consequences, as there are in any nutritional deficiencies. I refer to Dr. Michael Greger and Dr. Joel Fuhrman when trying to wrap my head around some of these nutritional nuances, and to learn more from their scientific mouths directly, check out the books, *How Not To Die* by Dr. Greger, and *Eat To Live* by Dr. Fuhrman. You can also reference Dr. Greger's acclaimed www.nutritionfacts.org website where you can search for seemingly any topic and find a helpful article or video addressing your area of interest, and Dr. Fuhrman's official website, aptly named, www.drfuhrman.com, where you can learn more about his successful 25-year professional career helping tens of thousands of patients achieve superior health with his *Eat To Live* approach.

Beyond what we eat and how we train, and whether or not we supplement or complement our diet with sports supplements, there are other principles that play a role in our success as we strive to achieve goals in areas of health and fitness. Sometimes we just need a reminder with some quick tips to get us right back on track to ensure we stay the course so we can get to the finish line.

UNDERSTAND THE ROLE NUTRITION PLAYS IN FITNESS

A common question that comes up among many people new to a plant-based diet is 'what do I eat?' It is quite clear which foods someone following a plant-based diet avoids, and that is all animal products. In the case of a whole-food, plant-based diet, oils and refined carbohydrates are also eliminated or greatly minimized for various health reasons, namely the reduction of the consumption of oil and high saturated fats and excess calories that may damage our artery walls and contribute to plaque build up, restricting blood flow in our vessels. As plant-based athletes, we incorporate more foods than we avoid but many still wonder about how to get adequate nutrition, especially protein. This question often piques further curiosity from the athletic-minded individual. I've been down this road for decades, helping people understand the fundamentals, which I will now share with you.

The human requirement for protein is so low (5-10 percent of our total caloric intake) that as long as you consume adequate calories based on your individual caloric needs, it is impossible to have a protein deficiency. You would experience a calorie deficiency before you would experience a protein deficiency, and both are relatively unheard of in first world societies. To determine your own personal caloric needs, simply search 'Harris-Benedict calculator' online and input your data. This will reveal your average caloric expenditure, which will guide your caloric intake needs based on your goals to maintain weight, build muscle, or burn fat. Once you determine your daily calorie target, aim to get about 10 percent of your total calories coming from protein, and that's all you need to do to put the protein intake worry to rest. The Harris-Benedict calculator factors in your Basal Metabolic Rate based on your gender, age, height, and weight, combined with your actual daily activity to determine how many calories you truly expend on an average day. This is incredibly helpful information to know about yourself, and can transform and influence how you eat and exercise moving forward.

When it comes to what to eat, know that your options are boundless with ample varieties of fruits, vegetables, legumes, grains, nuts, and seeds. Simply choose the foods you like the most, and eat meals throughout the day so you are constantly nourished, avoiding under eating or overeating. This way, you will have sufficient fuel to work out anytime, rather than feeling too hungry, too full, or too tired to exercise. The two biggest obstacles keeping people from exercising regularly are shortages of time and energy. You can now put the energy issue to rest and work on time management to ensure regular exercise is part of your routine.

EAT FOR NOURISHMENT

Nobody is fueled by kale, so don't fool yourself into thinking you will get sufficient energy to perform athletic activities from eating leafy greens, which contain only about 100 calories per pound. Consume more calorically dense complex carbohydrates for long-lasting fuel, such as potatoes, beans, lentils, squash, brown rice, oats, quinoa, and other starchy vegetables, legumes, and grains. Fruits are also an excellent source of fuel, especially right before exercise because they digest quickly and will not weigh heavily in your stomach during cardiovascular exercise. When you consume an abundance of whole, plant-based foods you not only get the fuel, but the macro and micronutrients, antioxidants, fiber, water, and other important components found in foods in their whole, unprocessed state that help you perform at your best.

Since most whole plant foods (aside from primarily nuts and seeds) contain 500 or fewer calories per pound, you can eat a lot of food, experiencing many flavors and textures, and the volume will fill you up before you overdose on calories, which is easy to do when consuming isolated nutrients and processed foods. By consuming high nutrient-dense and low calorie-dense plant foods, you can support energy production and muscle recovery without excess fat gain, while avoiding the energy-sucking process of digesting refined foods.

PERFORMANCE NUTRITION

When I am focused on burning fat I won't eat during my workout, but when my goal is building muscle, I will often eat a couple of pieces of fruit or a Lara Bar or two during my actual workout to add more fuel (i.e., more calories) and to get the muscle-repair process started right away, even while I'm still training. I reserve fasted exercise for cardiovascular training, often first thing in the morning when fat burning is a high priority. My preference is to use the Stairmaster and then follow my fasted cardiovascular workout with lots of fluids, fruits, and then heavier, more satiating starchy legumes, grains, and vegetables. The reason for my post-workout nutrition approach is to replenish nutrients lost through exercise: electrolytes, glycogen, carbohydrates, and of course overall calories and water. Drinking water with fruit replenishes fluids and electrolytes lost through exercise, and eating starchy legumes, grains, and vegetables replenishes glycogen burned up as fuel, calories expended through exercise, and helps get amino acids to work, repairing and growing muscle tissue to expedite post-exercise recovery.

The primary difference between my overall nutrition approach when I am focused on fat burning versus muscle building is my total caloric intake, and secondarily, the timing of my meals. With a fat burning approach I will consume fewer total calories and will avoid eating immediately before, and during a workout, and will restrict my calories late in the evening to avoid excess fat gain. When bulking up is an objective, my total calories increase and I don't restrict calories before or during exercise, or late in the evenings. I just make sure I am eating enough total calories to support my workouts and muscle-building efforts.

Blackberries, raspberries, and kumquats

Chapter 7

OUR CURRENT PLANT-BASED MEAL PLANS

Quinoa, chia, peanut butter, hemp seeds, banana, and cinnamon

Robert

Since our approaches to plant-based nutrition change from time to time, we labeled these as our *current* plant-based meal plans. Clearly my nutrition plan is different when I am running half marathons than when I am building muscle mass and strength. A running objective would see me consuming fewer calories to stay at a lighter bodyweight for performance, and a weight training approach would see an increase in overall calories to repair, replenish, and grow muscle tissue to add muscle mass. Since I am back to weight training at the time of this writing, my current meal plans will reflect those goals. Vanessa's approach remains a constant as she is in continuous pursuit of building quality muscle.

It is also important to note that Vanessa takes a much more calculated and precise approach to nutrition than I do. For example, she will often weigh or measure food intake to specific grams, cups, tablespoons, or other desired measuring units. I don't measure anything, and I only occasionally record my nutrient intake using a program such as Cronometer to check how many calories I am consuming and to evaluate my macronutrient breakdown. The last time I checked my calorie and nutrition intake and expenditure for any substantial amount of time, which was in early 2017, I was averaging about 3,000 calories consumed per day, with a breakdown of roughly 70 percent of my calories coming from carbohydrates, 20 percent from fats, and just 10 percent from protein. I was also expending slightly fewer than 3,000 calories per day on average during this time of tracking and evaluating nutrition and exercise (during a 4-week period).

Vanessa doesn't count her total calorie intake, or her macronutrient breakdown, but she measures food in portion size and micronutrient content – with a special emphasis on high vitamin, mineral, and antioxidant content, and high fiber foods.

Plant-Based Meal Plans
Vanessa

MONDAY

4:00AM
Cup of Matcha tea with lemon

6:00AM
Breakfast:
½ cup cooked quinoa
2 tablespoons peanut butter
2 tablespoons chia
1 banana
1 tablespoon cinnamon
2 tablespoons hemp seeds

*709 calories, 85g carbohydrates,
27g protein, 29g fat, 21g of fiber*

8:00AM
2 pieces of fruit with Matcha
green tea

*97 calories, 23g carbohydrates,
0.5g protein, 0.3g fat, 4.4g fiber*

10:00AM
Workout

12:00PM
Post-workout:
Powerootz brand protein shake
with 1 cup of almond milk/ice/
water

Spirulina and chlorella tablets
*211 calories, 13g carbohydrates,
24g protein, 7g fat, 5g fiber*

1:00PM
Lunch:
½ block tofu
½ cup sweet potatoes
1 cup Brussels sprouts/butternut
squash
Flavor God brand seasoning

*445 calories, 55g carbohydrates,
24g protein, 14.3g fat, 15g fiber*

3:00PM
Snack:
1 cup dried peas

*93 calories, 14g carbohydrates, 8g
protein, 0.6g fat, 6g fiber*

4:00PM
Dinner:
½ block tofu
½ cup black lentils
½ avocado

*296 calories, 42g carbohydrates,
23g protein, 4g fat, 12g fiber*

6:00PM
Snack:
2 homemade pumpkin muffins or
Powerootz brand protein shake

*211 calories, 13g carbohydrates,
24g protein, 7g fat, 5g fiber*

TOTALS:

2,062 calories, 245g carbohydrates, 130.5g, protein, 62.2g fat, 68.4 grams fiber

Tofu, avocado, and lentils

TUESDAY

4:00AM

Cup of Matcha green tea with lemon

6:00AM

Breakfast:

½ cup dry oats soaked overnight with ½ cup of almond milk, 2 tablespoon of chia

Add the next morning:

2 tablespoons peanut butter

1 banana

1 tablespoon cinnamon

2 tablespoons hemp seeds

627 calories, 72g carbohydrates, 23g protein, 27g fat, 20g fiber

8:00AM

Rawxies brand food bar with a cup of coffee

130 calories, 16g carbohydrates, 3g protein, 6g fat, 3g fiber

10:00AM

Workout

12:00PM

Post-workout:

Powerootz brand protein shake with 1 cup of almond milk/ice/water

Spirulina and chlorella tablets

211 calories, 13g carbohydrates, 24g protein, 7g fat, 5g fiber

1:00PM

Lunch:

½ block tofu

½ cup sweet potatoes

1 Hilary's brand black bean burger

Flavor God brand seasoning

502 calories, 70g carbohydrates, 24g protein, 14g fat, 15g fiber

3:00PM

Snack:

1 cup dried peas

93 calories, 14g carbohydrates, 8g protein, 0.6g fat, 6g fiber

4:00PM

Dinner:

Kale and spinach salad

½ cup black lentils

Cucumber, tomatoes, onion, carrots, avocado, cauliflower, marjoram, dill, and pepper

2 tablespoons balsamic vinegar

149 calories, 24g carbohydrates, 11g protein, 1g fat, 13g fiber

6:00PM

Snack:

Powerootz brand protein shake with 1 cup of almond milk/ice/water

211 calories, 13g carbohydrates, 24g protein, 7g fat, 5g fiber

TOTALS
1,923 calories, 222g carbohydrates, 117g protein, 62.6g fat, 73g fiber

Matcha green tea with lemon

WEDNESDAY

4:00AM
Cup of Matcha green tea with lemon

6:00AM
Breakfast:
½ cup cooked quinoa
2 tablespoons peanut butter
2 tablespoons chia
1 banana
1 tablespoon cinnamon
2 tablespoons hemp seeds

709 calories, 85g carbohydrates, 27g protein, 29g fat, 21g of fiber

8:00AM
Lara Bar and Powerootz brand protein shake with 1 cup of almond milk/ice/water

441 calories, 36g carbohydrates, 30g protein, 20g fat, 8g fiber

10:00AM
Workout
Spirulina and chlorella tablets

192 calories, 26g carbohydrates, 4g, protein, 8g fat, 3g fiber

11:00AM
Lunch:
3oz tempeh
½ cup sweet potatoes
½ cup Brussels sprouts
1 cup dried peas

528 calories, 69g carbohydrates, 32g protein, 14g fat, 16g fiber

3:00PM
Snack:
Celery and carrots with hummus

78 calories, 9g carbohydrates, 2g protein, 3.8g fat, 2g fiber

4:00PM
Dinner:
½ block tofu
½ cup black rice
½ avocado
½ cup salsa

483 calories, 29g carbohydrates, 22g protein, 31g fat, 11g fiber

6:00PM
Snack:
Powerootz brand protein shake with 1 cup of almond milk/ice/water and 2 pumpkin muffins

452 calories, 38g carbohydrates, 30g protein, 20g fat, 9g fiber

TOTALS
2,883 calories, 292g carbohydrates, 147g protein, 125.8g fat, 70g fiber

Chlorella tablets

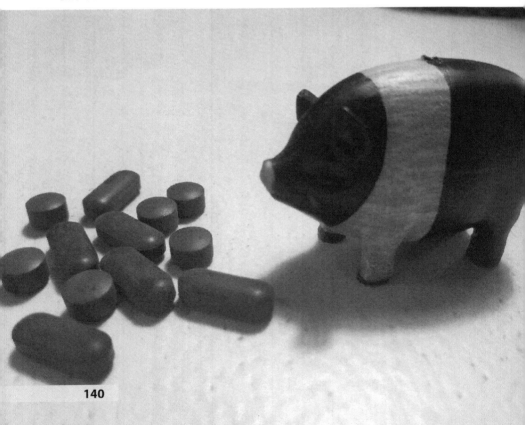

THURSDAY

4:00AM
Cup of Matcha green tea with lemon

6:00AM
Breakfast:
½ cup dry oats, soaked overnight with ½ cup of almond milk and 2 tablespoons of chia
The next morning, add:
2 tablespoons peanut butter
1 banana
1 tablespoon cinnamon
2 tablespoons hemp seeds

623 calories, 72g carbohydrates, 23g protein, 27g fat, 20g fiber

8:00AM
Rawxies brand food bar with a cup of coffee

103 calories, 16g carbohydrates, 3g protein, 3g fat, 6g fiber

10:00AM
Workout

12:00PM
Post-workout:
Powerootz brand protein shake with 1 cup of almond milk/ice/water

211 calories, 13g carbohydrates, 24g protein, 7g fat, 5g fiber

1:00PM
Lunch:
½ block tofu
½ cup sweet potatoes
1 Hilary's brand black bean burger
Flavor God brand seasoning

502 calories, 70g carbohydrates, 24g protein, 14g fat, 15g fiber

3:00PM
Snack:
1 cup of dried peas

93 calories, 14g carbohydrates, 8g protein, 0.6g fat, 6g fiber

4:00PM
Dinner:
Kale and spinach salad
½ cup black lentils
Cucumber, tomatoes, onion, carrots, avocado, cauliflower, marjoram, dill, and pepper
2 tablespoons balsamic vinegar

149 calories, 24g carbohydrates, 11g protein, 1g fat, 13g fiber

6:00PM
Snack:
Powerootz brand protein shake with 1 cup of almond milk/ice/water

211 calories, 13g carbohydrates, 24g protein, 7g fat, 5g fiber

TOTALS

1,892 calories, 222g carbohydrates, 117g protein, 59.6g fat, 70g fiber

Dried peas

FRIDAY

4:00AM

Cup of Matcha green tea with lemon

6:00AM

Breakfast:

½ cup dry oats, soaked overnight with ½ cup of almond milk and 2 tablespoons of chia
The next morning, add:
2 tablespoons peanut butter
1 banana
1 tablespoon cinnamon
2 tablespoons hemp seeds

623 calories, 72g carbohydrates, 23g protein, 27g fat, 20g fiber

8:00AM

Smoothie:
4 tablespoons Powerootz brand protein powder
1 cup almond milk
1 cup water
Blueberries, frozen banana, strawberries, spinach

433 calories, 69g carbohydrates, 28g protein, 5g fat, 15g fiber

10:00AM

Workout

12:00PM

Post-workout:
1 scoop Powerootz brand protein shake with 1 cup of almond milk/ice/water

211 calories, 13g carbohydrates, 24g protein, 7g fat, 5g fiber

1:00PM

Lunch:
1 cup black rice
1 cup lentils
Broccoli sprouts
Sprinkled nutritional yeast
Flavor God brand seasoning

278 calories, 52g carbohydrates, 13g protein, 2g fat, 11g fiber

3:00PM

Snack:
1 cup dried peas

93 calories, 14g carbohydrates, 8g protein, 0.6g fat, 6g fiber

4:00PM

Dinner:
BBQ jackfruit on top of lentils, red, green, and yellow peppers, onion
Sprinkled nutritional yeast

284 calories, 50g carbohydrates, 12g protein, 4g fat, 23g fiber

6:00PM

Snack:
1 scoop Powerootz brand protein shake with 1 cup of almond milk/ice/water

211 calories, 13g carbohydrates, 24g protein, 7g fat, 5g fiber

TOTALS
2,133 calories, 283g carbohydrates, 132g protein, 52.6g fat,
85g grams fiber

SATURDAY

4:00AM
Cup of Matcha tea with lemon

6:00AM
Breakfast:
½ cup cooked quinoa
2 tablespoons peanut butter
2 tablespoons chia
1 banana
1 tablespoon cinnamon
2 tablespoons hemp seeds

709 calories, 85g carbohydrates, 27g protein, 29g fat, 21g of fiber

8:00AM
2 pieces of fruit with Matcha green tea

97 calories, 23g carbohydrates, 0.5g protein, 0.3g fat, 4.4g fiber

10:00AM
Workout

12:00PM
Post-workout:
1 scoop Powerootz brand protein shake with 1 cup of almond milk/ice/water
Spirulina and chlorella tablets

211 calories, 13g carbohydrates, 24g protein, 7g fat, 5g fiber

1:00PM
Lunch:
½ block tofu
Dr. Praeger's brand burger
1 cup Brussels sprouts/butternut squash
Flavor God brand seasoning

496 calories, 66g carbohydrates, 26g protein, 14.3g fat, 17g fiber

3:00PM
Snack:
1 cup of dried peas

93 calories, 14g carbohydrates, 8g protein, 0.6g fat, 6g fiber

4:00PM
Dinner:
½ block tofu
Hilary's brand burger
½ cup of lentils
1 cup broccoli and cauliflower

483 calories, 69g carbohydrates, 27g protein, 11g fat, 16g fiber

6:00PM
Snack:
2 homemade pumpkin muffins or Powerootz brand protein shake

211 calories, 13g carbohydrates, 24g protein, 7g fat, 5g fiber

TOTALS:
2,300 calories, 283g carbohydrates, 136.5g, protein, 69.2g fat, 74.4 grams fiber

Broccoli, lentils, wild rice, and plant-based burger patty

146

SUNDAY

4:00AM

Cup of Matcha green tea with lemon

6:00AM

Breakfast:

2 slices 12-grain bread
2 tablespoons peanut butter
1 banana
1 tablespoon cinnamon
2 tablespoons hemp seeds

623 calories, 72g carbohydrates, 23g protein, 27g fat, 20g fiber

8:00AM

Smoothie:

1 cup almond milk
1 cup water
1 scoop Powerootz brand protein shake
Blueberries, frozen banana, strawberries, spinach

433 calories, 69g carbohydrates, 28g protein, 5g fat, 15g fiber

10:00AM

Workout

12:00PM

Post-workout:

1 scoop Powerootz brand protein shake with 1 cup of almond milk/ice/water

211 calories, 13g carbohydrates, 24g protein, 7g fat, 5g fiber

1:00PM

Lunch:

½ block tofu
1 cup cabbage and Brussels sprouts
Broccoli sprouts
Flavor God brand seasoning

290 calories, 52g carbohydrates, 16g protein, 2g fat, 11g fiber

3:00PM

Snack:

1 cup dried peas

93 calories, 14g carbohydrates, 8g protein, 0.6g fat, 6g fiber

4:00PM

Dinner:

1 Beyond Burger brand patty
½ cup lentils
½ cup wild rice
1 cup broccoli

764 calories, 89g carbohydrates, 43g protein, 26.2g fat, 18g fiber

6:00PM

Snack:

Powerootz brand protein shake with 1 cup of almond milk/ice/water

211 calories, 13g carbohydrates, 24g protein, 7g fat, 5g fiber

TOTALS

2,625 calories, 322g carbohydrates, 166g protein, 74.8g fat, 80g grams fiber

Plant-Based Meal Plans
Robert

Though I don't believe an extremely diverse diet is *necessary* for good health, I do believe that increased variety makes any nutrition plan more fun and exciting. One could be quite healthy eating the same fruits every day, the same starchy vegetables, the same leafy greens, and the same legumes and grains day in and day out. What makes an eating plan typically more desirable is having lots of options. How do these foods sound? Vegan sushi, Pad Thai, yellow curry, Aloo Gobi, Chana Masala, vegetable Tom Kha soup, cheese-less vegetable pizza, Ethiopian veggie platter, vegan burrito, vegetable pho, lentil Shepherd's Pie, vegan potato salad, falafel wrap, vegan lasagna, and much, much more. It sounds pretty good, right? Those are certainly not all whole foods, but they are some pretty tasty plant-based meals,

Salad greens with green beans and peppers

to be sure. At the end of the day, fruit is my favorite food, and having a wide variety of fruits at home and when I travel is not only a key to good health, vitality, and high energy, but also a tasty way to enhance any nutrition plan. Even while flying on a plane, I'll have a tote bag filled with fruit, especially bananas, apples, oranges, berries, and grapes – just don't place the bananas at the bottom of the bag – a lesson it seems I would have learned the first time. At home, my fruit collection is far more diverse.

Calling upon my desire for diversity in my nutrition program, I will share with you my weekly nutrition plan. You will notice that some foods are consumed nearly every single day, such as bananas, oranges, oats, brown rice, and beans. Other foods may be less common but are still considered to be staples in my diet, such as potatoes, yams, lentils, leafy greens, and avocado. International cuisine is also part of my weekly diet, especially when traveling.

Unlike Vanessa, I don't measure my foods or count serving sizes. I eat "plates" and "bowls" and "handfuls" of foods when I consume snacks and meals. It would be disingenuous for me to suggest otherwise. Since I don't weigh or measure foods I consume, I will not include specific serving sizes of my meals. I don't eat at particular times either. I have listed my meals as "meal 1, meal 2," etc., because I generally eat when I'm hungry, and I eat for athletic performance. If I am planning a weight-training workout, I'll eat a pre-workout meal or snack, even if I'm not particularly hungry at the time. I want the extra fuel, power, and strength to carry me through a tough weight-training workout, so I'll eat anyway. The same goes for following a workout. Even if I'm not particularly hungry, I know I need to start consuming nutrition after training to replenish, rebuild, and recover, so I'll eat something, even if just a small snack until I am ready for a larger meal. Other times, I'll eat when I'm hungry, and I will just continue on with my day if I'm not hungry, therefore I don't always have a set number of meals in a day either, but for simplicity, I will list seven meals per day, which could be a good average for me on any given day.

Weekly Nutrition Plan

MONDAY

MEAL 1

Breakfast:
16 ounces yerba mate tea
3 bananas
Bowl of oats with berries and walnuts

MEAL 2

Lunch:
Lentil wrap with beans, vegetables, lentils, and a vegan dipping sauce
Small green salad with mixed leafy greens, cucumbers, tomatoes, artichoke hearts
12 ounces water

MEAL 3

Snack:
2 sliced Pink Lady apples

MEAL 4
(final heavy meal before workout)

Snack:
Plate of Yukon gold potato wedges with ketchup
8 ounces yerba mate tea

MEAL 5
(light pre-workout)

Pre-workout snack:
2 bananas
2 clementine oranges

MEAL 6
(dinner/post-workout meal)

Dinner:
Burrito bowl – Brown rice, pinto beans, refried beans, black beans, avocado, lettuce, tomato, jalapeño peppers, olives
Green salad with romaine lettuce, spinach, carrots, beets, broccoli
12 ounces water

MEAL 7

Snack:
Orange
Small bowl of raspberries

Oatmeal with walnuts, blueberries, and raspberries

TUESDAY

MEAL 1

Breakfast:
8 ounces yerba mate tea
2 bananas
Bowl of oats with berries or other fruit

MEAL 2

Lunch:
2 avocado sushi rolls (8-12 pieces)
12 ounces water

MEAL 3

Snack:
Mary's Gone Crackers brand gluten-free, organic crackers with hummus
12 ounces water

MEAL 4
(final heavy meal before workout)

Snack:
2 sweet potatoes with broccoli
16 ounces yerba mate tea

MEAL 5
(light pre-workout)

Snack:
3 bananas
8 ounces water

MEAL 6
(dinner/post-workout meal)

Dinner:
Polenta plate with polenta, collard greens, barley, and tomato sauce
Large green salad with a mixture of leafy green vegetables, broccoli, cauliflower, chickpeas, kidney beans, and olives
12 ounces chocolate almond milk
12 ounces water

MEAL 7

Snack:
Bowl of strawberries
2 clementine oranges

Vegetable sushi

WEDNESDAY

MEAL 1

Breakfast:
12 ounces water
3 bananas
Bowl of oats with berries and walnuts

MEAL 2

Lunch:
Large bowl of lentil soup with chunks of potatoes over brown rice
Beanfield's brand vegan bean and rice chips for dipping into soup
12 ounces water

MEAL 3

Snack:
Fruit salad consisting of chopped honeydew and cantaloupe melons, sliced blood oranges, blueberries and strawberries
12 ounces water

MEAL 4
(final heavy meal before workout)

Snack:
Plate of Pad Thai noodles with vegetables and tofu
Bowl of fried rice with peas, corn, tomatoes, cucumber and bamboo shoots
12 ounces water

MEAL 5
(light pre-workout)

Snack:
2 bananas
2 clementine oranges

MEAL 6
(dinner/post-workout meal)

Dinner:
Plate of lasagna with tofu, spinach, olives, and tomato sauce
Small green salad with romaine lettuce, beets, carrots, cucumber, and radishes
12 ounces water

MEAL 7

Snack:
Handful of blackberries, blueberries, or other seasonal berries/fruit

THURSDAY

MEAL 1

Breakfast:
8 ounces yerba mate tea
2 bananas
Bowl of oats with berries and walnuts

MEAL 2

Lunch:
Bowl of soup (vegetable, lentil, pea, or other)
Burrito with beans, rice, avocado, lettuce, tomato and salsa
12 ounces water

MEAL 3

Snack:
3 large carrots

MEAL 4
(final heavy meal before workout)

Snack:
3 vegetable samosas
Bowl of brown rice with curried vegetables
12 ounces water

MEAL 5
(light pre-workout)

Snack:
8 ounces yerba mate tea
2 bananas
2 oranges

MEAL 6
(dinner/post-workout meal)

Dinner:
Pasta with vegetables, tomato sauce and olives
Small spinach salad with artichoke hearts, garbanzo beans and blueberries
12 ounces water

MEAL 7

Snack:
2 oranges

FRIDAY

MEAL 1

Breakfast:
12 ounces water
3 bananas
Bowl of oats with berries and walnuts

MEAL 2

Snack:
2 Larabars
12 ounces water

MEAL 3

Snack:
Tempeh Ruben sandwich with small side salad
16 ounces water

MEAL 4
(final heavy meal before workout)

Snack:
Bowl of lentils and brown rice
12 ounces sparkling water

MEAL 5
(light pre-workout)

Snack:
6 small clementine oranges
8 ounces yerba mate tea

MEAL 6
(dinner/post-workout meal)

Dinner:
Plate of aloo mutter (Indian dish with peas and potatoes)
Bowl of brown rice
24 ounces water

MEAL 7

Snack:
Bowl of sliced mango
Bowl of cherries

Tempeh Reuben sandwich

SATURDAY

MEAL 1

Breakfast:
8 ounces sparkling water
2 bananas
Bowl of oats with berries or other fruit

MEAL 2

Snack:
4 vegetable spring rolls
12 ounces water

MEAL 3

Snack:
Bowl of mixed nuts
1 snack bar
24 ounces water

MEAL 4
(final heavy meal before workout)

Snack:
Large leafy green salad with mixed greens, dolmas, artichoke hearts, and sunflower seeds
12 ounces water

MEAL 5
(light pre-workout)

Snack:
2 bananas
Apple

MEAL 6
(dinner/post-workout meal)

Dinner:
Gnocchi pasta bowl with baby spinach, tomato sauce, and black olives
Green side salad with mixed greens, peppers, pickles, and purple cabbage
16 ounces coconut water

MEAL 7

Snack:
Bowl of blueberries

SUNDAY

MEAL 1

Breakfast:

12 ounces orange juice

Bowl of mixed berries

Tofu scramble with seasoned tofu, sautéed green and red bell peppers, spinach, onions, and cubed potatoes

MEAL 2

Snack:

Bowl of vegetable soup with spring rolls

12 ounces water

MEAL 3

Snack:

3 pieces of whole fruit

Snack bar:

12 ounces water

MEAL 4 (FINAL HEAVY MEAL BEFORE WORKOUT)

Snack:

3 bean burgers (no bun) on a plate with ketchup, mustard, and a pickle

12 ounces sparkling water

MEAL 5 (LIGHT PRE-WORKOUT)

Snack:

2 bananas

2 mandarin oranges

MEAL 6 (DINNER/POST-WORKOUT MEAL)

Dinner:

Burrito bowl with brown rice, pinto beans, black beans, avocado, lettuce, tomato, olives, peppers, pickle, and salsa

24 ounces water

MEAL 7

Snack:

Bowl of grapes

Vegetable soup over brown rice

You can use online apps such as MyFitnessPal or Cronometer to track your daily food intake. Any type of nutrition journal can be helpful to reveal what you're really eating. By knowing what types of foods, and how many calories you're consuming each day, you can control your caloric intake and expenditure, or alter your caloric intake/expenditure in order to meet fat loss or muscle building goals. I find it to be incredibly helpful to document meals for a full week a couple of times a year to evaluate and compare current habits with previous records. As an example, for the entire month of November 2016, I documented every calorie I consumed, and every ounce of water I drank. For good measure, I also tracked every calorie burned through exercise and metabolism, and every minute of sleep for the entire month. The week-by-week summaries with totals like this for the entire month of November, 2016 can be found on www.robertcheeke.net/blog:

The November Project

Week 1 totals:
Total calories consumed = 20,878
Average calories per day = 2,983
Average percentage from carbohydrates = 73%
Average percentage from protein = 10%
Average percentage from fat = 17%
Total water intake = 477 ounces
Average water per day = 68 ounces (slightly more than half a gallon)
Total calories expended = 21,762
Average calories expended per day = 3,109
Average net calorie intake/expenditure = 126-calorie deficit per day
Total time spent exercising = 15 hours, 48 minutes
Average time spent exercising per day = 2 hours, 15 minutes per day
Total amount of sleep = 57 hours, 45 minutes
Average sleep per night = 8 hours, 15 minutes

I blogged about my experiences of transparently documenting my complete nutrition intake and exercise schedule for that month-long period, and some of my own observations and realizations were rather profound and very helpful to me as I evaluated my actual habits and behaviors, many of which I was unaware of until that month of accountability.

This is an excerpt of my own report I wrote in the weeks following the month of tracking data:

"I discovered something I'd like to share with you: For the entire month of November, I documented every meal I ate and every workout I did, along with other details, and I posted weekly updates publicly here (RobertCheeke.net/blog), and along the way, I discovered something pretty cool. I didn't have any specific goals of muscle building or fat burning, I simply wanted to share an inside look into the life of a vegan athlete, meal by meal, and workout by workout, with full transparency.

Though I didn't have specific goals, I wanted to maintain my roughly 200-pound size, while also getting a bit leaner, coming off a few months of inactivity in late spring and most of the summer due to an injury. I decided to document all of my health and fitness actions for an entire month to help readers understand what I do on a daily basis to maintain muscle size and strength as a 21-year vegan athlete, currently aged 36 years, but I also did it to help keep myself accountable. You see, I know the power of documenting actions honestly and transparently, because I have done this many times during my bodybuilding career – and while I was a competitive distance runner. I also know full well what can happen if I conveniently avoid acknowledging what I am eating, and carelessly remain clueless of my actual activity level. When I eat poorly for a period of time, and avoid exercise, naturally, I want to forget about these actions, as if they never happened. The problem is our bodies don't forget about our careless actions, and those actions have health and fitness consequences – whether we want to acknowledge that or not. Like undesirable actions, positive actions produce results and outcomes too. Discovering more of those helpful actions is one key to health and fitness success.

While I was spending part of spring, all of summer, and part of fall, recovering from a torn disc in my lower back and a case of sciatica on the left side of my entire lower body, I reached an all-time high in body fat and body weight. I peaked at 208 pounds with 23% body fat, exactly three times the body fat percentage I had when I was a competitive bodybuilder at 7.8% body fat. I could still flex and display a level of muscle size, especially from favorable angles, but I found myself in a position I had never been in before: out of shape. Taking nearly half of 2016 off from exercise (and healthy eating) took a toll on me mentally, emotionally, and physically – likely in that order.

Though I am the author of a bestselling book about burning fat and building muscle on a whole-food, plant-based diet (Shred It!)*, I stopped following my own advice because I was feeling down. I was in a lot of pain and wasn't able to exercise. I got frustrated and didn't want to lose a bunch of weight after working so hard to build from 165 to 205 pounds over the course of 18 months, following a year of distance running, so I kept eating a lot, even though I wasn't exercising. And I wasn't exclusively sticking to whole foods. I was in the process of moving to a new state, buying a house for the first time, and was recently engaged, and I allowed myself to feel pretty stressed out. Consequently, I ate a lot of frozen vegan meals. I loaded up on Amy's frozen foods like vegan burritos, mac and* cheese, Thai noodles and curry, and more. I prided myself on the fact that I maintained my 200+ pound frame, but then I experienced some new territories as a result of my enthusiasm to maintain weight. Clothes stopped fitting – everything from boxers that had their elastic band stretched and ruined, to size large and even a few XL shirts that just wouldn't fit anymore, including some that used to be baggy on me. I literally went from being a 165-pound distance runner to a 205-pound weight lifter in less than two years, and then a few months later I became a 208-pound inactive person. *My clothes changed as fast as my mood, and it was a challenge unlike anything I have gone through. I was still on tour and still trying to spread the vegan fitness message, but I didn't feel comfortable with myself, knowing I had abandoned my own advice and I was suffering internally and externally. It was time for a change. Enter the November Project.*

I thought of the November Project one day in late October while I was sitting in the sauna at the gym. I had been pain-free for most of September and for all of October, and since I was training 4-5 days a week again, I figured it would be interesting to share my training and nutrition programs with others. I was basically starting over, only doing cable and machine exercises, but I was being consistent again, and my diet was starting to get back on track too. I was motivated, happy, and feeling positive again for the first time in a while. When I was required through my own discipline to document all of my actions, it was really eye opening to see what I was really eating on a daily and weekly basis, and how often I was actually exercising. By documenting these actions, I was able to alter my meals to focus more on whole foods, while avoiding certain processed foods, and I could gauge my activity level and boost it at any time if I felt the need to burn more calories or build more muscle. I also discovered some secret weapons, like using the Stairmaster for an hour at a time, performing fasted cardio, burning 500+ calories during a single session, creating puddles of sweat on the machine, while simultaneously melting off fat and toning muscles. By documenting all of these things, I was able to change my health, fitness, and my mood in a very short amount of time.

My journey is still a work in progress, and I continue to do rehabilitation exercises for my back, and I am still working on including more whole foods into my diet (especially salad greens), while eliminating as many processed foods as I can, fighting addictions along the way."

The reason why I share that here is because I am still at odds with some of the minutiae, the daily ins and outs of a truly healthy relationship with food and fitness. As the expression goes, "the struggle is real." Though my overall objective is to share my knowledge, experiences, and decades of lessons learned as a plant-based athlete, and I think I am in a better position than most to do this, writing and sharing is therapeutic for me too. Thank you for allowing me to indulge over the past few paragraphs. I would love to provide exclusively *Shred It!*-approved whole, plant-based meal plans in the recommendations above, and I still believe in that core concept, but it just isn't an accurate representation of where I am right now with my nutrition program. What I am saying is, things don't have to be perfect to work. My diet isn't perfect, nor is the diet of many of the greatest athletes on Earth – Olympic and elite professional athletes alike. Perfection in nutrition, though a noble goal to strive for, is all but elusive, even for the nutrition experts, doctors, athletes, and practitioners subscribing to a specific nutritional dogma. I don't mean for this to sound like a "do the best you can" cop out, loosening the reins on a highly important topic – one that can be truly life altering in its practice. Rather, I am making clear the sentiment that a state of perfection in diet is unlikely to be achieved by any of us in the real world. In essence, aim to eat the healthiest foods you can, but give yourself a break, and don't be too hard on yourself when you enjoy a bowl of vegan ice cream on a hot summer's day. Just put a little cherry on top and call it a fruit dessert. In all seriousness though, allow yourself to live a little and try some of the amazing plant-based (processed) international cuisine out there, but work hard to incorporate large quantities of healthy, whole plant foods into your nutrition plan too.

In the forthcoming chapter, Vanessa will construct nutrition programs for you to achieve specific objectives – building muscle or burning fat, and improving aerobic conditioning, which collectively tend to be by-products of a high complex carbohydrate diet, coupled with a consistent schedule of aerobic exercise. Note that the meals are primarily whole-food based, but there is an option, per Vanessa's personal preference, for a protein drink for those who prefer to consume a shake as a snack.

Chapter 8

PLANT-BASED MEAL PLANS FOR MUSCLE BUILDING AND FAT BURNING

Vegetable fried rice with tofu and broccoli

Vanessa explains different approaches for men and women

In general, if you put men and women on the same muscle-building program, men will typically experience results at a faster rate, due to having more testosterone and a more efficient muscle-building machine (body) with which to work. When it comes to building muscle or burning fat, men will typically have an advantage, largely due to genetics. That being said, women can experience effective and efficient muscle building as well, with the right approach. Consistent resistance training coupled with adequate nutrition over a period of time does the trick. I didn't build the muscular physique I have now overnight, and you shouldn't expect to be able to either, as a man or as a woman. As a result of my consistent effort, intensity, and because of the type of training and attitude I have had over the past 15 years, I have built a more muscular physique than most men with a similar frame. That is by design. I didn't take shortcuts, expect quick results, nor give up or make excuses. I just went to work day after day doing what I loved to do – lift weights – and progress took place over time. Now I have nearly two decades of experience as a weight lifter to be able to help clients understand how to achieve their goals.

If you are a woman, starting a training program from the same beginning stages as a man, don't get discouraged if your results take a little more time. That's the nature of the challenge women are up against, and something that we can rise to the occasion and overcome through persistence, drive, and desire to achieve our own meaningful goals.

* If you follow a soy-free or gluten-free diet, or have any other food allergies or strong preferences, please substitute any potential allergens listed for foods of similar nutritional value. If you avoid soybeans for example, replace a meal that calls for tofu or tempeh

with kidney beans, lentils, or black beans. The same goes for any allergen. Find a suitable replacement, and continue on with the meal plans.

Muscle Building Meal Plans 4-Week Guide by Vanessa

In each of the following weeks, use the described meals as a sample to structure your food prep for the full week. Use Vanessa's meal plans as a template, or follow them exactly, making changes based on preferences, accessibility, and other factors such as meal prep time, as you deem necessary. These meal planning guides will provide you with a different set of meals for each week, meaning that for efficiency of batch cooking bulk quantities, you will eat the same thing each day for a week before moving on to week number two. It is impractical to create an entirely new menu each day when meal prepping due to the time investment and because of the effectiveness of making staple foods in bulk to last for most of the week, or for perhaps the entire week. This also creates a very consistent plan to eat roughly the same foods, same quantities, and same calories each day for up to seven consecutive days.

Before you construct your personal muscle building meal plans, determine through the Harris-Benedict calculator, what your true calorie expenditure is in order to create a daily meal plan that has a calorie count that is conducive to building muscle when combined with exercise. In essence, if muscle building is your goal, you need to consume more calories than you expend (from mostly healthy whole foods – not refined flours, sugars, and oils), therefore knowing your calorie expenditure will help you determine your calorie intake, which will help you construct your meal plans to meet your goals.

* Optional protein drinks not factored into calorie and nutrition calculations

WEEK 1

Breakfast:

1 cup cooked quinoa
1 tablespoon peanut or almond butter
2 tablespoons chia
1 banana
1 teaspoon cinnamon
1 tablespoon hemp seeds

699 calories, 96g carbohydrates, 23.8g protein, 24.4g fat, 20g fiber

Snack:

Apple and 1 tablespoon peanut butter

Calories 275, 31g carbohydrates, 7.5g protein, 15.3g fat, 6.4g fiber

Optional protein shake in place of the snack listed above:

Vegan protein shake with 1 cup unsweetened almond milk, water, and ice

211 calories, 13g carbohydrates, 24g protein, 7g fat, 5g fiber

Lunch

6 ounces baked tofu using different types of seasoning
½ cup sweet potatoes
2 cups roasted or steamed veggies

698 calories, 62g carbohydrates, 45g protein, 30g fat, 5g fiber

Snack:

Raw veggies of any kind (I like to keep chopped up celery, carrots, cucumbers, and radishes in the fridge)
2 tablespoons hummus

78 calories, 9g carbohydrates, 2g protein, 3.8g fat, 2g fiber

Snack:

Handful raw nuts and seeds (no oil or salt): peanuts, walnuts, pecans, cashews, Brazil nuts, macadamia nuts, pine nuts, sunflower and pumpkin seeds (pepitas)

441 calories, 14g carbohydrates, 15.2g protein, 36g fat, 9g fiber

Dinner:

Black Bean Bowl
1 cup black beans
1 cup cooked brown basmati or black rice, farro or quinoa
½ avocado, diced
½ cup salsa of your choice
Sprinkle nutritional yeast
Mix together in a bowl.

658 calories, 96.6g carbohydrates, 27g protein, 18.3g fat, 26.2g fiber

Snack:

1 cup strawberries and 1 cup blueberries

122 calories, 28g carbohydrates, 2g protein, 0g fat, 6g fiber

*Optional protein shake in place of the snack listed above:

Vegan protein shake with 1 cup unsweetened almond milk, water, and ice

211 calories, 13g carbohydrates, 24g protein, 7g fat, 5g fiber

TOTALS

2,971 calories,
336.6g carbohydrates,
122.5g protein,
127.8 fat,
74.6g fiber

WEEK 2

Breakfast:

1 cup oats and 2 tablespoons chia seeds, combined and soaked overnight in ½ cup unsweetened non-dairy milk of your choice
Before eating the oats, add in the following:
½ cup of berries
1 sliced banana
1 teaspoon cinnamon
1 tablespoon hemp seeds

477 calories, 46g carbohydrates, 20.3g protein, 23.6g fat, 19g fiber

Snack:

1 cup roasted peas

320 calories, 44g carbohydrates, 20g protein, 6g fat, 12g fiber

Optional protein shake in place of the snack listed above:

Vegan protein shake with 1 cup unsweetened almond milk, water, and ice

211 calories, 13g carbohydrates, 24g protein, 7g fat, 5g fiber

Snack:

Apple or pear or any type of fruit you like

97 calories, 23g carbohydrates, 0.5g protein, 0.3g fat, 4.4g fiber

Lunch:

Lentil Bowl
1 cup cooked brown lentils
½ cup cooked navy beans
1 cup cooked broccoli
½ cup peas
2 tablespoons nutritional yeast
Mix together in a bowl.

320 calories, 51g carbohydrates, 24.5g protein, 2g fat, 22.6g fiber

Snack:

Raw veggies of any kind: celery, cucumbers, carrots, radishes, etc. spread with 2 tablespoons hummus

78 calories, 9g carbohydrates, 2g protein, 3.8g fat, 2g fiber

Dinner:

5 ounces tempeh, cubed
1 cup green beans
½ avocado, diced
2 cups chopped red, green, yellow, and orange peppers
2 tablespoons nutritional yeast
Toss everything together in a bowl.

612 calories, 41g carbohydrates, 40g protein, 32g fat, 3g fiber

Snack:

½ cup almonds

273 calories, 9.3g carbohydrates, 10g protein, 23.9g fat, 5.6g fiber

*Optional protein shake in place of the snack listed above:

2 banana protein muffins and vegan protein shake with 1 cup unsweetened almond milk, water, and ice

470 calories, 47.8g carbohydrates, 34.4g protein, 21.8g fat, 10.6g fiber

TOTALS

2,177 calories,
223.3g carbohydrates,
117.3g protein,
91.6g fat,
68.6g fiber

Dried peas

175

WEEK 3

Breakfast:

1 cup cooked spelt
2 tablespoons sunflower butter
1 tablespoon raisins
1 teaspoon cinnamon
1 sliced banana
Mix together in a bowl.

634 calories, 95g carbohydrates, 17.6g protein, 20.4g fat, 14g fiber

Snack:

1 cup edamame

189 calories, 15g carbohydrates, 17g protein, 8g fat, 8g fiber

Optional protein shake in place of the snack listed above:

Vegan protein shake with 1 cup unsweetened almond milk, water, and ice

211 calories, 13g carbohydrates, 24g protein, 7g fat, 5g fiber

Snack:

2 cups blueberries, strawberries, raspberries or any combination of the three

92 calories, 20g carbohydrates, 3g protein, 0g fat, 3g fiber

Lunch:

Spinach and Kale Salad
1 cup raw spinach
1 cup raw kale
½ cup cooked brown lentils
Any type of veggies you like
1 tablespoon sunflower seeds
1 tablespoon pumpkin seeds (pepitas)
½ cooked sweet potato
2 tablespoons Follow Your Heart brand vegan honey mustard dressing

495 calories, 71g carbohydrates, 16g protein, 16.3g fat, 12.3g fiber

Snack:

Handful of raw nuts and seeds (no oil or salt): peanuts, walnuts, pecans, cashews, Brazil nuts, macadamia nuts, pine nuts, sunflower, and pumpkin seeds (pepitas)

441 calories, 14g carbohydrates, 15.2g protein, 36g fat, 9g fiber

Dinner

½ cup cooked black rice
½ cup chickpeas
1 tablespoon pine nuts
1 tablespoon hemp seeds
1 cup cooked broccoli or asparagus
2 tablespoons nutritional yeast
Mix together on a plate.

343 calories, 64g carbohydrates, 15g protein , 3g fat, 10g fiber

Snack:

2 banana protein muffins

259 calories, 34.8g carbohydrates, 10.4g protein, 14.8g fat, 5.6g fiber

TOTALS

2,521 calories,
319g carbohydrates,
108.8g protein,
91.1g fat,
64.3g fiber

WEEK 4

Breakfast:

1 cup cooked kamut
1 tablespoon peanut or almond butter
2 tablespoons chia
1 banana
1 teaspoon cinnamon
1 tablespoon hemp seeds
Mix together in a bowl.

632 calories, 88g carbohydrates, 23.8g protein, 20.5g fat, 7.4g fiber

Snack:

3 tablespoons pumpkin seeds (pepitas) and 1 tablespoon raisins

400 calories, 42.9g carbohydrates, 12.1g protein, 23.8g fat, 6.6g fiber

Optional protein shake in place of the snack listed above:

Vegan protein shake with 1 cup unsweetened almond milk, water, and ice

211 calories, 13g carbohydrates, 24g protein, 7g fat, 5g fiber

Snack:

2 cups strawberries or sliced kiwifruit

92 calories, 20g carbohydrates, 3g protein, 0g fat, 3g fiber

Lunch:

6 ounces baked tofu
½ cup cooked beans
½ cup cooked basmati rice
1 cup vegetables of your choice
Serve together on a plate.

552 calories, 63g carbohydrates, 39g protein 16g fat, 16g fiber

Snack:

1 cup roasted peas or edamame

200 calories, 15g carbohydrates, 17g protein, 8g fat, 8g fiber

Dinner:

1 cup cooked jackfruit, chopped
½ cup cooked chickpeas
½ cup cooked brown lentils
1 cup cooked broccoli

442 calories, 76g carbohydrates, 21g protein, 6g fat, 31g fiber

Snack:

1 slice Dave's Killer 21-grain bread and 1 tablespoon almond butter

218 calories, 25g carbohydrates, 8.4g protein, 11g fat, 6.6g fiber

*Optional protein shake in place of the snack listed above:

Vegan protein shake with 1 cup unsweetened almond milk, water, and ice

211 calories, 13g carbohydrates, 24g protein, 7 grams fat, 5 grams fiber

TOTALS

*2,506 calories,
329.9g carbohydrates,
124.3g protein,
85.3g fat,
78.6g fiber*

Pumpkin seeds (pepitas) and raisins

Fat Burning Meal Plans 4-Week Guide by Vanessa

In each of the following weeks, use the described meals as a sample to build your food prep for the full week. Use Vanessa's meal plans as a template making changes based on preferences, accessibility, and other factors such as meal prep time, as you deem necessary, or follow them exactly. These meal planning guides will provide you with a different set of meals for each week, meaning that for efficiency of batch cooking bulk quantities, you will eat the same thing each day for a week before moving on to week number two. It is impractical to create an entirely new menu each day when meal prepping due to the time investment and because of the effectiveness of making staple foods in bulk to last for most of the week, or for perhaps the entire week. This also creates a very consistent plan to eat roughly the same foods, same quantities, and same calories each day for up to seven consecutive days.

Before you construct your personal fat-burning meal plans, determine through the Harris-Benedict calculator, what your true calorie expenditure is in order to create a daily meal plan that has a calorie count that is conducive to burning fat when combined with exercise. In essence, if fat burning is your goal, you need to burn more calories than you consume, therefore knowing your calorie expenditure will help you determine your calorie intake, which will help you construct your meal plans to meet your goals.

Optional protein drinks not factored into calorie and nutrition calculations

WEEK 1

Breakfast:

½ cup cooked quinoa
1 tablespoon peanut or almond butter
2 tablespoons chia
1 banana
1 teaspoon cinnamon
1 tablespoon hemp seeds
Mix together in a bowl.

545 calories, 69g carbohydrates, 18.8g protein, 21.5g fat, 19g fiber

Snack:

1 Pear

102 calories, 27g carbohydrates, 0.6g protein, 0.2g fat, 6g fiber

Optional protein shake in place of the snack listed above:

Vegan protein shake with 1 cup unsweetened almond milk, water, and ice

211 calories, 13g carbohydrates, 24g protein, 7g fat, 5g fiber

Lunch:

6 ounces baked tofu
½ cup cooked sweet potatoes, chopped
1 cup roasted or steamed veggies
Seasonings of your choice
Mix together and serve on a plate.

171 calories, 9g carbohydrates, 18g protein, 7g fat, 6g fiber

Snack:

Raw veggies of any kind: celery, carrots, cucumbers, radishes, etc., spread with 2 tablespoons hummus

78 calories, 9g carbohydrates, 2g protein, 3.8g fat, 2g fiber

Dinner:

Black Bean Bowl
1 cup cooked black beans, drained and rinsed
1 cup cooked brown basmati or black rice, farro, or quinoa
½ avocado, sliced
½ cup salsa of your choice
1 tablespoon nutritional yeast
Mix together in a bowl.

528 calories, 73.9g carbohydrates, 22g protein, 16g fat, 18g fiber

TOTALS
1,424 calories, 187.9g carbohydrates, 61.4g protein, 48.5g fat, 51g fiber

Sweet potato, tofu, and Brussels sprouts

WEEK 2

Breakfast:

1 cup oats and 2 tablespoons chia seeds, combined and soaked overnight in ½ cup unsweetened non-dairy milk of your choice
Before eating the oats, add in the following:
1 teaspoon cinnamon
1 tablespoon hemp seeds

399 calories, 34g carbohydrates, 17.3g protein, 21.6g fat, 17g fiber

Snack:

1 cup blueberries and 1 cup raspberries

150 calories, 37g carbohydrates, 3.5g protein, 1.3g fat, 11.6g fiber

Optional protein shake in place of the snack listed above:

Vegan protein shake with 1 cup unsweetened almond milk, water, and ice

211 calories, 13g carbohydrates, 24g protein, 7g fat, 5g fiber

Snack:

Apple or pear

78 calories, 9g carbohydrates, 2g protein, 3.8g fat, 2g fiber

Lunch:

6 pieces Beyond Meat brand plant-based chicken
½ cup chickpeas
1 cup Brussels sprouts or veggies of your choice
Mix together in a bowl.

368 calories, 35g carbohydrates, 30g protein, 12g fat, 12g fiber

Snack:

1 cup roasted peas

140 calories, 14g carbohydrates, 12g protein, 4g fat, 6g fiber

Dinner:

5 ounces tempeh, sliced
½ cup cooked brown lentils
½ avocado, sliced
1 cup red, green, yellow and orange peppers, chopped
1 tablespoon nutritional yeast
Combine and serve on a plate.

479 calories, 41g carbohydrates, 27g protein, 23g fat, 2.4g fiber

TOTALS
1,614 calories, 170g carbohydrates, 91.8g protein, 65.7g fat, 51g fiber

Raspberries and blueberries

WEEK 3

Breakfast:

Tofu Scramble
6 ounces tofu
½ cup chopped mushrooms
½ cup red or green peppers
Handful spinach
Pinch turmeric
Pinch paprika
Sprinkle onion and garlic granules, optional
Chopped cilantro for garnish
Mix together and serve on a plate.

340 calories, 48g carbohydrates, 27g protein, 4.4g fat, 10g fiber

Snack:

Banana spread with 1 tablespoon sunflower butter

205 calories, 30.5g carbohydrates, 4.5g protein, 8.4g fat, 5g fiber

*Optional protein shake in place of the snack listed above:

Vegan protein shake with 1 cup unsweetened almond milk, water, and ice

211 calories, 13g carbohydrates, 24g protein, 7g fat, 5g fiber

Snack:

2 cups blueberries, strawberries, raspberries or a combination of the three

92 calories, 20g carbohydrates, 3g protein, 0g fat, 3g fiber

Lunch:

Spinach and Kale Salad
1 cup raw spinach
1 cup raw kale
½ cup cooked brown lentils
1 cup mixed veggies of your choice
2 tablespoons Follow Your Heart brand vegan honey mustard dressing
Combine together into a bowl.

288 calories, 27g carbohydrates, 12.3g protein, 14.6g fat, 11g fiber

Snack:

Handful raw nuts/seeds (no oil or salt): peanuts, walnuts, pecans, cashews, Brazil nuts, macadamia nuts, pine nuts, sunflower and pumpkin seeds (pepitas)

441 calories, 14g carbohydrates, 15.2g protein, 36g fat, 9g fiber

Dinner:

½ cup basmati rice
½ cup chickpeas
1 cup cooked broccoli or asparagus
1 tablespoon sprinkled nutritional yeast
Mix together and serve on a plate.

321 calories, 64g carbohydrates, 15g protein, 3g fat, 10g fiber

TOTALS
1,657 calories, 203.5g carbohydrates, 77.2g protein, 66.4g fat, 48g fiber

Mixed nuts and seeds

WEEK 4

Breakfast:

½ cup cooked kamut
1 tablespoon peanut or almond butter
2 tablespoons chia
1 banana
1 teaspoon cinnamon
1 tablespoon hemp seeds
Mix together in a bowl.

510 calories, 65g carbohydrates, 18.8g protein, 19.5g fat, 18.7g fiber

Snack:

2 kiwis and 1 cup strawberries

164 calories, 39g carbohydrates, 2.6g protein, 0g fat, 5.2g fiber

*Optional protein shake in place of the snack listed above:

Vegan protein shake with 1 cup unsweetened almond milk, water, and ice

211 calories, 13g carbohydrates, 24g protein, 7g fat, 5g fiber

Snack:

Raw veggies of any kind: celery, carrots, cucumbers, radishes, etc., spread with 2 tablespoons hummus

78 calories, 9g carbohydrates, 2g protein, 3.8g fat, 2g fiber

Lunch:

6 ounces tofu
½ cup cooked beans of your choice
1 cup vegetables of your choice
Mix together in a bowl.

275 calories, 27g carbohydrates, 26g protein, 7g fat, 15g fiber

Snack:

1 cup edamame

209 calories, 15g carbohydrates, 17g protein, 9g fat, 6g fiber

Dinner:

1 Sunshine brand burger (or tofu or tempeh)
½ cup chickpeas
½ cup lentils
1 cup broccoli
Serve on a plate.

321 calories, 32g carbohydrates, 28g protein, 9g fat, 12g fiber

TOTALS

1,557 calories, 187g carbohydrates, 94.4g, protein, 48.3g fat, 58.9g fiber

Tofu, lentils, Brussels sprouts, butternut squash, and purple cabbage

188

If you keep within these general guidelines whether following these meal plans exactly, or making your own alterations and adaptations to them, while also supporting your efforts with a consistent exercise program, you can expect to experience positive results over time.

A few key points to keep in mind are to determine the foods that you actually like, that you will actually eat. That could take some experimentation, but it could open up doors to foods you never thought you'd try, such as vegan Ethiopian food, vegetable sushi, exotic fruits, and a variety of different types of leafy green vegetables. Additionally, find some sort of accurate way to track your accountability, at least for a period of time, even if just for a few days or a week. Know and understand what you are truly eating, in what quantities, and determine your total caloric intake in relation to your total caloric expenditure over a given period. Know that in areas of nutrition, just as in areas of fitness, there will be ups and downs. Embrace the road ahead and take it in stride.

Chapter 9

PLANT-BASED
PERFORMANCE RECIPES

Assortment of potatoes at Sprouts Farmers Market

Robert

If you have been inspired by the meal plans Vanessa has outlined, and have wondered how to make some of her favorite dishes, this chapter will satisfy your hunger. From a jackfruit bowl to performance cookies, she'll have you well fueled with tasty treats to boost your athletic performance.

One thing that we want to make abundantly clear is that neither Vanessa nor I make a lot of recipes – we primarily make meals. We combine our favorite foods together into healthy meals but we don't follow a lot of recipes. Therefore, our "recipes" will be fairly basic, because our focus is on eating the foods we like, in healthy quantities, without having to spend a lot of time looking up ingredients and following recipe instructions. We both largely subscribe to the opinion that the more recipes you make, the less healthy foods you are likely consuming (due to the inclusion of oils, flours, sugars, added fats, and processed ingredients). Furthermore, given the fact that there are only 1,440 minutes per day, the more time you spend shopping for ingredients, preparing ingredients, following recipes, and cooking more elaborate dishes, the less time you have for exercise, basic meal prep, down time and recovery from exercise, sleep, or other healthy lifestyle actions that could be performed to further support your overall health and fitness goals.

Since we know time is a limiting factor preventing many of us from spending as much time exercising, or resting, recovering, and lowering stress as we would like in an ideal situation, it seems practical to want to reduce our time spent preparing more complicated foods and meals. It seems especially logical to avoid spending an exorbitant amount of time preparing those meals with a long list of ingredients, including oils which should largely be avoided, when our time could be spent eating fresh, whole fruits, vegetables, salad greens, and prepared staples we have in bulk quantities, such as brown rice, beans, lentils, oats, and potatoes. So don't get *too* excited about the forthcoming recipes, but you do have some delicious and easy to make recipes to look forward to. Our recipes are deceptively simple, by design – in order to be quick and efficient, aiding in assisting with sports performance and exercise recovery. But fear not, we have links and resources to some truly awesome and diverse whole-food, plant-based recipes for those who care to indulge in the process of making more complex meals.

Neither one of us is a chef, or a baker, or even close to being able to play one on TV. You're about as likely to find me in the kitchen looking up measurements for recipes, as you are to find me celebrating my birthday at a steakhouse. If you see me using a more advanced kitchen tool than a can opener, you can politely ask, "who are you, and what have you done with Robert?" Vanessa, on the other hand, is a big step up from my culinary skillset, but you will also be unlikely to find her following many specific recipes, though she does all of her own meal prep, which means she is making meals comprised of the staple foods in her diet. Though we don't make a lot of our own recipes, we do have a number of suggestions for you to find beautifully constructed whole-food, plant-based recipes online. Some of the usual suspects will likely come to mind for you, such as Forks Over Knives, Engine 2, Dreena Burton, anyone with the last name Esselstyn, and a family of Campbells (not of the famed soup variety – but rather Dr. T. Colin Campbell and his family).

Some helpful links for healthy, primarily whole-food, plant-based recipes include:

- forksoverknives.com

- engine2diet.com

- plantpoweredkitchen.com

- nutritionstudies.org/recipes

- straightupfood.com

You can find some outstanding recipes to follow on the links above, but for those interested in knowing precisely what Vanessa eats at home, the following recipes will be rather interesting to you. Mine, probably not so much, because I eat for simplicity, a bit of emphasis on flavor, personal preference and for performance, without an emphasis on intricacy. Nonetheless, you will get a feel for the types of staples that I eat at home as well, and how I combine those staple foods to make a plant-based performance meal.

Vanessa's Plant-Based Performance Recipes:

BANANA PROTEIN MUFFINS (OR COOKIES)

4 bananas
1 cup dry rolled oats
2 scoops protein powder
½ cup coconut flakes
½ cup walnuts
¼ cup vegan chocolate chips

Preheat the oven to 350 degrees Fahrenheit. In a large bowl, mash the bananas. Mix in the remaining ingredients until thoroughly combined. Form into 12 balls and place on a cookie sheet (if making cookies), or pour into a muffin tin. Bake for 20 minutes.

Nutrition information:

Entire batch makes 12 muffins
1,554 calories, 209g carbohydrates, 62g protein, 88.8g fat, 33g fiber

For one banana muffins:
129.5 calories, 17.4g carbohydrates, 5.2g protein, 7.4g fat, 2.8g fiber

PUMPKIN PROTEIN MUFFINS

1 can pumpkin
2 tablespoons pumpkin spice
½ cup unsweetened applesauce
½ cup walnuts
2 scoops protein powder
1 ½ cup dry rolled oats
¼ cup vegan chocolate chips or raisins

Preheat the over to 350 degrees Fahrenheit. In a large bowl, thoroughly combine all the ingredients. Pour into a 12-muffin tin. Bake for 30 minutes.

Nutrition information:

Entire batch makes 12 muffins
1,305 calories, 135.7g carbohydrates, 67.5g protein, 63.6g fat, 24.9g fiber *factors in chocolate chips rather than raisins in calorie count

For one pumpkin protein muffin:
108.8 calories, 17.4g carbohydrates, 5.6g protein, 5.3g fat, 2.1g fiber

GRANOLA

1 cup coconut flakes
1 cup sliced almonds
1 cup sunflower seeds
1 cup pumpkin seeds
¼ cup coconut oil, melted
¼ cup Enjoy Life brand mini vegan chocolate chips

Preheat oven to 350 degrees Fahrenheit. In a large bowl, combine the dry ingredients. Melt the coconut oil and toss with the dry ingredients. Spread out on a cookie sheet. Bake for 30 minutes. Remove from the oven, and after cooling, top with chocolate chips.

Nutrition information:

3,138 calories, 85g carbohydrates, 98g protein, 275g fat, 42g fiber

SOAKED OATS

Overnight soak
½ cup dry rolled oats mixed with 1 tablespoon chia
1 cup unsweetened almond milk
½ cup fresh fruit of your choice
1 tablespoon peanut or almond butter

Soak the oats and chia seeds in the almond milk overnight. Just before serving, stir in the fresh fruit and peanut or almond butter. Combine everything in a mason jar for a meal you can take with you in the morning.

Nutrition information:

364 calories, 34g carbohydrates, 17.3g protein, 21.6g fat, 17g fiber

QUINOA BOWL

1 cup cooked quinoa
1 tablespoon peanut butter
1 tablespoon hemp seeds
1 tablespoon chia
1 teaspoon cinnamon
1 teaspoon cacao chips (not pictured)
1 banana, sliced

Once the quinoa is done cooking, but while it is still hot, combine all the ingredients in a bowl.

Nutrition information:

683 calories, 85g carbohydrates, 27g protein, 29g fat, 21g fiber

JACKFRUIT BOWL

1 cup Upton's Naturals brand Bar-B-Que jackfruit
½ cup cooked black rice
1 onion, diced
1 cup red, green, yellow, orange peppers, chopped

In a large dry skillet over medium-high heat, sauté the onion and peppers until the onions brown, about 6 to 7 minutes. Reduce the heat to medium and add the jackfruit, cooking it for 1 to 2 minutes to warm through. Serve over cooked rice.

Nutrition information:

412 calories, 86.7g carbohydrates, 12.8g protein, 6.7g fat, 23.5g fiber

MEXICAN SWEET RICE

This recipe is one of my favorite pre-workout snacks. I like to use farro or spelt rice because it has more fiber and protein in it, but rice works just fine in a pinch.

2 cups farro, spelt, or rice of your choice
2 (14-ounce) cans coconut milk
1 teaspoon vanilla extract
1 teaspoon cinnamon
½ cup raisins or dried cranberries
Sweetener to taste, optional

Combine all the ingredients in a bowl, cover with plastic wrap, and refrigerate overnight.

Nutrition information:

1 cup
530 calories, 63g carbohydrates, 11g protein, 26g fat, 8g fiber

BAKED TOFU

16-ounce block firm tofu, sliced into ½-inch thick strips
Nutritional yeast or seasoning mix of your choice

Preheat the over to 425 degrees Fahrenheit. Line a cookie sheet with parchment paper and lay the strips of tofu on the parchment. Sprinkle with nutritional yeast or your favorite seasoning. Bake for 25 to 30 minutes until golden brown.

Nutrition information:

3 ounces
72 calories, 2g carbohydrates, 8g protein, 3.5g fat, 2g fiber

ROASTED VEGGIES

You can roast almost any vegetable. My favorite vegetables to meal prep every week are: Brussels sprouts, butternut squash, cauliflower, broccoli, red beets, and sweet potatoes. I pour vegetable broth on the vegetables in a large bowl, massage with my hands, mixing thoroughly, put them on a cookie sheet and then bake them.

2 cups sliced or chopped veggies of your choice
¼ cup veggie broth

Preheat the over to 350 degrees Fahrenheit. Toss the veggies with the veggie broth. Transfer to a cookie sheet. Bake for 45 to 60 minutes, until the veggies are well-browned.

Nutrition information:
256 calories, 52g carbohydrates, 11g protein, 0.4g fat, 17g fiber

ACINI DI PEPE (GRAINS OF PEPPERCORNS) FRUIT SALAD

"Cheat meal snack"

1 package (about 2 cups) acini di pepe pasta, cooked according to package directions
2 tubs So Delicious brand coconut whip cream
I can diced pineapple, drained
1 can mandarin oranges, drained
1 cup Dandies brand mini-vanilla marshmallows

In a mixing bowl, combine all the ingredients. Cover with plastic wrap and refrigerate until chilled, at least 2 hours. Serve chilled.

Nutrition information:

1 cup
375 calories, 71g carbohydrates, 7g protein, 7g fat, 4g fiber

Robert's Plant-Based Performance "Recipes" (Meal Ideas)

As mentioned previously, I don't really make "recipes," but rather, I eat the foods that I enjoy most, and/or which give me the best nutritional and sports performance benefit, in meals that I assemble, or which my fiancée, Karen, prepares. In fact, Karen suggested that I call these "meal ideas" rather than "recipes." In the possible scenario that you skipped right to this section and missed the preface at the beginning of this chapter, I want to clearly explain why you likely won't associate the word "chef" with any of my particular meals ideas. I aim to eat based on preference, simplicity, efficiency (in preparation time, cost of ingredients, etc.), and in relation to my lifestyle and exercise schedule. Essentially, I eat a fairly basic plant-based diet and rarely consume meals made from "recipes."

ROBERT'S BURRITO BOWL

1 cup cooked brown rice
½ cup cooked pinto beans
½ cup cooked black beans
1 avocado, sliced
1 tomato, sliced
1 handful romaine lettuce
1 jalapeño, sliced
1 pepperoncini, sliced

Combine the cooked rice and beans, then top with other ingredients to make your burrito bowl.

Nutrition information:

735 calories, 112g carbohydrates, 23.5g protein, 24.8g fat, 30g fiber

GNOCCHI WITH SPINACH AND OLIVES

1 (16-ounce) package eggless gnocchi, preferably whole wheat or potato gnocchi
1 cup packed raw spinach leaves
2 tablespoons sliced black or Kalamata olives
½ cup tomato sauce or marinara of your choice
1 tablespoon nutritional yeast

Bring a pot of water to a boil. Boil the gnocchi until it floats. Immediately drain, but do not rinse. While hot, toss with the sauce, spinach, and olives. Mix together in a serving bowl and top with nutritional yeast.

Note that some gnocchi has eggs, but you can find wheat and potato gnocchi at stores like Trader Joes, for example.

Nutrition information:

659 calories, 80g carbohydrates, 16g protein, 33g fat, 11g fiber

GREEN POWER SALAD

2 cups leafy green vegetables
½ cup kidney beans
1 cup brown rice
1 cup mixed vegetables
2 tablespoons sunflower seeds
1 tablespoon balsamic vinegar

Go to a salad bar at your local Whole Foods Market, Sprouts Farmer's Market, Sweet Tomatoes, or other build-your-own salad buffet. Select a handful of two or three of your favorite leafy greens to be the base of your salad. Add a legume such as kidney beans, chickpeas, soybeans, or black beans in a desired amount. Add a grain such as brown rice, quinoa, or barley in a desired amount. Add two or three vegetables such as broccoli, carrots, beets, cucumbers, artichoke hearts, zucchini, cauliflower, peppers, or radishes. Top it off with nuts or seeds such as walnuts or sunflower seeds. Use an oil-free dressing such as balsamic vinegar, or simply squeeze pepperoncini, tomatoes, or lemon as a dressing.

Mix into a large salad bowl.
To add more bulk to your salad, consider adding cubes of yams, potatoes, tofu, or avocado – or all of them.

Nutrition information:

514 calories, 84.7g carbohydrates, 19.5g protein, 12g fat, 13.5g fiber

FRUIT SMOOTHIE WITH GREENS

1 cup water
1 cup frozen blueberries
1 cup frozen mangoes
1 cup spinach
1 cup kale
½ cup ice

Pour one cup of water into a powerful blender such as a Blendtec or Vitamix.

Select a handful or two of your favorite frozen fruits such as blueberries, cherries, mangoes, raspberries, or strawberries and put them in the blender. Select a handful or two of your favorite leafy greens such as spinach, kale, or romaine and put it in the blender.

Add a handful of ice, blend it up, and serve chilled.

Nutrition information:

222 calories, 51.5g carbohydrates, 3.5g protein, 1.7g fat, 9.4g fiber

MIXED FRUIT SALAD

This is especially good before a workout for a burst of energy, or immediately following a workout to replenish fluids, electrolytes, and carbohydrates used up and lost during exercise. It makes a colorful, flavorful, antioxidant-rich meal.

2 mangoes, sliced
1 cup blackberries
1 cup raspberries

Mix together in a big bowl.

Nutrition information:

529 calories, 129.2g carbohydrates, 9g protein, 4.1g fat, 26.4g fiber

Whether you try some of Vanessa's creative recipes, some of my very simple whole-food recipes, or you visit one of the outstanding resources listed above such as Forks Over Knives, know that plant-based recipes can be as intricate or as simple as you like, and can be very tasty and satisfying. There is nothing you have to "give up" in order to fuel your body for optimal performance with plants. In fact, by eating closer to nature you can cut out some of the excess calories that come from oil (pure fat) that is used in nearly all prepared food, and often in salads, snacks, or processed treats. By focusing on plant-based whole foods, especially large amounts of fruits and vegetables, you will ensure you are getting optimal amounts of vitamins, minerals, antioxidants, fiber, and more, all in nourishing, flavorful, satiating plant-based meals.

Chapter 10

GROCERY SHOPPING TIPS FOR OPTIMAL ROI

Robert

My biggest shopping tip, which supersedes many other aspects of grocery shopping, is simply asking the question, "what will this do for me?" when considering any food purchase. This question can help make the difference between spending money on junk foods or investing into health-promoting foods. Imagine asking yourself this question, "What will this do for me?" when standing in front of an aisle filled with packaged cookies and chips, compared to standing in the produce department. There are profound differences in health outcomes when you buy and consume fresh fruits and vegetables versus cans of soda or containers of ice cream. As I've said before, there is still room for processed or junk foods in a nutrition program, if the true foundation of the nutrition intake is real, whole, plant foods. In fact, these days, I eat some breads, some processed spreads, burritos and wraps, and plenty of processed international cuisine such as samosas, curry dishes, noodle-based entrees, and fried rice, as outlined already. Though I do try to limit oil intake, when possible, consuming popular dishes such as Pad Thai. Vanessa includes cookies and muffins in her nutrition program, but they are made from real foods and she makes them herself. They aren't filled with refined sugars, flours, and filler ingredients. We both enjoy some non-dairy ice cream, sorbet, and other vegan treats from time to time, but the question posed above, in general, can be incredibly helpful and influential when determining how to spend your hard-earned money on food.

For many consumers, whole plant foods are not the foundation of their nutrition plan, so each additional processed or junk food included in their diet reduces the overall percentage of real food intake. This could even mean that the *majority* of calorie intake in one's diet could be comprised of junk foods, making that the *actual foundation* of their nutrition program. The true essence of our real nutritional intake is not what we *think* we consume, but it is the sum of, and the macronutrient and micronutrient breakdown of the calories we *actually* consume, and this compounds over time whether we're aware of it or not. When we get the mathematical majority of our calories (rather than estimates based on intuition or instinct or memory) consumed coming from oily foods, sugary drinks, processed and refined carbohydrates, and food-like products typically categorized as "junk foods" we fall into a calorie-rich, nutrient-poor trap that creates an environment destined to struggle, and unlikely to thrive in areas of real health. This doesn't bode well for overall wellness and is not conducive to achieving fitness goals. But it is quite common, and the reality that many people consume the majority of their calories from calorie-rich but nutrient-poor foods is likely the biggest factor resulting in the obesity epidemic that is sweeping the Western world. Lack of exercise and general physical activity are factors as well, but nothing contributes more to weight gain and poor health than excess consumption of low-quality calories. Before we proceed to suggest specific national chain stores, recommended brands for anything that isn't a whole food, and techniques to save money by finding sale items during specific times from specific stores (such as Sprout's 35% off plant-based protein sales), we want to ensure we communicate our favorite shopping tip right up front, which is to simply ask yourself if you are about to make a healthful investment, or throw money away.

GENERAL GROCERY SHOPPING TIPS FOR COMMON GROCERY STORES

Salad bar at Whole Foods Market, Austin, TX

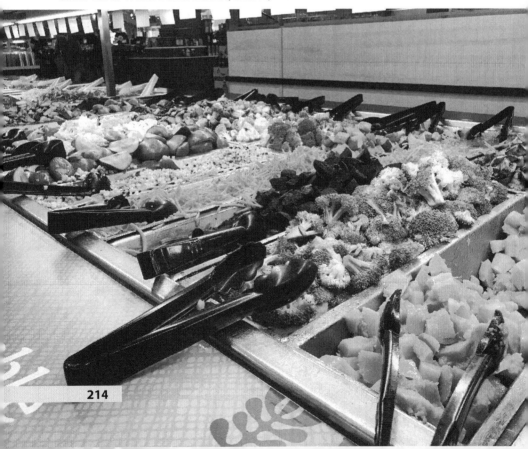

For those living in the USA (and other locations that have these stores), here are some tips regarding specific grocery store chains including Whole Foods Market, Sprouts, Natural Grocers, Trader Joe's, Costco, and Kroger, among others:

- Many Whole Foods Market locations have a discount on their hot food bar on Wednesdays. Inquire at your local Whole Foods Market store about Wednesday hot food bar savings.

- Sprouts Farmers Market has 35% off sales on plant-based products during certain times of the year. Ask your local Sprouts about their promotional calendar to plan out your purchases.

- Sprouts Farmers Market has Buy 1, Get 1 Free sales throughout the year on products such as Gardein and Hillary's brand vegan frozen foods, which can save you literally half your budget for plant-based frozen food items.

- Sprouts Farmers Market has 25% off vitamin department sales every three months. Four times throughout the year you can get ¼ off your favorite nutrition bars, vitamins, and sports supplements – and even toothpastes, deodorants, soaps, and more. Since these sales are frequent, every 12 weeks, one could plan their shopping to buy bulk quantities of certain items to last for three months, and only buy at 25% off year-round, without having to spend a lot up front (compared to sales that are only once or twice per year).

- Trader Joe's has some of the cheapest prices of all national chains that focus on health foods. They have bottles of water for 17 cents, bananas for less than a quarter, and full-serving sizes of prepared vegan foods like lentil or vegetable wraps, tofu spring rolls, and more, for less than five dollars each.

- Trader Joe's has plenty of packaged and prepared ready-to-eat plant-based meals, such as those mentioned above, as well as hummus, quinoa, and even an Indian-spiced cauliflower meal to take to go. They have bottled juices and smoothies and other ready-to-drink snacks. It is very much a grab-and-go type of store in addition to a grocery store that is known for their unique and quirky offerings (such as chocolate covered anything-you-can-think-of), Japanese-style fried rice, sorbets, and dumplings – as well as international foods and beverages, sweets, and often the best value on some non-food items, such as Tom's of Maine brand dental products, and their own Trader Joe's brand of soaps, shampoos, and beauty products that are not tested on animals and vegan approved.

- Natural Grocers sells only organic produce, and if that is a priority for you, it is a great store to consider. They have competitive pricing on packaged plant-based foods too. From Thai spring rolls to burritos, you can find prepared foods, and plenty of snack foods at low prices, such as tofu jerky, plant-based yogurts, frozen entrees, and a wide variety of plant-based nutritional supplements and products. They offer in-store demos for sampling and frequent sales on nutritional products. Half their store is dedicated to vitamins and supplements so their variety is sufficient and their deals are impressive. They also often have a discount bin for products that are going to expire soon. You can typically find popular plant-based brands such as Vega on sale for 50% off if an expiration date is approaching. These discount/clearance bins, racks, and shelves can really make a difference when looking to save on high-dollar items such as sports nutrition products.

- Kroger is the largest grocery chain in America, just ahead of Albertsons, which owns Safeway (fun fact for those like me – Robert – who like strange, interesting, but not always super useful fun facts), and offers a wide variety of plant-based frozen foods, fresh vegetable sushi, non-dairy beverages, dairy-free products, and standard grocery store produce at low prices. They have their "natural products" sections clearly marked from the breakfast cereal aisle to the frozen food sections and all throughout the store. Kroger, like Safeway, has a fuel partnership program, so as you purchase groceries you accumulate a discount on a future fuel purchase. They also have periods where they offer 2x points per dollar for additional savings at the pump. Just don't get carried away and spend hundreds of dollars in a given month just to get 40 cents off per gallon, which saves like $8 (been there, done that, learned from it, and get carried away less now – though I still save 10-20 cents per gallon per month)

• Costco is a great place to buy bulk produce, frozen foods, organic foods, plant-based burgers, and other frozen and packaged foods from popular brands. Costco is perhaps the best overall bang-for-your-buck store to shop at, especially if you don't mind buying large/bulk size quantities of whatever you are purchasing (which is what they offer and are known for). Want a case of 16 plant-based burgers? Sure you do! Put 'em in the cart. How about a gallon of salsa? Why not? In need of a 20-pound bag of potatoes, or oranges, or other produce? Bring it on! 100-serving container of mixed nuts? You get the idea….

• On the West coast, Winco Foods is considered a "low price leader." If cost is an issue or a topic for consideration when you're shopping for food, Winco has some of the lowest prices on produce that I have seen anywhere in the USA. They also carry tofu and soy products, frozen foods, non-dairy alternatives, and plenty of other plant-based foods like any major grocery store chain.

• The Dollar Store has plenty of all plant-based, vegan certified foods, for you guessed it, just a buck. Most fall into the junk food category such as bags of chips, frozen meals, jars of salted nuts, orange juice from concentrate, and crackers, but there are some good deals to be had, and nearly every town as a Dollar Store, Dollar Tree, General Dollar, or 99 Cent Store. Stop in and discover that there are some hidden gems to be found – occasionally a totally mainstream vegan brand of frozen foods typically three or four dollars somewhere, else for only a dollar at one of these dollar-themed stores.

- Publix is a popular grocery store in the southeastern USA, with well over 1,000 locations. They remind me of a slightly more progressive Albertsons and tend to have more plant-based specialty items such as vegan mayo, plant-based cheeses, non-dairy drinks, trendy brands of kombucha and probiotic beverages. They also have some GreenWise Market locations that focus even more on natural and organic products, which means more products that are not tested on animals, and inherently more vegan and plant-based options, especially with their emphasis on specialty foods.

- If budget is an important factor for you, keeping tabs on produce sales at Kroger, Sprouts, Safeway, Natural Grocers, Publix, Albertsons, and Whole Foods Market is a good way to ensure you get the best deals if you live or work in close proximity to a number of these national chains. Many of these stores have newsletters you can sign up for, apps for additional savings, and social media accounts to follow to get a heads up on current sales.

- Amazon can be an outstanding place to find awesome deals on products such as protein and energy bars, sports supplements, and other specialty food items, as well as kitchen appliances such as high-powered blenders, Instant Pots, and the most diverse collection of plant-based cookbooks available. They hold a large piece of the online market share, even in grocery type items like vitamins and supplements, and with Amazon Prime ($99 annual membership) you can get free shipping on every order, often within two business days. Amazon also hosts "Prime Day" once per year, an event that celebrates their anniversary when they offer Amazon Prime members "flash sales" and "lightening deals" that only last for a few hours, as well as day-long sales on thousands of items. Like many retailers, Amazon is also notorious for their Black Friday sales, so keep Amazon on your radar for some of the best deals with a diverse catalog of plant-based offerings. Amazon now owns Whole Foods Market as of June 2017, so there may be some changes coming in the near future as Amazon takes over the helm of the natural product leader.

- Asian food markets near Chinatown in major US cities are outstanding places to get exotic fruits typically found in places like China, Thailand, Indonesia, and throughout Southeast Asia. Prices are usually low and variety is sufficient. You will also find many soy products, noodles, exotic green vegetables, and other plant-based foods you may not have seen before – especially in the frozen food section and even in the leafy green vegetable section of the produce department. Whether it is Chinatown, Koreatown, Thaitown, or any other Asian-influenced district in your city, you will likely find great variety of super antioxidant-rich foods and good prices. Shopping in Asian markets is one easy way to add healthy diversity to your nutrition program with great tasting, often unique and exotic produce.

- In addition to the national chains, international food stores, similar to the Asian markets I mentioned above, are a great place to find diverse plant foods. Check out Indian, Mexican, Mediterranean, and African food stores, among others for diverse plant-based bulk and packaged foods as well as interesting and unique produce from various global regions (though some common global produce items often found elsewhere can also be grown locally, such as rice from California versus grown in China or Indonesia or Japanese Sweet Potatoes grown next door).

- Many health food stores like Whole Foods Market have hot food and salad bars, as mentioned earlier. These can be great for convenience, but they can be very expensive, paying for food by the pound. Many healthy foods that make up the staple of a plant-based diet, such as potatoes, yams, beans, rice, and tofu are very heavy and are typically very inexpensive foods – but not at the salad or hot food bar. These heavy foods – potatoes, tofu, artichoke hearts, broccoli, beans of all types, and heavy vegetables – can really add up, so be aware of that when you stop by the salad bar. Make the base of your bowl lightweight leafy greens, and go from there.

- Many grocery store chains offer membership programs, such as Kroger, Albertsons/Safeway, and Natural Grocers. These membership programs can get you special savings, discounts, and even help you earn and accumulate rewards to save on future shopping or on affiliated fuel stations as discussed earlier. If you can be part of a number of loyalty programs you can compare prices relatively quickly online, in person, and from ads mailed directly to you. Staying up to date on all the buy one, get one free sales, the 25 and 35 percent off sales, and clearance items at one store or another, can pay huge dividends on the long run. Implementing these purchasing strategies could save a family hundreds or even thousands of dollars per year.

- Savvy grocery stores, and savvy shoppers may use online or mobile apps for additional coupons, savings, or for product locators to save time. As they say, time is money, so if you know what you're looking for, where to find it, and how to get it quickly, that helps your bottom line as you maximize the 1,440 minutes you have each day, while also getting the most value for your hard-earned dollar. Either become familiar with your local stores, including where their clearance and discount racks are, their sales calendars and seasonal specials, or keep abreast on these events with mobile apps to stay connected.

- In stores such as Whole Foods Market, Sprouts, Natural Grocers and Costco, you might find product demos taking place within the store. This gives you an opportunity to try foods for free to see if you like them before purchasing them. These product demos are especially popular at Whole Foods Market and Costco, and at the former you're very likely to see plenty of plant-based products sampled out to customers, and at the latter you might just get lucky and see a plant-based burger or protein drink being sampled out to the masses.

- Cooperative markets are a great place to become a member-owner and get monthly or everyday discounts when you shop. You can also have some sort of say in the products that are being carried, or ones you'd rather not see at the co-op and it can be an empowering feeling. Co-op grocery stores seem to be inherently vegan-friendly and organic-friendly, while also carrying local products grown, made, or handcrafted in your own community. If your city has a co-op, I highly recommend checking it out, if just for the initial experience, the tea and vegan muffin, and the free wi-fi.

- Farmers markets are another great option for shopping, especially for fresh produce, if you have any in your area. Many farming communities and metropolitan cities alike have farmers markets sprouting up all over town on certain days of the week, often Wednesdays and Saturdays. Some cities, such as Los Angeles, boast dozens of farmers markets in different parts of the city, so common that they have at least one farmers market open every day of the week, and dozens open on weekends. Shopping at farmers markets gives you a unique opportunity to buy produce directly from the farmer. This can be a rewarding experience, as well as an opportunity to learn more about where food comes from, how it is grown, and perhaps a chance to arrange special deals when buying in bulk. Building relationships with farmers can also provide opportunities to visit farms for U-pick days, where you can select your own produce for discounted prices, while getting to experience the harvesting of farm fresh produce first hand. I highly recommend picking your own fresh produce directly from the farm, if given the opportunity.

- If you shop online, and have a desire to support all vegan stores, there are a number of great options, including Vegan Essentials and Vegan Proteins. Since I am long-time friends with both store owners, I even have some coupons for you to use. If you shop from www.veganessentials.com, use code VBB to save 10% on your entire order (one-time use). If you are a first-time customer, living in the USA, shopping at www.veganproteins.com, use code VBBFNEW for free shipping (one-time use). There are a number of other all-vegan online stores and a simple Internet search will help you discover a variety of online vegan retailers. Again, just like with brick and mortar stores in your areas, you can sign up for online newsletters, follow the online vegan stores on social media such as Twitter and Instagram and keep up the latest sales, promotions, closeout items, and seasonal products and discounts.

- If after reading Vanessa's recommendations for Powerootz, her honest to goodness favorite plant-based sports supplement, you decide to order it, you can save 20% when you use code VANESSA, ordering from powerootz.com. You can also order directly from the link on plantbasedmuscles.com where the discount has already been applied, no coupon code necessary.

Shopping at Sprouts Farmers Market

VITAMIN & BODY CARE
EXTRAVAGANZA
25% OFF
regular retail

Limited to stock on hand. Not to be combined with other promotional discounts in effect.

We truly hope that this has been a helpful and educational chapter. It sure was a fun one to write. When you eat to build plant-based muscle, it often requires a high volume of food since plant-based foods are so low in calories. Therefore, it becomes that much more important to have a strategy, a budget, and a plan to get the most bang for your buck, and the highest return on your investment. We believe the strategies explained above will help you achieve your goals of getting the most out of your health-promoting, time-saving, strategic planning, money-saving trips to the market, the store, the co-op, or your couch (when you order online). Happy saving, in every sense of the word (time, money, health, animal lives)

Chapter 11

ACTIVISM IN ACTION THROUGH SPORTS

Clockwise from top left: Tricia Byers, Simone Collins, Vanessa Espinoza, Mindy Collette

Robert

One of the main messages we aim to convey with this book is for you to use your talents, your skills, your achievements, and your body built by plants as positive activism. Once you are equipped with the knowledge to build your body on a plant-based diet, actually building your body into a walking billboard for your cause makes a powerful statement. Whether that means you burn fat, tone muscle, increase your energy, or improve your overall health in a measureable and visual way, you are often automatically a role model or inspiration for others around you. I have witnessed this for decades, and Vanessa epitomizes this notion. She literally wears veganism and animal rights on her sleeve (in the form of tattoos) and is a walking billboard for plant-based muscle with her strong, muscular body. Whether we're in the gym, or out to dinner together, men and women alike stop her in awe of her physique. When people learn that she is a compassionate plant-based athlete, it gives people a certain perception of what a plant-based athlete looks like. Perhaps they already envisioned a strong, healthy body when associating the plant-based lifestyle with fitness, but possibly not. As a walking billboard for plant-based muscle, we have an opportunity to write that script and tell our story.

This is not to say that everyone needs to or should look a certain way, and I want to make that abundantly clear. I'm going to go ahead and plant this flag here for you to see it and reference it. There is absolutely no requirement or obligation to look a certain way when promoting the plant-based-muscle lifestyle. We all have our own unique journeys, stories, challenges, obstacles, transformations, and successes that go with the ups and downs that life brings us. There are all kinds of different body types from those of powerlifters to bikini models, and from runners to non-athletes, and everything and everyone in between. My main point is that the more you build your body with plant-based muscle, the louder statement it tends to make to the mainstream masses who still collectively question whether someone can adequately build muscle when abstaining from all animal products.

Does that mean it is *your* responsibility to carry that message and figuratively or literally wear it on *your* sleeve? Of course not; it's just a concept to think about. This potential positive influence on others in the form of activism in action through sports is something I have been observant of over the past couple of decades. When I have been at my biggest and most muscular self while wearing a vegan themed t-shirt, tank top, or hoodie, the feedback I received from the mainstream public was one of surprise that I could build so much muscle without eating animals. People have been especially impressed when I discuss the longevity of my vegan lifestyle. Of course, we can't just take anecdotal praise, feedback, or criticism from strangers on the street or strangers in the gym as our only sample size. But when we put our plant-based-muscle images online in photos and videos, for an Internet mass audience to see, the online feedback typically resonates with the mass audience feedback we get in person. The question is, what message are we sending to the general public about what a plant-based athlete might look like, train like, and eat like? One could argue, "who cares what other people think?" But if we truly have the ability to positively influence others – those we know and those we don't know – then clearly we have an opportunity to save a lot of lives, human and non-human animals alike. That's really the whole point of activism in action, from my perspective. It's not about setting specific physique expectations or body shaming those who don't represent a specific look, but it's about using leverage from hard-earned work in the gym and in the kitchen to have a positive influence on others, and subsequently save lives. We realize that not every vegan, nor every athlete following a plant-based diet needs to or wants to put an emphasis on promoting the plant-based muscle lifestyle in an outgoing way. Certainly some people have more of an outgoing personality and demeanor than others, but the potential influence and impact is there for those who have an interest in actively, consciously, spreading the compassionate plant-based fitness message.

I spend hours each day online promoting the plant-based-athlete lifestyle, which is likely how you found out about this book. Though I spend hours online promoting photos, videos, answering questions, and sharing information about the plant-based-athlete lifestyle, unless I use paid advertising or unique collaborations with others, I am mostly reaching fellow vegans and plant-based diet enthusiasts with my message (those who follow me on social media platforms or subscribe to my website). What is perhaps more effective is when I go to the gym wearing vegan-themed clothing while being a strong and fit representative of the plant-based-muscle lifestyle – or even when I'm shopping at Costco, or attending a live sports event. I'm that guy who wears vegan-themed clothing to the grocery store, to airports, on airplanes, to the gym, and pretty much everywhere I go. It's not to be obnoxious or annoying, or self-promoting (I wear many brands besides my own), but it's to encourage others to think about the plant-based lifestyle in a new way. When you're wearing a vegan/plant-based-themed shirt while grocery shopping, it could pique the interest of others to look in your cart. What does a vegan eat, anyway? When you're in your spin class or doing yoga, it's another great way to use subtle forms of activism, just by wearing clothing that identifies you as a plant-based athlete.

For the past two decades I have been labeled many things, including a vegan, a vegan athlete, a vegetarian, a plant-based athlete, an activist, an author, a marketer, and many other labels. So I understand that adding more labels to ourselves or identifying by particular labels can be a bit overwhelming and undesirable. Therefore, it's up to us as to whether we'll pursue this type of activism in action. I simply want to argue the case that when it comes to equating some sort of positivity to the plant-based-athlete lifestyle, I think there is some merit in this pursuit.

I'm old school enough to know what it was like being a plant-based athlete in the '90s before the Internet came around, when it was a fringe lifestyle. We didn't have the platforms we have today, and we didn't have the awareness of what a vegan was back then either. That's why I am so passionate about promoting the plant-based-athlete lifestyle in effective ways today, because for so many years it was a struggle to share this compassionate and life-saving message with others outside of my inner circle of family, friends, teammates, and co-workers. If activism or outreach of any kind is not something you're interested in, one very simple way I encourage each of you to quietly promote the plant-based lifestyle, simply through your daily lives, is to follow the fat-burning, muscle-building, and energy-boosting principles in this book. As you make forward progress in areas of health and fitness, people around you tend to take notice and will often ask questions. That is your non-invasive, non-aggressive, compassionate, and transparent opportunity to share your lifestyle with others, without even having to initiate a conversation. I have witnessed this casual approach of leading by example time and time again in the Forks Over Knives and Engine 2 communities, which are full of amazing body, health, and lifestyle transformations. I'm not even referring to people who built muscle in these cases, but to those who improved their overall health in a noticeable way by switching from an omnivorous diet to a plant-based diet, and subsequently impacted those around them.

Furthermore, success stories such as the health transformations Forks Over Knives shares regularly to an audience greater than one million on Facebook alone, are distributed far and wide online too, reaching exponentially more people. Body and health transformations are inherently inspiring to many people, and therefore, they are a positive by-product of making forward progress as you pursue your health and fitness goals, while sharing your success. This is what I like to refer to as a win-win-win, or even a win-win-win-win, where you, those around you, the animals, and the planet all win as a result of your activism in action through your personal health and fitness journey. Never underestimate the power of your own positive actions.

One of the things I admire so much about Vanessa is that she is always in top shape. She is a walking billboard for plant-based muscle at all times and it is so encouraging and inspiring. In addition to making ourselves walking billboards for plant-based muscle, there are myriad other ways to put activism in action. Here's a specific campaign I created that has made some waves over the years, and has no doubt saved a lot of lives simply through imagery combined with words presented on social media platforms.

No Meat, No Problem

In 2013, I created a social media campaign using the slogan No Meat, No Problem that was paired with an image of a strong and muscular plant-based athlete in what could be considered to be a social media "meme" of sorts. I used many different plant-based athletes as examples in these images and shared them on popular social media platforms and pages. This has been overwhelmingly my most popular slogan campaign I've ever used throughout social media in 15 years promoting my Vegan Bodybuilding & Fitness brand. I encourage you to consider sharing this message as well, especially with your non-vegan friends. The concept behind No Meat, No Problem is simple: the combination of the images and words you see in one succinct message challenges what many people think about vegans in relation to strength. Of course, many of you reading this are already on board and understand that vegans can build muscular, strong bodies. But this type of messaging is largely for those who still associate the plant-based and vegan lifestyles with characteristics that are not accurate representations of the current plant-based-athlete community. If you have your own personal success story, create your own images, wording, and show some before and after photos, highlighting some of your challenges and successes.

Another form of activism in action is through your success and achievements in sports. If you win a race or competition of any kind, you might consider writing an article about it and submitting it to your local newspaper, to a website or blog, or to a magazine that is related to your sport. Many media outlets are looking for news stories to share, especially local news. I have been on the front page of my hometown's newspaper (*Corvallis Gazette-Times*) several times, and have been featured in many newspapers and magazines worldwide because I shared an inspiring story with them. The same can be done by anyone; it just takes a little bit of effort. When journalists are researching a topic and see interviews with specific people in existing content from previous published work, it makes it easier for them to find you, if you have already had your stories published, and it gives you another opportunity and platform to share your message.

At the end of the day, determine what message you want to convey to an audience and decide what the most effective methods for conveying that message are. It certainly isn't for every plant-based athlete or individual to put themselves out there, and these days there are more of us to carry the weight than there has ever been, but if you are so inspired, we hope some of these ideas and suggestions in this chapter help spark some of your own ideas for activism in action. The animals you save as a result of your activism will likely never have the opportunity to thank you. So, if we may, just for a moment, speak for them, we personally thank you for making a difference in the lives of the innocent among us who share our same desire to live lives free of fear, pain, and suffering. Thank you for being a champion for peace and compassion as a plant-based athlete.

RESOURCES

BOOKS REFERENCED IN *PLANT-BASED MUSCLE:*

Shred It!

How Not To Die

Eat To Live

The No Meat Athlete Cookbook

Forks Over Knives Cookbook

WEBSITES REFERENCED IN *PLANT-BASED MUSCLE*:

plantbasedmuscles.com

veganbodybuilding.com

nutritionfacts.org

nomeatathlete.com

forksoverknives.com

drfuhrman.com

veganessentials.com

veganproteins.com

engine2diet.com

plantpoweredkitchen.com

nutritionstudies.org/recipes

straightupfood.com

ACKNOWLEDGEMENTS

Vanessa

First I would like to thank my parents and my sister for being my inspirations and believing in me no matter what new adventure I stumble upon. Even though my father is no longer with us, I know he is always by my side guiding me through life. And thank you to my mother for showing me how to love and respect all living creatures; she is the one that inspired my compassionate lifestyle and my love of lifting weights.

I would also like to thank Robert. He was my biggest inspiration when I started out on my vegan journey and he is still my biggest inspiration to this day. If it weren't for Robert, the vegan bodybuilding community would not be where it is today. When everyone doubted me for being a vegan athlete, his website and book confirmed that I was doing the best thing for my health and performance, but most importantly, doing the best thing for the animals. I am so very lucky that our paths have crossed; I truly know we were meant to meet.

Also, thank you to Karen Oxley for being such a wonderful friend, and for being so patient with us during this process. I appreciate you and love you very much. We are family forever!

Last but not least, thank you to Jessica Smothermon for taking on this huge project of editing our book. You have been so easy to work with, and I am so thankful to have worked with you. I hope to continue to work together in the future.

Robert

First and foremost, I want to thank my fiancée, Karen Oxley, for contributing to this book in so many ways – from photography and feedback, to preparing countless meals for me while I focused on writing and editing for months on end. She has been by my side during this entire process. Karen, I love you, and I appreciate all of your contributions to this very meaningful project. Keeping it in the family for a moment, I'd also like to thank our dogs, Benny and Ellie, for literally being by my side when I spent many long days and nights writing and editing, brainstorming, and putting this book together. I'd also like to thank my parents and siblings for believing in my goals and dreams of becoming an author, and for helping me along this literary adventure over the years.

I'd like to thank Vanessa for embarking on this journey with me. I didn't know that when I asked her to co-author a book with me that it would take us two years to complete it, but I have been inspired, motivated, and have learned so much along the way, and I feel immense gratitude for her. Vanessa, thank you for sharing your knowledge, your wisdom, and your heart with our readers and me.

This book would not have come together so well without the help of our editor, Jessica Smothermon. Jessica, thank you for not only helping me learn when to hyphenate and when not to, but for your insight, your creativity, and your incredible work ethic. You played such an important role in this book, and I am so deeply appreciative.

I would also like to thank our book cover photographer, Trevor Grayston, who provided a number of professional photos throughout the book. I would like to thank our design team led by Art Gorodetsky. And I would like to thank Jennifer Schumacher for her creative influence with format and style. Thank you all for bringing our vision to life!

There are a few other people I want to give a special thanks to, including Giacomo Marchese and Dani Taylor. Giacomo and Dani, thank you for assuming the role of managing the Vegan Bodybuilding & Fitness Facebook group I had been running for nearly a decade, something that might seem like a small task, but it completely freed up my schedule, time, and responsibilities, which made putting the requisite amount of time into this book possible. Thank you so much. I love you two. You're family to me, and I have so much respect, love, and appreciation for you. Thank you for keeping the community going and growing while I've been working away on this book.

I'd like to thank Charles Chang for giving me some of the most incredible opportunities of my life, including hiring me for my 10-year career with Vega that opened up more doors than I could imagine. Charles, thank you so much for believing in me when I was a 25-year-old kid with a go-getter attitude, and a bit too much arrogance and confidence for my lack of success at the time. You must have seen a diamond in the rough, and you truly helped shape my professional career and mentored me into adulthood as I grew my own brand and business. I sincerely thank you and your family for everything. It has been an amazing ride. Thanks for sticking with RC 2.0 for all these years.

I want to extend a special thank you to Dr. T. Colin Campbell, Dr. Caldwell B. Esselstyn, Jr., Dr. Michael Greger, Dr. Joel Fuhrman, Brian Wendel, Matt Frazier, and Chris Rowe for having a positive influence on my approach to this book, bringing reason, evidence, and science into the forefront of my current approach to nutrition and training.

I'd like to thank my childhood friend, Jordan Baskerville, whom I've known since preschool. Jordan has helped me with each one of my books in some meaningful way, from editing, to advice, to critical feedback and suggestions. A few months into the writing of this book, Jordan challenged me to make this my best work yet. I took that challenge, and I hope I have succeeded.

Additionally, I would like to thank Will Tucker for providing The Yard as a gym for Vanessa and I to use for book photos and videos. I would also like to thank Chef Jason Wyrick for the incredibly helpful feedback with the structure and layout of the meal plans and recipes, literally while we were in book production. It made a huge difference, and we thank you very much. Along with Will and Jason, I would like to thank each and every person that endorsed this book. It means a lot that you would put your name on a recommendation of our work. Thank you so much. We don't take this responsibility lightly, and we aim to make you all proud of our work in this field.

Lastly, I'd like to thank all of you, the readers. It is cliché to say I couldn't do it without you, or that I wouldn't be here without your support, but that sentiment tends to ring true in a very fundamental sense. Writing books is a passion of mine, but sharing my passion with readers is what makes this process fulfilling. Thank you for encouraging me, for challenging me, and for motivating me to test my creative spirit. I truly thank each and every one of you for reading our collaboration, and for supporting our passion for compassion.

ABOUT THE AUTHORS

Vanessa Espinoza

Vanessa was born and raised in Denver, Colorado. She adopted a plant-based lifestyle in 2003, at age 22. Today she owns a personal training business, specializing in strength and conditioning, boxing, and basketball skills.

As one of the top 10 point guards in the U.S. coming out of high school, Vanessa was awarded a full basketball scholarship to Colorado State University. She was drafted to play professionally in the WNBA. Due to her father's passing during that time, Vanessa declined the offer to play in the WNBA and took up boxing, honoring her father who was a professional boxer. Vanessa became a 3-time Colorado Golden Glove state boxing champion.

Along with Vanessa's in-home personal training business, she offers personalized nutrition and training programs on www.plantbasedmuscles.com. She is a regular contributor to *Vegan Health & Fitness Magazine,* has been vegan for over 15 years, and aims to inspire others, showing that you don't need to harm animals to have a muscular physique.

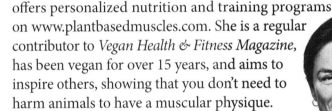

Robert Cheeke

Robert grew up on a farm in Corvallis, Oregon, where he adopted a vegan lifestyle in 1995 at age 15. Today he is the best-selling author of the books, *Vegan Bodybuilding & Fitness* and *Shred It!*.

As a two-time natural bodybuilding champion, Robert is considered one of *VegNews* magazine's Most Influential Vegan Athletes. He tours around the world, sharing his story of transformation from a skinny farm kid to champion vegan bodybuilder.

Robert is the founder and president of Vegan Bodybuilding & Fitness. He writes books, gives lectures around the world, and maintains the popular website, VeganBodybuilding.com. He is a regular contributor to *Vegan Health & Fitness Magazine*, *Naked Food Magazine*, *Forks Over Knives*, and *The Dr. T. Colin Campbell Center For Nutrition Studies*, is a multi-sport athlete, entrepreneur, and has followed a plant-based diet for more than 20 years.

Thank you!

Dear Reader,

Thank you so much for reading this collaboration that we enjoyed putting together to help you become your personal best. If you want to follow our continued progress and endeavors as long-time plant-based athletes and training partners, please follow our Instagram pages for regular updates:

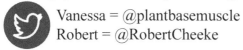
Vanessa = @plantbasedmuscle
Robert = @veganbodybuildingandfitness

And to engage with us with quick dialog, find us on Twitter here:

Vanessa = @plantbasemuscle
Robert = @RobertCheeke

Sincerely,
Robert & Vanessa

Made in the USA
San Bernardino, CA
28 June 2018